D. H. Miller

MW01103655

ADVANCE PRAISE FOR OVERLOOKED

James Robertson does what few can do, and that is to tell a good story, engage with popular culture, and teach Christian history all at the same time. This witty and insightful book provides a helpful and hopeful guide for Canadian Christians who wonder how the past has led to the present and a few words of challenge as they think about the future.

— **Gordon L. Heath**

FRHistS, Professor of Christian History and Centenary Chair in World Christianity, McMaster Divinity College, Hamilton, Ontario

The history lesson I wish I'd had in Sunday School!

— **Tara Jean Stevens**

Podcaster, Host of "Heaven Bent"

A kind revisionist historical look at some of the missing narratives of the Canadian Christian story, James Robertson offers a glimpse into a few of the prevalent themes that help readers organize our Canadian Christian roots. As a local church pastor, I found this to be eye-opening and mind-bending for its significance in shaping our Canadianism. With a witty, organized and challenging way, Robertson paints the historical picture that sheds light on what shaped our imaginations and serves as a cautionary tale for the future. Definitely a must-read of 2022!

— **Bernard Tam**

Pastor of The Living Room Church, Toronto, & New Ventures Implementor

As the Canadian Christian church finds itself at yet another threshold moment in history, *Overlooked* offers a timely and much-needed perspective. This book should be at the top of the 'must-read' list for those who sense the transformative potential this threshold moment holds and who actually care!

With equal parts seriousness, lightheartedness and gentle irreverence, Dr. Robertson masterfully weaves together seemingly disparate threads to reveal a complex 'tapestry' of the Canadian Christian Church over the last 250 years. These threads - stories of specific people, places and events - invite Canadian Christians to see and embrace the gift of being overlooked. Both evocative and provocative, *Overlooked* provides an accessible historical exegesis of how and why the Canadian church is where it is; and suggests that what has always been most true about Canadian Christianity is possibly the key to finding a humble, conciliatory and faithful way forward.

— **Jan & Jeff Steckley**

Threshold Commons

There's something indiscernible about Canadian identity. Doubly so for Canadian Christian identity. One can feel lost, much like driving through a snowstorm. Thank God we've got James Tyler Robertson riding shotgun, reminding us that the only way to understand where we are is to look in the rearview mirror. As our country experiences seismic shifts, the church in Canada finds herself in unfamiliar terrain. James reminds us how we got into this storm, and orients us in the right direction through stories that are heartbreaking, revitalizing, and always brutally hopeful. And like a good road-trip buddy, he's funny too.

— **Kevin Makins**

Author of Why Would Anyone Go to Church? and Pastor of Eucharist Church, Hamilton, ON

Peace!
JoCorB

Congrats Bennett,
this is a great
achievement, we're proud
of you, and wish you
all of God's love +
grace for the future.
— Colm

Congrats Bennett,
may our God continue
to use you & bless
you! Keep smiling
for Jesus!
(Phil 4:8-9)
Alize K.

So proud of
you Bennett!
Professor
Syl

Live deeply
Eph 3:14-19
Rue George

OVERLOOKED

THE FORGOTTEN ORIGIN STORIES OF CANADIAN CHRISTIANITY

by james tyler robertson
foreword by gary v. nelson

publishing@newleafnetwork.ca
newleafnetwork.ca
435 Kingsmere Blvd,
Saskatoon, SK S7J 3T9

James Tyler Robertson
Overlooked: The Forgotten Origin Stories of Canadian Christianity

Cover Design by: James Kingsley

ISBN: 978-0-9953054-4-1 [print book]

*Dedicated to my Grandmas, both of whom taught me
to respect the past*

And to

*S. & S. both of whom show me love in the present
and give me hope for the future.*

TABLE OF CONTENTS

ACKNOWLEDGEMENTS

Reading the acknowledgments of a book is akin to reading the credits at the end of the movie. Unlike the Marvel movies, this acknowledgment has no cool, story-advancing Easter egg in the middle. Knowing that, I still want to acknowledge my debt to those who helped create and correct the work you are about to read. Writing a book is a very isolating experience but it is also a team sport in many respects as well. This book wouldn't have existed were it not for the support and care of many others. Here are the thanks I would like to offer, in an after-movies-credit-type-of-style:

Jared Siebert - Conversationalist/Creative Thinker/ Canadian context guru

Elle Pyke - My guide through my own wandering thoughts

Amy Bratton - Editor extraordinaire/hero of this work

Tim Bratton - Jesus People aficionado/Creative director

Gordon L. Heath - My personal hero/Canadian history mentor/unfortunate Bruins fan

Taylor Murray - Atlantic Canadian faith correspondent/excellent collaborator

Scott McLaren - 19th century Methodist & book culture expert

Linda Ambrose - Heroic critic and guide into the world of Pentecostalism

Bruce Douville - Piano genius and guide through the crazy 1960s and 1970s Christians

Evan Habkirk - Kept me from the minefields in the Reconciliation chapter/ beyond insightful and compassionate/ corrector of my careless words.

Dina and Kris - Location providers (I wrote a HUGE section of this in their cottage...without dipping into an "All work and no play makes Jack a dull boy" mentality)

Doug Holt - Best friend/ "You can't write everything so just write something" mantra provider

Andrea - My hero and my champion

Mountsberg and Westover Baptist Churches- My faith families

Gary Nelson - Fantastic Boss/ Foreword Writer/ Fellow eggnog and Ginger Ale evangelist

Alicia Wilson - The person who titled this book

New Leaf Writing Circle - Creative muses who helped shape and discuss the early work

My folks - Cheerleaders/meal cookers/question askers/ support givers. I love you both...sorry I am such a grump sometimes.

My boys - Self-starters/hilarious/better children than I

deserve/ my everything...the best thing I ever had a part in making!

Finally, I want to thank you, gentle reader for taking the time to read this. I hope you like it and I really do hope it gives you some insights and hope.

All of you are brilliant and kind scholars and you each transformed my ideas into something more cogent. Anything of excellence found in this book is thanks to you — the deficits remain mine alone.

Sincerely,
James Tyler Robertson

FOREWORD

It was a 'by invitation only' meeting organized by former President Jimmy Carter. The denomination that he had grown up in (the Southern Baptist Convention in the United States) was in the midst of a rhetorical and political take over by what he considered to be the fundamentalist of the movement. All who attended the meeting had come to discuss the need to gather Baptists together to present a more unified and progressive voice. As the only Canadian present, I found the dialogue fascinating. Unexamined assumptions and undefined stereotypes were thrown around as accepted truth. Foundational themes, so confidently asserted, left me in a state of confusion and perplexity.

I realized that we, the attendants, had been invited because of those unexamined foundations. Their naïve, and frankly superficial beliefs, were jaw dropping, and also because their stereotypes were shared fully by all around the table of conversation; stereotypes which framed a socio-political and religious bounded set which has shaped American Christianity from its early beginnings. I was a fish out of water, invited because the denomination I represented in Canada was part of the Baptist World Alliance and therefore part of the North American Baptist Fellowship, but I didn't fit their assumptions.

With trepidation, I entered the conversation. I told them that I felt like the 'neighbour' looking over the fence as a family squabble was taking place. I was not comfortable amidst the tensions they were feeling because the foundational boundaries of Republican and Democratic Christianity were not of my home. I told them that I was a Western Canadian having grown up on the prairies in the land of Tommy Douglas and William Aberhart. Like many of my Canadian Baptist sisters and brothers, I believed in the complex beauty of a faith which was 'evangelical in its flavour, committed to the universal health care of a social network, prolife, anti-war, egalitarian in approach to leadership in the church and profoundly committed to evangelism and social justice.' I could find no resting place, no home in their unexamined polarizing definitions.

The result of my conversational foray into their discussion was blank stares. Once again I experienced the deeply isolating 'habitus' as described by James in this book you are about to read. It is an experience I have felt many times. I have had the privilege of working locally, regionally, nationally and globally. This experienced feeling of dislocation has too often been my reality. I used to believe that it was simply me—I am an odd and peculiar person of faith after all. However, I came to realize that this feeling was about so much more than that. I am Canadian, and as strange and general as that statement might be, it explains so much of my experience in the religious dialogues I have entered into over the years.

Kathleen Norris in her book *Dakota* alludes to this. She realized that if you come to understand the land that you grew up in, you will see the shape of your soul. Somehow we are an amalgam of our lived experiences, geography, history and faith experiences. I have come to realize that they shape us in mysterious ways. They do so often without any self-examination or reflection. It affects the way we think, relate, and experience spirituality and faithfulness. Even what we value. It shapes our souls.

This is why for so many years I have pleaded for the discovery of our Canadian Voice as Christians. Both for self understanding but also for knowing how our voice might influence in conversations.

Canadians are an odd and strange people. Lovers of two games played on ice that most people do not understand—curling and hockey—and of a football game that looks like chaos to NFL lovers.

We hold a strange mixture of insecurity and apology that has for so long hindered us from forming our own voices. Robertson

Davies one time stated: "We Canadians are an insecure people but one thing we are sure of—we are not Americans!" What happens when our whole identity is formed around what we are *not*?

We are a people uniquely shaped by a history profoundly different for our neighbours to the South but yet intricately interwoven together because of proximity. Having built our national identity around a value of collective, good governance and peace, the rugged individualism exhibited by our neighbours to the South is at one point suspect and on the other strangely appealing. Seeking an answer to the congregational decline that has overtaken the church of the last 20 years, we look for our solutions to the South, while holding in tension a certain wariness about its influence.

We study their trends and responses but suffer from an uneasy dissonance or nagging doubt about whether or not it speaks to our world as Canadians. The dissonance is real but it has not always led to more contextual responses by the church in Canada.

At the peak of the 'Attractional-Church-Seeker-Sensitive' movement in the US, I attended a conference where related ideas and strategies were being unpacked. So much of what was discussed emerged from a strong belief in the US that most people have experienced church at some point in their life. The strategy could be boiled down to one simple phrase – if you've 'had a bad experience in church growing up, we can give you a more relevant and better experience.'

I, however, was coming from a secularized Canada where from the 60's on, a slow eroding and decline of apathy toward the church has taken place. This decline has not been angry response to a bad experience of life in the church, but rather it has been an apathetic and slow moving away from an institution that no longer appears relevant. Ample studies clearly show that Canadians are in fact quite interested in exploring spirituality. They are just not so sure that the institutional church can be a place where that search and exploration could or should take place. In fact, in conversations I have had over the years, I have constantly been surprised that many searching people had not even considered the church. In truth our *Canadian* strategy would be better stated in this way: 'Exploring spirituality, never had an experience in church, maybe you might want to consider that the church might be a safe place to explore those questions.'

Church historian James Robertson describes this experience of apathy and migration away from the church through the journey of Tara Jean Stevens. He notes she no longer self-identifies as Christian not because she is angry, bitter or dismissive but simply because she can no longer live with the disconnect between the church's teaching and her lived experiences. They were too substantial to overlook.

This is a book that needed to be written. It needed, however, to be written by someone who understands the dissonance but is imaginative enough to look at our church history in a new way. I confess to having a deep respect for James Robertson. Who else could help us understand our story more clearly, this wonderful historian who sees the wide sweep of culture and is not afraid to explore it in ways that helps us understand ourselves as Canadian?

I have long admired his wit and wisdom. After reading this book, I now know how insightful he truly is. So it is no wonder that he concludes the book with strong Christ-like hope for the church: "To see the freedom, the beauty and the power in being overlooked...to see that as a Christian virtue." Maybe, just maybe this is the unique voice we have to offer as Canadian people of faith. Read on and be challenged.

Gary V Nelson,
Former President of Tyndale University
Author of *Borderland Churches*

INTRODUCTION:
FAUX PAS

"You can't be fond of living in the past
'Cause if you are then there's no way
that you're going to last"

— "Wheat Kings,"
The Tragically Hip

"History does not repeat, but it does instruct."

— Timothy Snyder,
On Tyranny

"Contemporary societies — not just North American — are no longer
used to looking at where they have come from. They are far more fix-
ated on...what comes next. Rather than use the past to help determine
where they are on the trail of life in relation to where they started,
they plunge ahead, frequently blindly, expecting that the future will
correct any mistakes they make in navigation."

— Terry LeBlanc,
Walking in Reconciled Relationships

Picture yourself arriving at a party.

The door opens and you hand your host a large, brownish box containing a mixed assortment of doughnuts from a hockey-player-inspired Canadian franchise. Before you enter into their home you lean against the outside of the doorframe and kick the toe of your boot against the ground to dislodge stubborn remnants of snow. You enter while exchanging pleasant greetings. You tuck your gloves into the pocket of your winter coat before removing it; you unfurl your scarf and stuff it into one of the sleeves as you place the coat on a hanger. You bend over and undo the laces of your boots and then use the classic toe-to heel- maneuver to remove your boots without touching them with your hands; you finish by placing the now dripping footwear on a rubber mat near the door. You stand up, adjust your sweater, and survey the gathering already in progress, pleased to see that this is a warm room full of friends. You find a small clique of people, again exchange greetings, and take some time to warm up both physically and socially.

After a few moments, and emboldened by the blood returning to your cold limbs, you make a slightly risqué joke, the content of which is admittedly controversial but, given your familiarity with the group, you are confident that your calculated risk will produce a laugh.

And then it happens.

Your joke yields only awkward silence. The eyes of your friends widen in shock and then firmly avoid any contact with you. The other members of the group share horrified glances with each other; there are shoulder shrugs, pursed lips, and non-committal head nods in your direction. Your stomach clenches and though you were in the cold only moments ago, you feel sweat roll down your back. You came late to the group and your first words effectively killed a conversation. It's all the more unsettling because you don't know why. If you have ever been in this type of situation, you know what it is to discover culture.

Social norms agreed upon by certain collections of people

is one way we can understand the term "culture." Not the written down elements of society that are discoverable through careful study. Rather, the equally important unwritten rules that govern social interaction. Culture dictates human responses to a myriad of elements including race, religion, gender, time, family dynamics, conflict, priorities, parenting, friendship, humour, etc. and can be problematic because culture creates norms as well as taboos. One of the most awkward ways of discovering a norm is by saying—or becoming—something taboo.

This is what anthropologist Pierre Bourdieu calls the "habitus," the repeated interactions within our various spheres that socialize us into acting in acceptable ways. This is also how we navigate in certain "fields" like parties, school, or the office. We find ways of minimizing perceived imbalances (like the joke) because these create uncomfortable experiences. These invisible social constructs are complex and as subtle as they are powerful. As Bordieu explains, these are "neither a result of free will, nor determined by structures, but created by a kind of interplay between the two over time: dispositions that are both shaped by past events and structures, and that shape current practices and structures."[1]

You are a decent person (I mean, you brought doughnuts for crying out loud) and, had you been at the party even five minutes earlier, you would have learned that one member of the collective just celebrated five years in programming for the CBC. Having known that, you would have chosen to focus on the engaging, new content rather than quipping that the network is a government-funded graveyard for creativity. You were an immigrant to that party community, you misread social and cultural cues but, most importantly, you were ignorant of the stories that helped shape that community; and your ignorance proved costly.

Hopefully, one friend in the party puts an arm around

---

1 Pierre Bourdieu, *The Field of Cultural Production: Essays on Art and Literature.* (New York: Columbia University Press, 1993), 170.

you, escorts you momentarily from the maligned group, and explains to you what happened before you arrived. Properly informed, you can make the necessary adjustments (probably should apologize and explain that *Schitt$ Creek* is, honestly, one of the best shows you have ever seen) and rejoin the group to contribute in acceptable ways.

Learning the stories that create a culture is my way of explaining the relevance of knowing history. This book is my attempt to put an arm around anyone who feels like their religious and spiritual beliefs are akin to a party foul within the larger Canadian context. An attempt to walk away from the concerned looks of fellow party-goers and explain some of the pertinent stories of Canadian Christianity that, I think, many of us have overlooked.

CAUSES FOR CONCERN

This book tells stories about the Christian faith in Canada that many of us have overlooked. It examines these overlooked accounts in order to challenge the belief that something is wrong with the church in present-day Canada. I want us to challenge the interpretive lens that speaks about secularity and post-Christendom as if they are indisputable facts. They are not. These are just words and, like all words, contain meanings that shift depending on *who* is saying them, *where* they are saying them, *why* they are saying them, and *when* they are saying them.

There are many different ways to interpret the word secularization but, for the sake of clarity, I find Robert Choquette's definition adequate to the task at hand. He writes that secularization, as a development of modernity, is, "the gradual emancipation of this world from the *other* world." In a more practical definition he goes on to state that secularization "was a process whereby segments of society and culture were withdrawn from the authority of religious institutions and symbols."[2] Ramsay Cook is also helpful at this juncture as he

---

2 Robert Choquette. *Canada's Religions*. (Ottawa, University of Ottawa, 2004),

explains secularization as "the shift" from a religious explanation of people's "behavior [sic] and relationships to a non-religious one."[3] Such definitions tend to support the concerns of those who believe the Canadian church is in trouble. However, I wanted to put these terms here to show you that I do acknowledge the reality of the world we inhabit. I don't want you to think I am being purposefully provocative or naïve but I do want to argue similar definitions have existed in other Canadian time periods.

I am writing to those who are concerned about the future of Christianity in Canada. But I also hope that those who are simply curious about religion or Canada will reap some benefit from this work (though I harbour no illusion that a historical book about Canadian religion will draw in a wide audience). For those who are more concerned than curious, the conversation tends to boil down to three parts:

The concern: numbers in regular church attendance are declining and the church has very little influence in society (the "we used to pray in school" argument).

The culprit: the church has failed to hold fast to the Gospel and has betrayed the message of God; and/or the nation is losing its faith due to a variety of issues related to generational differences, immigration, government policies, and cultural shifts; and/or the church has become irrelevant.

The plan of attack: Once we return to the "faith of our fathers" the bounty of souls will also return; and/or once we find ways to communicate the true power of the Gospel without the trappings of outdated religious modes people will find the benefit of church community once again.

From a statistical point of view, the drop in regular church attendance is a quantifiable fact. However, even the criteria for attendance are interesting and need to be read contextually, as we will see in a future chapter.

Those who believe the church has lost its way tend to point

353.

3 Ramsay Cook. *The Regenerators: Social Criticism in Late Victorian English Canada* (Toronto: University of Toronto Press, 1985), 5.

to the increasing numbers of more theologically conservative churches like the Pentecostal Assemblies of Canada (PAOC) and the declining numbers of more liberal churches like the United Church of Canada (UCC) as evidence that such a stance is correct. Again, such beliefs need to be scrutinized because they don't tell the full story and set up false myths about the nature of a successful church.

Others see earthlier reasons like irrelevant teaching, outdated music, cult-like rituals, hypocritical moralizing, or the relentless scheduling demands of modern life as the true issues. But how do we address such concerns without throwing away ancient Christian practices? Whatever the concern, many Canadians feel we are losing something precious and fear what that could mean for this place we call home.

THE POINT OF THIS BOOK

A few years ago I was asked to bring a historical understanding to the topic of growing secularity in Canada. I provided a one-hour talk about the developments of Christianity in this land (some of those stories are in this book). As I prepared to write the book, based on this talk, a trend I had not previously considered began to emerge. A trend that, despite all my study in this area, I had overlooked: secularization is actually nothing new.

The remainder of this book is dedicated to explaining what I mean by that, and why that is a good thing.

Secularization—if we accept the definitions listed above—is not new phenomena. Sure, the ways in which the "other world" of faith have been minimized in recent years are very modern and wouldn't have existed in previous generations. However, I want to caution readers against such a narrow understanding of secularization because history reveals a different picture.

This books shows that even the religiously cataclysmic decade of the 1960s is better understood as a natural outworking of previous trends; some of them centuries old. Secularization is a term used by religious people who are currently experiencing a perceived loss. It argues there was a time when a Christian worldview was more dominant than it is today. It is a term of lament and loss, a term that describes a feeling of powerlessness the religious are facing and want to correct. It is a term steeped in beliefs about what is, what was, and what could be again.

Such definitions set Canadian Christians up for a very specific kind of failure, a kind of failure that is unique to this country. While terms like post-Christendom, secularization, or loaded questions like "What happened to the Christian character of Canada?" can seem scary and unique to this time in history, this book challenges that this is something new or, perhaps, even something to worry about.

Each generation in this land from the 1500s and on has dealt with challenges to established religious worldviews and the perceived lack of Christian influence over this place. The who, what, when, where, and why are different but the outcomes and responses were noticeably similar. Even in a country as young as Canada, there have always been those who lamented and feared the loss of time-tested Christianity.

This was part of the missionary days in the 16th century; it happened in the pre-Christendom Canada when Christianity was the dominant interpretive paradigm; it happened during the heyday of Canadian Christianity when the church hit the pinnacle of power and influence; it happened in the 1950s and 1960s when everyone went to church; and it happened in the 1980s when the Seeker Sensitive movement hit full stride; and it is present yet again in this age. It is up to you, gentle reader, to discern what is unique about your time and place. But make no mistake, when it comes to the struggles of declining Christianity, Canada has been here before.

CANADA: OVERLOOKING AND OVERLOOKED

Before I can explain the unique and ultimately surprising characteristics of Canadian Christianity, I need to spend some time talking about the land itself. First, we need to address the enormity of the land.

The geography of Canada is one of the main characters of this book. The pages to follow demonstrate how the sheer size of this land impacted the theologies that were born and developed here. Other than missionaries, church-planters, or immigrants, few people seem aware of how much location influences beliefs and practices. This is problematic for a variety of reasons. As it pertains to Canada, the vastness of Canadian territory meant that numerous faith communities grew and developed over generations with little awareness of other faith communities that equally and simultaneously claimed Canada as their home. Canada struggled to define itself with little ability to communicate internally until the advent of the railroad in the late 19th century. In a land this big, it was and still is very easy to overlook fellow inhabitants.

Added to such internal realities is the ongoing historic connection of Canada to the Old World of the British Empire. Which brings us to our second point: Canada, as a nation, is often overlooked on the global stage. At least that is what many Canadians feel. This nation struggled to define itself not only internally, but as a distant colony nestled on the shoulder of the New World giant located immediately to the south. Scholars call this the Atlantic triangle because Canada leaned on both America and the Empire to help define itself.[4] Combining these external influences with an internal dissonance brought on by massive distance and you have a people whose ideas about faith were as vast and varied as the land they called home.

CANADIAN CHRISTIANS

Therefore, when I talk about a "Canadian Christian" or "Canadian Christianity" I don't want you to see the first word indicating a country, while the second term denotes a religion. I rely on Benedict Anderson's *Imagined Communities* to help me understand and explain what I mean by this.[5] Nations are

4 John Webster Grant. *A Profusion of Spires: Religion in Nineteenth-Century Ontario*. (Toronto: University of Toronto Press, 1988), 68-84.

5 As Anderson puts it: "The nation is imagined as limited because even the largest

not just places in an atlas; they are also agreed upon concepts contained within the minds of numerous people with some connection to a specific geographical locale. Both "Canadian" and "Christian" indicate a series of beliefs held in common by a collection of otherwise different people.

The term "Canadian" is a construct built around shared, though nuanced, beliefs rooted in the land, languages, rituals, and stories that were developed in this place. The term "Christian" is different only insofar as it is not as connected to geography (theoretically anyway, again this entire book argues that *where* and *when* you believe shapes *what* you believe). Christianity is equally tied to ideologies, languages, rituals, and stories that create meaning. This is important to note because Christianity helped create the "Canada" I am talking about in this book but that Canada also influenced how Christianity came to be understood.

Let me offer myself as an example: I grew up in Western Canada (B.C. and Alberta), but have lived in Ontario for almost two decades. Despite this move, I still cheer for the Calgary Flames whenever they play against the Toronto Maple Leafs, even if I am vastly outnumbered by Leafs fans. However, if the Leafs are playing any other team, I will cheer for *them* as loud as any native-born Torontonian. If geography was the only issue, I would have changed teams the moment I crossed the border of Ontario. I didn't because strong personal ideologies—be they perceived loyalty to my place of origin, some form of nostalgia, a desire for distinctness, or the simple fact that Calgary has actually won a Stanley Cup in my lifetime—can transcend physical distance. However, geography does play a role because I never would have cheered for Toronto had I remained in the

of them...have finite, if elastic, boundaries, beyond which live other nations...it is imagined as a community, because, regardless of the actual inequality and exploitation that may prevail in each, the nation is always conceived as a deep, horizontal comradeship." Benedict Anderson, *Imagined Communities: Reflections on the Origin and Spread of Nationalism*. (New York: Verso Press, 2016), 7. Italics part of the original quote.

west. That example, while specific to me, gets at the concept I want you to remember as we go forward.

Here is a national example of this concept from recent history: in 1989, Baltej Singh Dhillon incurred the rancour of numerous fellow Canadians when he appealed to RCMP leadership regarding dress code. Dhillon's Sikh faith called him to grow a beard and wear a turban, a direct conflict with Mountie regulations regarding headwear and a prohibition against beards. When his appeal was granted (similar changes had been made in the 1970s to allow female officers to wear skirts and heels) cries that this ancient Canadian institution was being destroyed by a foreigner rang from coast to coast. Racism obviously played a major part in that controversy and that is one lamentable lesson we need to take from this encounter. Dhillon's non-Christian faith may not have precluded him from acceptance as a Canadian, but such tolerance turned to rage the moment his faith questioned a Canadian symbol, perceived to be sacred and unalterable. I would argue that a bearded Mountie in a turban is the epitome of historical Canadian values, not the end of them. Dhillon—now a decades-long veteran of the RCMP who has served with quiet distinction—clearly supported the values of his Canadian home (and risked his life to uphold them). He also valued his ancestors and his faith. That tension between honouring ancestral and modern homes is a much more foundational element of Canadian culture than even the iconic RCMP hat.

Fittingly, Linda Colley explains such tensions by using the allegory of hats in her brilliant work on Britons during the zenith of the British Empire.[6] A Welshman or an Irishman who self-identified as a Briton wore different social and cultural "hats" at different times in order to best embody his imperial identity in ways that were faithful to the land in which he lived. The same was true of early settlers in Canada. They were not Canadians

---

6 Linda Colley. *Britons: Forging the Nation, 1707-1837*. Revised Edition (New Haven: Yale University, 2009.)

per se, even if they used that word. They are better understood more distinctly as English, French, Irish, Scottish, American, German, and Eastern Europeans living in British lands and figuring out what it meant to be a Briton on the edges of the Empire. Frequently that meant bringing important elements of their previous home and blending them with the demands of their new home.

The same can be said for the later addition of Russian, Chinese, Korean, Japanese, African, Indian and other immigrants. Despite the differences of these culturally diverse people, they shared a desire to remain connected to former homes in ways that made sense with their new home. Though far from their respective ancestral lands, they never stopped "cheering for the Flames" and the mashing together of Old World Empires, new world Republicanism, and Indigenous influences provided the building blocks of early Canadian culture.

Such multi-generational adaptations, conflicts, and evolutions also helped contribute to the lack of a clear Canadian self-identity. Figuring out what a Canadian is proves just as tricky for Canadians as it does for anyone else (not that anyone else really pays us much mind). The stereotype of Canada being the polite, hockey-loving, beer-drinking, maple-syrup-pouring, friendly, and gentle teddy bear of the world may be enjoyable and helpful to tourism, but it doesn't stand up to any intentional scrutiny. I've been on enough C-Trains (Calgarian term for an LRT) leaving downtown Calgary after a long and cold workday to easily dispel the myth of the polite and cheerful Canadian. As it pertains to hockey, such stereotypes don't take our growing immigrant population into account either, many of whom have alternate sports connected to a place of origin, which they prefer over Canada's unofficial national sport.[7]

This matters because, historically speaking, Canada's distinctness doesn't come from novel ideas or innovations necessarily, but in its somewhat unique ability to blend

---

7 Our actual official national sport is lacrosse, not hockey.

seemingly contrary ideas together to make them work. We are, in some respects, a nation of mixed media artists taking pieces of other nations' ideas, mixing them with some practical realities of this place, and making everything slightly different; but something that can rightfully be called Canadian. That cultural mixology happens in Canada because even though we chose to remain engaged with the global world via the British Empire, we don't command the attention of the world. This has freed Canadians to experiment in relative obscurity. That is an important characteristic of Canada especially when compared to our closest neighbour, a country whose every idea is trotted out onto the world's stage.

A BIRD'S-EYE VIEW

Such complexities must be taken into account and as I do that I am reminded of the profound shortcomings of this work. This is a bird's eye view of some overlooked stories from this land with a focus on the role Christianity played within those stories. Because this book's perspective is sweeping, the stories herein sometimes lack certain nuances that makes the academic in me cringe. This work also overlooks important smaller, regional differences in favour of larger concepts. In other words, I describe the size and shape of the Canadian Christian forest but spend precious little time describing the individual trees. Whereas you, the reader, have a more grounded perspective of what is around you but, perhaps, lack a sense of the larger woods within which your specific trees grow.

I have tried to capture stories from as many different parts of this land as possible but, as you will see, individuals from certain places wrote more and, therefore, feature more in this work. My own home provinces of B.C. and Alberta factor in less than my regional pride desires. The unique spirit and religious expressions of Atlantic Canada are addressed but their nationalism has all sorts of regional characteristics that are unique and valuable. Most disappointing to me is the fact that this book adds to the isolation of our brothers and sisters in the Territories. I simply could not find enough sources to truly explain their religious landscape. For that I sincerely apologize. If you are reading this and you live there, please feel free to contact me because the lack of stories from your part of our land remains a noticeable and painful absence to me. I am genuinely sorry for overlooking you.

Most exciting about the vastness of this land is that I could write this book every year for the rest of my career and never tell the same story twice. For every choice I have made and every story I am about to tell, there are numerous other stories that would be equally valid. I am attempting to discern patterns with one eye toward history and another eye turned toward the period in time we currently inhabit. It is my hope that the situations and stories I have included have some particular relevance for you as they do for me. These are not the only stories I can tell but they are the stories that I chose. And I do hope that you find the stories amusing, insightful, and, most importantly, helpful.

CANADIAN FAITH IS NEW

In late 2019 Don Cherry, the iconic broadcasting personality of Hockey Night in Canada, was unceremoniously dropped from the Canadian Broadcasting Company for comments deemed offensive to certain Canadians. While debate raged around this issue, few people saw this for what I think it was: proof of a fundamental shift in the Canadian ethos. A shift that was not as noticeable only a few short years ago. The incident is proof positive that so-called traditional Canadian values are once again yielding to undefined new ones.

While most people simply debated whether or not he should have been let go, the deeper point is the one I raised in the beginning of this introduction. Don Cherry thought he knew the norms of this nation, the norms of his audience. Don Cherry thought he could offer a risqué opinion and get away with it; he was wrong. He committed a party foul, he became taboo, and this TV icon of Canada's most iconic sport made a comment one Saturday night—a comment similar to countless others he had made before—and was out in the cold by Monday. The careful observer of faith would do well to pay heed to this for it is indicative of the Canada we now inhabit. The concerned observer of Canadian Christianity might fear what this means for our own time-honoured traditions. However, the wise observer will see the new world forming and take a few moments to ask: "why *now*?"

Aaron Hughes rightly argues that religion "is imagined, constructed, and situated within specific national frames of reference."[8] Canada is a child of the modern period and Christianity helped determine what the nation became. Canada is too big to unite its inhabitants with geographical proximity alone. It is better to see our national identity as a collection of regionalisms attached to each other through flexible and elastic boundaries tethered to certain understandings enforced by language, history, and law. Specific to this book are the elastically bounded understandings of the Christian faith that shaped, and were shaped by, modern ideas of nation. Although it might seem antithetical to use history to talk about something new, that is exactly what I want to do (that rhyme was unintentional). It is important to see Canadian Christianity as a vast collection of thoughts related to Jesus, but it is also important to see those ideas as new ones.

Christians can fall into the trap of thinking the messages, thoughts, and expressions of the faith are timeless given the belief in Jesus' divinity. However, it serves us better to see how we frame our beliefs within a particular time and space. If the size and underpopulated nature of Canada contributed to the multiplicity of Canadian Christian beliefs, then the comparatively short amount of time Canada has existed reveals how young such multiple beliefs actually are.

This book begins in the 18th century looking at the faith of

---

8 Aaron W. Hughes. *From Seminary to University: An Institutional History of the Study of Religion in Canada.* (Toronto: University of Toronto, 2020.), 173.

immigrants who arrived in a land already inhabited by others. At first look, this downplays the importance and relevance of the Catholic missionaries and explorers who came to Canada's shores centuries earlier. While there are numerous relevant stories to these earlier encounters, I have chosen to begin this book when Protestants began to populate Canada as well. This is not meant to disparage or minimize the contributions of Catholicism to Canada. I hope that is clear because of the many stories of Catholic Canadian Christianity that are told in this book. However, for the sake of the major themes in this book, I thought it was better to begin our stories when immigrants from both of these branches of the faith were present and interacting with each other (although "interacting" is a *very* polite term as you will come to see).

Those immigrants introduced and adapted concepts from their former homes in order to build what they began to refer to as the "New World." As they bore children in their new homes, these settlers and immigrants handed their adapted concepts on to these children and other immigrants and created institutions to maintain, uphold, and enforce their new worldviews. Over the past 200 years, these institutions adapted the concepts further for subsequent generations of immigrants from even more remote places on earth. Those adaptations became the culture of what we now call Canada. And Christianity, more than any other religion, had a hand in such developments.

It also means that it is hard to say where Old World ends and New World begins in this country. That is also uniquely Canadian and also contributes to our national self-identity crisis. Arguably the greatest hindrance to Canadians' ability to concisely describe their national traits is the seemingly concerted lack of attention to Canadian history. To speak of a Canadian context without even a peripheral working knowledge of Canadian history is to repeat the blunder of the four blind men describing an elephant by feeling only that part which is within reach. We simply can't do a good job because my elephant is a wide and gnarled leg while yours is a flexible trunk, still another knows an elephant only by way of a tusk, and still another feels only the tail and assumes the animal to be quite tall and thin.

Most Canadians are pretty at ease when a person admits they attend church and see faith as an integral part of life. They will likely share a story of going to church when they were younger, ask some questions, talk briefly about how all religions are basically the same as long as they make people kinder (we'll see why that belief in kind faith is so common in a later chapter). Many will even listen to stories, smile at some of the programs offered by the church, and few have any issue with Jesus. However, if a Canadian Christian bring up salvation, eternity, or invites their neighbour to a service or something along those lines, watch how quickly the conversation will end as the person removes his or herself. That *laissez-faire* or indifferent attitude towards matters of faith (irrespective of which faith one practices) has more to do with the newness of this land rather than the vastness. Overlooking religion is a reality of the modern age that didn't exist only a few hundred years ago; and the exact same thing can be said about the nation of Canada.

HOPE IN THE OVERLOOKED

This book is all about the unique nature of Canadian Christianity and argues that this current experience is merely another in the ebbs and flows of historical faith in this land. Since the nation of Canada is a social experiment of the modern era, it only makes sense that the dominant religious voice of that experiment would also face certain modifications and adjustments along with the nation. The problem occurs when we don't see such modifications for what they are and, instead, ascribe to them meanings that fail to consider the Canadian context.

What you are about to discover in the pages to follow is that even these seemingly recent concerns are not harbingers of a doomed future, but are more the continuing echoes of a forgotten past. Historical ignorance narrows our perspective, creates cultural blind spots, and makes us prone to overlooking valuable lessons. When a forgotten ideology is re-discovered within the contemporary zeitgeist, our short-term cultural memory tends to label it as new. Even our so-called spiritual crisis is potentially something else entirely and that is why we find it so hard to define and correct.

I would like this book to help reframe concerns around secularism or post-Christendom Canada by offering a more full-orbed awareness of the actual history of Canadian Christianity. The current state of the church in Canada is not simply a result of religiously wayward Canadians or theologically unfaithful Christians. History shows us that big questions like this rarely have simple answers. They tend to be an amalgam of reasons that present us with equally complex and even competing potential solutions.

Now, I don't want you to fall under the misconception that simply hearing tales of Canadians of old facing (and, in some cases, conquering) their own religious struggles is going to somehow solve any perceived problems in our present world. It might, but that seems too lofty a goal to set. However, I do think this book can help us combat the nostalgic-laden myth that Canada is falling away from a golden age of Christianity into national apostasy. As with all things nostalgic, the reasons for this perceived calamity are rooted more in the issues and beliefs of this day being foisted upon the people of the past. What the past can actually offer us is the wisdom gained from experiences that didn't actually happen to us.

In order to do that, we have to take the time to root those people and what they were facing in *their* time and only after that can we gain clear insights. After rooting the people and events in their proper historical context, the historian interprets those people and events for contemporary audiences. This creates a tension as we examine a series of independent stories and somehow put them in step with each other. Sometimes it works in much the same way as a marching band with numerous independent instruments creating a unified sound; other times it is like herding cats. It is up to you to judge if this book is more akin to the synchronized music of the former or the howling cacophony of the latter. I don't want to bore you with the internal arguments many of us historians have about our own discipline save to say that we are very aware of such realities but still see history capable of helping.

So, as you venture further into this book, please know that this is intended to be a hope-filled tool to inspire dialogue and discussion around the role of faith in the Canadian *milieu*. In all my conversations I have had on this topic I have yet to find a truly angry or combative person. Most have firmly held beliefs based on some research and genuine experience-based struggle; others base their arguments on prejudices, misunderstandings, memes, or myths. This is true of those who want Christianity to return and those who don't care. Although admittedly anecdotal, I am pleased to report that those I have spoken with over the years seem kind and willing to share their views with relative grace, ease, humour, and candour.

Most Canadian Christians tend to be pretty decent people.

Most Canadian critics of Christianity tend to be pretty decent people as well.

That's a pretty good place to start.

THE RHYTHM

The chapters of this book reveal the rhythm of Canadian Christianity in a fairly—though not exclusively—chronological manner. For the most part I want to introduce you to the events in the order they happened to help you see the patterns for yourself. However, as I already mentioned, there will be times when I will have to jump backward and forward to help land a point I think is important. For example, even though this book starts in the mid-1700s, there will be times when we go back centuries earlier to show the importance of the Catholic nature of this land.

The first idea addressed is that of power because Canadian power dynamics are unique amongst the global community and need to be understood before we move forward. The Canadian nation has always possessed a unique relationship with power and the churches of that time had to find their way in a strange new land unlike any other in many respects.

Next, we look at rivalry to see how the religious landscape was formed and how many of those early decisions shaped our context for generations to come. Denominational battles and feuds proved remarkably resilient to cultural change and damaging to unity, despite the myth that Canadians are pleasant and cooperative. This chapter will also show how 19th century Christians reversed the surprising statistical reality that almost 20% of Canadians in their day considered themselves secular.

What should be noted about these chapters is that they take place in a time when Christianity was the dominant expression of the day. Issues like Darwinism, biblical criticism, and scientific discoveries had yet to appear as challengers to the ancient interpretations of the faith. Even in such a blatantly Christian world, concerns that closely echo present-day discussions involving increased secularity in Canada were present.

Next, we see the church truly influencing what would become Canada. Confederation and the advent of the railway did little for church engagement but the idea of Canada as a Dominion (a purposefully biblical word) lit the fire under many Canadian churches. We will be able to see the nature of Canadian Christendom in all its power and influence and then judge its efficacy as well as its legacy.

Many of you might be tempted to move past these early times as less relevant or archaic but I strongly caution you not to do so. After all, if the Marvel Cinematic Universe has taught us anything, it is the importance of origin stories.

Next we tackle the 20th century and look at how language created new tensions in response to growing concerns about the faith. Old tensions continued and grew as English and French Canadians vied for control. New voices appeared on the landscape as the newly formed Fundamentalist Christians began to speak and shape significant portions of Canada. Pentecostalism was born in Canada in this century and while always a small denomination, its influence over both Canadian and global Christianity belies its numerical size.

The increased freedom brought about by the 1960s ushered in a world-changing epoch with a legacy so large that we still live in its shadow. We will witness the end of the Canadian Christendom experiment 100 years, almost to the day, after it began. We will explore Quebec's Revolution, affordable housing's impact on churches, Canadian interpretations of the Bible, how padded pews ruined church, how money both helps and hinders ministry, and discover an overlooked culprit of secularization.

Building on that, we will then examine the reality all these events and ideas created to argue that they were neither accidental nor mysterious, but a natural—and fairly predictable—outworking of cultural trends. In this chapter we will see how women saved the church, how birth control shaped theology, how televangelism changed the nature of worship, how a Toronto church changed the world, the beautifully skeptical faith of Gen-X, and discover what Canadians really believed on the eve of the 21st century.

Reconciliation is at the heart of much of Christian theology but it tends to be more difficult than any other element of lived faith. The second-last chapter of this book deals exclusively with the story of Christianity and the people who lived here long before the first explorers ever set eyes upon the shores. Simply put: Indigenous peoples' history with Christianity is a terrible one. Responding to these tales is one of the most visible and obvious ways the followers of Jesus can embody the reconciliatory spirit lauded throughout the New Testament. The legacy of First Nations cripples some people with guilt, and creates new opportunities for systemic racism in others. The solutions are complex and not readily forthcoming but I can think of no greater hindrance to the faith in Canada than this and, because of that reason, Christianity's interactions with Indigenous peoples in Canada deserves its own chapter.

This book will stop in the early 2000s, and that might

be upsetting to some of you. I didn't do this because I believe nothing of merit has taken place since then, but I did choose that time specifically. First, this is meant to be a history book and I believe its examination should conclude well in the past so that I don't accidentally stumble into the realms of sociology or anthropology, two disciplines that are well beyond my abilities. That distance allows us to, hopefully, gain some perspective on situations not too far removed from our current world.

Second, I make the argument that 1990-2001 was a much more secular period in time than our current one. If we measure secularization based solely on numbers, you might have a problem with such a statement. If you measure it based on cultural significance, the last two decades have shown a decisive and noticeable increase in religious discourse.

Each chapter will also end with a resource section that you can consult if you want to dig deeper into the topics covered in the chapter. At the end of that section, I will summarize one idea that I think you should carry with you as you head into the next chapter.

LOOKING AT THE OVERLOOKED

With these tales in mind, gentle reader, I hope you will feel more equipped to locate the struggles of today with an increased awareness of the rhythm of the Canadian Christian story. The final chapter will combine these histories and offer some practical critiques and examples of how churches in this nation can move forward with greater hope, clarity, and awareness of the Canadian context. I have found stories of the past to be messages of hope, reminding us that there is nothing new under the sun—despite changes to technology—and that we are not alone in our struggles.

I want to honour the concerns of those who believe losing Christianity would be detrimental to the life of everyone who calls Canada home. I want us to take some time and garner wisdom from our co-nationalists that have come before us. I want us to take seriously the indisputable fact that the times are, indeed, changing. But that is not cause for concern or panic; times always change, culture always shifts, values always evolve and devolve, and Canadians have perpetually lived in the tension between what was and what is yet to be. I hope to show that Canada, more than any other nation in the world, is uniquely gifted to handle this global ideological shift we call secularization.

As Canadian Christians we are uniquely situated to be part of something important that is both rooted in the ancient while engaging in the new; because that is historically how Canada has tended to operate. The Christian faith has always called its people to follow Jesus' teachings (past experience) throughout life while awaiting Jesus' return (future hope). I argue Canadians have built an entire national culture around reverence for the past blended with eager excitement for the future.

Canada is also, in the words of Tom Wayman, "A Country Not Considered," an idea that presents a unique and exciting recipe for a national religious expression. A humble antidote for the malaise, controversies, and triumphalism of 21st century western Christianity. A way forward that makes space for questions and concerns; a way forward that values a mustard seed mentality; a way forward that is both Christian *and* Canadian. A unique, surprising, and challenging path forward for those who have eyes to see it.

So, if it is okay with you, let's walk away from this party for a moment so that I can tell you some stories many of us have overlooked.

CHAPTER 1
POWER
1756 -

I had my hands in the river
My feet back up on the banks
Looked up to the Lord above
And said, "hey man thanks"

— "New Orleans is Sinking,"
The Tragically Hip

INTRODUCTION

Canadians have a difficult time expressing what we are.

However, we all know what we are not: we are not Americans. Rest assured, the irony that our first story begins in America is not lost on me.

It was a dark and stormy night in New Port, Rhode Island in the year 1756 and a young woman and her father were having a fight. Overwhelmed with shame, the young woman stood out in the rain and, screaming over the frequent peals of thunder, called for lightning to strike her and send her immediately to hell. While dramatic, this was no idle concern as several members of the community recently met their Maker in that very manner. What was the nature of her trespass? Who knows; it is best to forget about that (as we should forget many of the sins of youth) because this story is not about her. This story is about her little brother, eavesdropping on the argument from inside the family home. Caught up in the histrionics of his eldest sibling, the boy wondered what she meant by hell, what she did to deserve such a fate, and whether this was something he needed to worry about as well.

Schooled in religion, he began to reflect on the destination of the dammed. Curiosity became obsession and the child soon found himself unable to enjoy swimming for fear of drowning and winding up in hell. He removed himself from play for fear of neglecting personal reflection and penance. Occasionally, his boyish nature won the day and he played but, as soon as he was done, he felt even more worthy of the lake of fire than before. He found no rest from this topic. He found little peace in the simple joys that once filled his young life. His prayer life increased but he pictured God as a "hard hearted and cruel being" that needed to be placated with prayer in order to "get him pleased and get his favour." Four years of this spiritual torment went by and no amount of study alleviated his pre-adolescent mind. Then, at the age of twelve, his father informed the family they were moving to a newly-forming colony in the north.

Our tortured theologian was much relieved by this news,

believing the countryside would offer many wholesome distractions "to amuse [and make him] happy." Such happiness turned out to be an illusion as fear of travelling by sea and reports of vicious Natives in the region once again placed the dual spectres of death and hell before his eyes. Even the pleasantries of the countryside were tainted by fear. Any of the innumerable trees could fall on him or, as his sister had feared all those years earlier, "the next flash of lightning would be commissioned to cut me off." He found himself longing for the distractions of the city. Reporting on this in later life, the famous man stated this fearful phase to be a vital element of true religion. Every lost soul, he would write, "roving here and there" must remain a "poor, starving, wandering soul, until he finds the Lord Jesus Christ."

Piety unable to calm him, the young man indulged the desires of his "carnal passions" in order to earn the hell he believed awaited him. Sitting at the breakfast table after an especially raucous night, his mother scolded her wayward son that he alone was the trailblazer of his path to perdition. She warned him that if he refused her sage advice, he could blame only himself—not her—for his eternity in hell. Eyes wide and half-eaten food still in his mouth: "Those words were like pointed arrows to my inmost soul, and struck the greatest blow." Is there anything more powerful than mom-guilt?

However, conviction didn't turn to conversion until March in the year before the American Revolution began. The visions, research, trials, temptations, troubles, depressions, wanderings, and fears had done nothing to bring the now 27-year-old man closer to salvation. Grabbing the Bible and letting the book fall open, the words of Psalms 38 and 40 "seemed to go through my whole soul" in such a way that a near lifetime of fear was dispelled in mere moments:

> *My whole soul, that was a few minutes ago groaning under mountains of death, wading through storms of sorrow, racked with distressing fears, and crying to an unknown God for help, was now filled with immortal*

love, soaring on the wings of faith, freed from the chains of death and darkness, and crying out my Lord and my God; thou are my rock and my fortress, my shield and my high tower, [Ps. 18:2] my life, my joy, my present and my everlasting portion. O the astonishing wonders of his grace, and the boundless ocean of redeeming love.[1]

Henry Alline had come to an ecstatic and personal experience of salvation. In his room, by himself, a bright light appeared and brought him to a place of assurance in his salvation. Such assurance was based not on his own works but because of a loving and forgiving Christ who, "with one drop of...blood" atoned for even as great a sinner as Henry. For the first time since he was eight years old, flashes of light no longer conjured up the terror of a hard-hearted God sending him to hell. Rather, the light transformed into a sweet revelation of a tender-hearted Jesus bringing him into glory. Alline would dedicate the remainder of his life to sharing this message with his fellow colonists in the Township of Yarmouth. Then throughout the predominantly Protestant colony of Nova Scotia (which, at that time, also included the present-day province of New Brunswick). And that, gentle reader, is where I have chosen to begin our story.

The "Apostle of Nova Scotia," as he came to be known, began an itinerant ministry that would consume the remainder of his short life. By 1784 Alline was dead, but his legacy remains evident in Atlantic Canada to this day. In order to understand the impact of this man we must understand the world in which he lived. In order to do that, we must expand our view beyond the confines of Yarmouth for a moment and move ever out to gaze upon all of Nova Scotia as well as the New England colony of Henry's birth.

---

1 All previous quotes were from The Journal of Henry Alline. I didn't include them earlier because I was building to this reveal. Hopefully it worked. Alline's entire journal is also available for free at canadiana.ca

POWER

This chapter on power is about noting the unique dynamics that defined the early Canadian world. All stereotypes have origin stories and none of them are so pervasive to this place as the myth of the polite Canadian. Like all stereotypes, the secret to its success is rooted in its connection to a truth. Canadian power dynamics have some unique characteristics that have blended and softened over time into the polite Canadian meme. Going back through history reveals the character behind the caricature and the relevance that has for the development of Canadian Christianity.

John Webster Grant speaks of Canada as part of an Atlantic triangle of influence that helps explain the culture. The three points of the triangle are Britain, the U.S.A. and Canada. The last of those three would be the most passive recipient of the beliefs and culture of the other two. However, as we will come to see, there were moments when Canadian ideas were able to traverse the Atlantic Ocean and cross the American border and stimulate genuine change across the pond and south of the border. For the most part, Canadian culture borrows heavily from American and British/European sources and our look at Canadian Christianity needs to begin by taking that seriously.

Canada is the proud child of the largest and most influential empire the world has ever seen. It also shares an undefended border with the largest and most influential republic the world has ever seen. Despite the fact that the aforementioned Empire and Republic actually went to war against each other on a few occasions, Canada was able to somehow navigate those cataclysmic tensions and remain intact. Not only that, but it somehow remained independent from both as well. How was this seemingly miraculous feat achieved? That answer to that question changes generationally, but the foundation upon which those changes rest is Canada's strange relationship to power. A relationship that is neither American nor British, and we forget that at our own peril.

I began this chapter noting that if Canadians know one

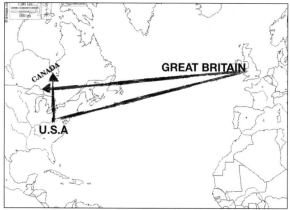

The Atlantic Triangle of Influence. Drawing by Author

thing about themselves it is that they are not American; but that's not entirely true is it? We are much more American than we may care to admit and historically the Republic has been the more dominant of our two main influences.

If you doubt the accuracy of what I am saying just think back to a time when you were watching an American TV show and it referenced a Canadian city. It kind of gives you a bit of a thrill to hear a Canadian city mentioned on an American show doesn't it? Or think about when someone talks about a famous athlete or celebrity and how quick we are to say, "Did you know that he or she is Canadian?" Don't feel bad, we all do it. Granted this kind of evidence won't stand up to any kind of academic critique, but it gets to the point I am making. In this chapter on power, I think it is important to talk about the birth of America because the Republic's understandings of power have impacted Canadian views. We need to see how we have inherited and altered the British and American definitions of power. Therefore, we begin in the time the Republic overthrew the power of the Empire.

In this chapter we are going to look at the following:
1. The American Revolution and revolutionary theology
2. The legacy of Henry Alline and early Canadian Evangelicalism
3. Issues with revivalism in Canada
4. Protestantism's arrival in Canada

5. Canada's interesting relationship with power
6. Canada: A nation of losers
7. Early Black Canadian Christians
8. Early Canadian Christianity
9. To cope or to conquer?

REVOLUTIONARY THEOLOGY

In 1776, the 13 American colonies declared independence from Great Britain and officially crossed over into rebellion. There were several prominent Nova Scotians who, like the Alline family, had been born and raised in the newly-rebellious colony of New England. This collection of merchants and farmers were influential and desired the maritime stronghold of Nova Scotia to join in the overthrowing of King George's government. Several trips to various rebel bases to meet none other than General George Washington had tremendous potential to align the people of Nova Scotia with the rebellion. These families even proposed that Washington invade, an offer he considered but eventually refused.

There were numerous valid complaints about the colonial government that could have won the province over to the revolutionary side. Many Nova Scotians retained close family and business connections to the colonies that would only sweeten the deal. Not to mention the fun and excitement at the idea of building a government by, and for, the people. Nova Scotia's loyalty hung in the balance and, in the early days of the rebellion, popular sentiment seemed to be sliding toward rebellion. However, by the final year of the Revolutionary War, sentiment had shifted decidedly back in the King's favour. That raises the questions: what happened and what does this have to do with Canadian Christianity or Henry Alline?

I don't want to overstate the case but there has been some good scholarship done by American Revolutionary historians to show the role of religion in providing some language for the Revolution. After all, the British Empire was a Christian Empire (a theme we'll return to again) and any colony that desired to overthrow such an Empire must question its allegiance to God. This was the Empire that had bested the Catholic Empires of Spain and France, this was the Empire that legislated only Protestants could sit on the throne, this was the Empire that gave birth to the anti-Catholic Church of England (are you detecting a certain anti-Catholicism? Good, you should have by now), this was the empire that raised up Protestant heroes like John Foxe, John Bunyan, and John Wesley (ironically, all of whom were considered enemies of the Church of England at one point or another).

However, it was another John—Jonathan Edwards—that has the most relevance to the topic at hand. His famous revivals throughout the 13 colonies influenced countless lives and made him a religious superstar throughout the Empire. He, and his much more charismatic contemporary George Whitefield, were able to catch theological lightning within a colonial bottle and create a somewhat uniquely American expression of faith. Such expressions were more emotive and dramatic and personal than even the most expressive versions back across the pond. This was colonial American faith and it was so successful that historians of the period call Whitefield America's first national celebrity. Given America's ongoing love affair with celebrities, I hope you are sensing the depth of his influence over the American colonial psyche.

Not only did the teachings of Whitefield and Edwards convict individual persons, they also contained compelling and emotive theology that brought low the institutions of the old world and elevated the importance of the individual in matters of salvation. There were numerous other reasons for the Revolutionary War but such ideas can clearly be seen in there as well. Whitefield spent his revivalist career in America and Scotland and his Calvinism created churches with strong senses of destiny and religious language for their separatist nationalism. In the case of America, such nationalism revolved around celebration of the individual that made rejection of the

Empire not only palatable but necessary. Britain had erred and, like the Israelites of old, become complacent in faith; it was time for the faithful in the New World to take over.

THE IMPACT OF HENRY ALLINE

Whatever your thoughts are on such theological matters, the point is that Edwards and Whitefield made theological arguments that influenced countless American Christians. Quebec's French Catholicism rendered such Protestant arguments irrelevant but why weren't the good Protestants of Nova Scotia swayed? The Apostle of Nova Scotia might offer an answer. Alline was raised in the theologies of these men and their Calvinist teachings go a long way to explain the young Henry's conviction of personal sin. However, Alline was also self-educated and he was unable to reconcile the character of the loving God he believed set him free from damnation with the harsh doctrines of Edwards' Calvinism. To Alline, God was a gracious and loving Lord who offered salvation to all creatures but, in His divine grace, also granted humans the ability to make the decision for themselves. That more nuanced and positive view of the human role in salvation resonated with the neutral Yankees of Nova Scotia.

Alline was so good at communicating to his fellow American-born colonists that historians credit him with inspiring Nova Scotia's Great Awakening. The differences between the Nova Scotia and New England Awakenings boils down to theology. The style and result of both were strikingly similar but Alline never utilized Edwards' *Sinners in the Hands of an Angry God* approach. He was so adamantly opposed to Calvinism that many of the early Maritime Baptist churches, themselves staunchly Calvinist, considered Alline an embarrassment due to his theology. These later 19th century churches decided to downplay Alline's influence, even though most traced their origins to his Awakening. This is why many Canadians have heard little about this influential preacher.

However, Alline's influence remains crucial for two very

important reasons: 1) Nova Scotia's isolated communities and rugged geography aided its neutrality throughout the revolution. Those who wanted to raise a concerted effort to overthrow the British simply could not get enough people together. Alline, on the other hand, was able to unite people together from the Minas Basin to the Bay of Fundy and over to the South Shore with such effectiveness that a concerted intellectual stream can be detected by the time of his death; 2) historians have convincingly argued that the Great Awakening was instrumental in preserving Nova Scotia's neutrality in the Revolution.

As the war dragged on, Maurice Armstrong argues Nova Scotians viewed Alline's revivals as a "retreat from the grim realities of the world...an escape from fear and divided loyalties." This is a theme we are going to see again in the next chapter because the harshness and isolation many of these colonists experienced was alleviated most effectively by travelling preachers like Alline. He gave, in Armstrong's words: "self-respect and satisfaction to people whose economic and political position was both humiliating and distressing"[2] as well as an alternative theological paradigm to Edwards' and Whitefield's America. Alline's legacy was that he brought revivalism without the addition of Republicanism. He ensured that Colonial American theology in Atlantic Canada remained faithfully wed to the first part of that title, and only flirted a little with the second part.

And that is how the Apostle of Nova Scotia received his second nickname: the first Nova Scotian. It was in Alline's ability to somewhat ignore or re-invent the New England traditions (like Calvinism) in which he was raised that made him able to create theology that suited his Nova Scotia home. It had similar language, it had similar enthusiasm, it had similar disregard for existing religious institutions (more on that later in this chapter), but it did not follow familiar New England teachings.

---

2 M. W. Armstrong, "Neutrality and Religion in Revolutionary Nova Scotia," *New England Quarterly* (Mar. 1946), 50-61.

This gave it an almost innovative appeal to these early colonists. The so-called Nova Scotia Yankees "turned to a religious rather than a political figure in their search for guidance on the many distressing problems produced by the war...Religious values that were specifically 'Nova Scotian' in character were beginning to emerge."[3]

Such intellectual trends were completely ignored in the rest of the world but that also provides an important element of Alline's influence. Henry was just as comfortable eschewing British ideas as he was the ideas of New England. Although we don't know much about rural Nova Scotia during this time, the lack of international attention made it quite easy for Henry and his New Light followers (as they came to be known) to jettison any Old World thinking that they didn't care to appropriate. Nova Scotia's Great Awakening looked like Edwards' Great Awakenings but contained within it teachings that rejected rebellious American sentiments and created a dominant religious climate just British enough to stay neutral.

If Canadian culture is a blending, and rejecting, of European and American ideologies into something that is a mix of both and neither than 18th century Nova Scotia might be the birth of Canada. And if Henry Alline is largely responsible for popularizing such sentiments then he might be more than the First Nova Scotian, he might be the first ever Canadian.

That's right, the first Canadian was born in America.

ISSUES WITH CANADIAN REVIVALISM

I want to introduce you to another person who will help us segue into a discussion on the nature and definition of power. The term would come to mean very different things depending on location. The United States and Canada have historically different interpretations of power due, in large part, to the historic journeys of these two similar but separate

---

3   Stewart, Gordon & Rawlyk, George. *A People Highly Favoured of God: The Nova Scotia Yankees and the American Revolution.* (Toronto: University of Toronto, 1972), 79-80.

nations. Often Canadian Christians fail to take such differences into account and among such oversights is the desire of some Canadian Christians for revival.

Revivalism in Canada has always been a beast of a different stripe when compared to America. For those who think that evangelical-style revivals might jump start the present-day Canadian Church I offer the following as the first of a few cautionary tales you will encounter in this book.

In May, the year before Alline died, an Irish Anglican living in New York was told of a clerical position opening in Nova Scotia. In August of 1787 the Bishopric of Nova Scotia, New Brunswick (a separate political identity from Nova Scotia since 1784), Prince Edward Island, Newfoundland, and Quebec was given to Charles Inglis. The 53-year-old would occupy this seat for the remaining 29 years of his life. Beginning in 1758, Inglis had served in Delaware and then New York until his loyalty to the Crown made his presence in the newly formed United States impossible.

During the war, Inglis lost an estimated $84,000 worth of property (that's in *18th century dollars*), one of his churches was burned by rebels, and he had been made a widower twice (his wives died of natural causes, can't blame the revolution for that). He left it all behind and preached his inaugural sermon at St. Paul's Halifax on October 28, 1787. Inglis began his bishopric in a land that was technically loyal but looked, from his vantage point at least, entirely too American. The man's personal experiences with the Revolution didn't equip him to handle Nova Scotian revivalism with much charity.

Although evangelical, the Baptists destined to hold such sway over Nova Scotia were also counted among Alline's detractors. Even though Alline and his New Lights are largely credited with bringing Baptist Churches to prominence, the man's theology was anything but Baptist. He didn't care about people's thoughts on child Baptism and believed all such arguments to be carnal and not spiritual. His already mentioned anti-Calvinism also did not enamour him to the Baptists. While his New Light communities and much of his evangelical style remained, his teachings and influence began to recede shortly after his death. The Baptists provide examples of those who were both evangelical and pro-revival, but still anti-Alline.

Inglis is an example of someone who was staunchly anti-revivalist and opposed to evangelicalism; and there were plenty more like him as you'll see. I bring this up because the New Lights and Alline would eventually be overshadowed by the Baptists in Atlantic Canada. It would take the research of later historians, working years after his death, to reclaim Alline as the father of Atlantic evangelical Christianity. The stories of Alline, the Baptists, and Inglis help explain Canada's more complex attitude towards revivalism.

While Canada has enjoyed revivals throughout its short history, Canadian revivalism as a mobilizing and unifying force simply doesn't have legs. True, there have been explosions of revivalism periodically in the nation's brief history (as we'll see) but the only denominations able to create longevity from such events are the ones who turned passion and excitement into order and organization. Alline created an experience of the heart and it won the day for a while, but it was the Baptists' ability to create an organization of the head that made them the victors in the end.

Historic figures like Bishop Charles Inglis also explain why Canada is a land in which revivalisms are measured much more modestly than some might think. The head of Nova Scotia's established church (the Church of England was established by the British government to be the only official church recognized in the land) failed to see Alline or his New Lights as anything other than "enthusiastics" who seemed too American in their manners. Such people and their practices constituted a threat to both the established English church in the colony and the colony's loyalty to the Crown. While Inglis remained oppositional to these travelling revivalists for the duration of his career, it should be noted that his rancor did not trickle down to the colonists in the pews.

This unique tension between official power and actual power must remain in your mind. Since inception, Canada has been a child of Empires (French and then English) and Empires are nothing if not organized. Governors always sought precision and yet the governed were comfortable evading official rules they deemed ill-fitting. Despite having the massive resources of the Empire at their disposal, officials like Inglis often found the implementation of their desires infuriatingly ignored. These early Canadians were able to side-step undesirable Imperial wishes without ever stepping into—or even admiring—the revolutionary spirit of America. Early Canadians founded a land that genuinely respected institutions of the Old World while still enjoying some exciting New World innovations. Balancing such tensions created a new nation even as it created some new problems as well.

From the Protestant Christian perspective, this tension created one of the many identity issues that plague Canadian Christianity to this day. Canadian evangelicals looked too conservative to American innovators but they also looked too enthusiastic for the tastes of the Imperial guard who actually had power in Canada. This strange balance is unique to Canada and strengthens the argument that sudden and dramatic outpourings of the Spirit have limited effect here. Controversial (or heretical) as that may sound, let me place this statement in a historical context to further explain what I mean and why this is so important to the Canadian dynamics of power.

PROTESTANTISM COMES TO CANADA

The French were the first substantive European presence in Northern America and they entered into numerous arrangements with the Indigenous people already living here. Despite the awareness of the evils of colonialism present today, the missionaries and merchants that built Nouveau France simply lacked the ability to force conformity onto the original inhabitants. I am not arguing that oppression didn't occur, but that is a more 19th century issue due to the material advancement this nation experienced during that time. The Jesuits desired conversion but also took the time to learn about the cultures, languages, and rituals of the people they were evangelizing. In the cases of Fathers Jean De Brebouf and Gabriele L'Alemant, some even died horrible deaths alongside the people whom they had grown to love.

Some of the Indigenous people early missionaries encountered accepted Christ as a new God, while others simply added the carpenter of Nazareth to an existing pantheon. Still others rejected Christianity outright, as a tool of a foreign invader. Those who accepted Catholic teachings tended to do better financially and became skilled with European technology and conversant in European language and culture. Those who remained more suspicious and remote lived in much the same fashion as before. The French government had uses for all of them and saw little point in aggravating such relations unless they threatened economic gains, which they rarely did. Forts were constructed and the timber and fur trades brought unbelievable wealth both to France and to the rugged lands such trees and animals called home. The relationship was so mutually beneficial that it came to the attention of the British. The British used their massive Atlantic naval presence and expelled a tremendous amount of energy to overthrow French claims.

After a long and complex struggle, the final battle between the English and the French was settled within earshot of Quebec City. In a battle on the Plains of Abraham that took less time to complete than the length of an average sitcom episode, the British finally took Quebec and the St. Lawrence from the French. They also recognized that Nova Scotia was the gate to this new land of opportunity, and the British were not going to allow potentially traitorous French Catholics to occupy such valuable real estate.

Henry's family moved north because, from 1755-1764, the British government was kicking French Catholic inhabitants out of Nova Scotia. The Expulsion of the Acadians (as this came to be known) freed up large tracts of land for loyal, English-speaking, Protestant colonists. Many Acadians died while others headed south to French lands in Louisiana (these Acadians, would become the "Cajun" population that remains to this day). While the Great Upheaval (another name it was given) in Nova Scotia was brutal, it also serves to highlight the strange clemency Britain displayed in other parts of the colony.

CANADA'S INTERESTING RELATIONSHIP WITH POWER

The origin story of Canada took place in the age of Empires, of which the British Empire was one among many. However, new ideas were gaining traction and Canada, as a newer version of a nation, was more amenable to the novelty of modern era diplomacy. While people groups have always conquered other people groups, the modern age was the first to genuinely view peaceful cohabitation between differing groups as a possibility.

Obviously, the ongoing wars of the modern period reveal the failure of people to genuinely treat peace as a virtue but that is not the point. Philosophers, political theorists, satirists, and authors had provided language and critiques for the unchecked love of violence they argued was normative of former, and less civilized, ages. Such teachings, along with the practical obstacles of the land itself, explain what is unique about Canada: the conquerors didn't force the conquered to become like them.

The Articles of Capitulation from 1759 and the subsequent Treaty of Paris in 1763 made it law that the inhabitants of Quebec (which encompassed both present day Quebec, south-western Ontario, and significant amounts of Michigan and Ohio) could maintain their property, language, and even their Catholic religion (Acadians of Nova Scotia and some others excepted) as long as they sent their wares to the British.

This chapter begins in 1760 because that decade saw massive change as well as solid continuity. 1760 was the first decade of British rule but it also was the 16th consecutive decade of French inhabitation. In such upheaval and stability, we see a microcosm of all the other shifts and changes we are going to explore in this book. Historically, even the most potentially cataclysmic changes tend to bring with them a sense of the old and familiar which has made them more palatable.

This land was handled with kid gloves when it first came over to British hands. By 1760 French Catholics had been transformed, with the swipe of a pen, into subjects of the British Protestant Crown. However, they also had rights that protected all that was important to them and that was very reassuring. With the exception of the Acadians, the power and might of Britain did not translate into tyranny and that had a lasting and beneficial effect on the people.

What Henry Alline was able to do for American-born, non-revolutionaries in the Maritimes, the Catholic priests were able to do for their French adherents farther up the St. Lawrence. Imperial policies toward British North America struck a balance that gave people freedom and autonomy as long as the colony remained profitable.

British North America came into being in an age of empires but also in an age of revolutions. America's success inspired the peasantry of France to revolt against their clergy and nobility. Since the Catholic Church was decimated in the French Revolution, French Canadian clergy would remain forever suspicious of revolutionary America. These priests and leaders literally thanked God for a British Empire that protected their faith through the rule of English law. The British were so good to the French that many historians have wondered why similar attitudes were not adopted for the English of the 13 colonies. Arguably, that would have prevented the Revolution from ever happening in the first place.

Thanks to British policies, Catholicism would remain the dominant form of Christianity in Canada. The unintended consequences of such policies also gave rise to the most violent, divisive, and formative threat in the Canadian story. I am going to leave that ominous statement hanging for now, but rest assured we will unpack that more later in this chapter.

No Canadian Protestant church has ever been as large or

as influential as the Catholic Church and that is something many Canadians tend to overlook. It also offers another explanation why revivalism has always been more of an American event than a Canadian one. Revivalism in the past few hundred years comes out of Protestant movements that made few inroads into Catholicism.

The origin story of America is one of adventure and thumbing noses at the powers that be and revival fits beautifully within that narrative. The more successful America became, the more influence its ideas garnered around the globe. The American story was quickly romanticized throughout Europe (even in England itself) and it became an admired nation where anyone could become anything; the notable and strange exception is that its closest neighbour and friend retained a much more nuanced perspective.

As the New World of America literally broke free from the Old World, the land that would become Canada forged another path, one that maintained Old World connections while building relationships with the New. America's audacious rejection of Empire necessitated its governmental inventiveness but that is not part of the Canadian story. Early Canadians chose a path more interested in peace and stability than innovation and political upheavals. John Quincy Adams, Alexis de Tocqueville, and the like had less pull over cities like Quebec, Montreal, or Halifax than they did in capitals like London, Paris, or Washington. These orators and champions of modern democracy meant even less in the lands of the Huron, Iroquois, and Hudson Bay fur trappers. That is not to say that early Canadians were ignorant of American philosophers and statesmen, but it is to say that cheap rent, low taxes, and fertile land proved more compelling than political philosophies.

Power dynamics across the globe were shifting as well in cataclysmic ways. The collection of Old World empires was collapsing into New World revolutionary and democratic states. These proto-Canadians were attempting to find their way in such messy and exciting times and they were attempting to do so as a collection of loyal(ish) Roman Catholics, Revivalist New Lights, Calvinist Baptists, fragmented Presbyterians, and overwhelmed Anglicans. But this chapter is not about rivalry (that's coming next); this chapter is about power. In order to continue our understanding of early Canadian culture we have to introduce the United Empire Loyalists and discover the most important and painful element of Canada as it pertains to power.

Canada, my gentle reader, is a nation of losers.

A NATION OF LOSERS

Now, if you are Canadian, I am sure that doesn't feel too good to read (I didn't enjoy writing it) but allow me some time to defend my position. In order to make my point, I need you to perform a simple action. Please put this book down, stand up, turn 180 degrees, and then take several steps away from the place you are currently residing (if you are in public you are excused from this exercise for obvious social reasons). Once you have completed that action, return to the book and continue reading.

Done? Good, you have now physically enacted the birth of English-speaking Upper Canada.

Upper Canada is a story of people who had to turn their back and walk away from all that they had known and begin again in a new land. This is not the story of the neutral New Englanders of Nova Scotia nor the faithful French Catholics of Quebec, this is the saga of the United Empire Loyalists (UEL) of what would come to be known as Ontario. This is as close as English Canada gets to a dramatic origin story (the 16th century French have a good one but we've already covered how that turned out). While the British had a strong Anglophone presence in Atlantic Canada, the province we call Ontario was destined to have even greater influence over the course of this nation. That is why we must look to the UEL to complete our picture of Canadian power dynamics.

It is a complex relationship because of the inhabitants' experience with loss. From the various First Nations people, to the French on the Plains of Abraham, to the Acadians allowed to remain in Nova Scotia, to the intake of British Loyalists in the wake of the Revolutionary War, Canada was predominantly filled with those who know what it means to lose. For all the rhetoric of British Imperial superiority, the lived experiences of those who called British North America home was one of defeat and humiliation, and that impacted the goals these people set for themselves.

By way of illustration I offer you this coin created a few decades after the period we are currently exploring (see image). This is the coin of the Loyal and Patriotic Society of Upper Canada. It was minted during the War of 1812 as a token of patriotism for those who had served in the war. Money was collected for the families of soldiers who had been killed or wounded and Anglican Rev. John Strachan (a character we'll meet in the next chapter) was one of the architects of this noble social outreach. These were given to soldiers and civilians alike who had served meritoriously on the field of battle or in their care for fellow Upper Canadians. I want you to note the imagery on the coin. The script is "Upper Canada Preserved" indicating the thwarting of America's ambitions during the 1812 war (the other side features a garland of leaves like those given to ancient Greek athletes and states: "For Merit. Presented by a Grateful Country"). A body of water bisects the coin and while there is some debate amongst Canadian scholars as to which body of water this represents, the point is that the water indicates the border between America and Upper

Picture of the Loyal and Patriotic Society of Upper Canada Medal. Images from fortyork.ca

Canada. On the American side is the Eagle, wings open and

clearly ready to pounce. On our side is an industrious beaver, minding its own business and literally too engrossed in the work of chewing a tree to be aware of the imminent danger. Thankfully for our hapless woodland creature, the great Lion of England sits nearby ever vigilant and on guard. Were it not for the Lion, clearly the beaver would be carried away by the aggressive bird of prey. This coin shows the condemnation of American aggression, the celebration of Upper Canadian industry, and the protection of England. More to the point, this is Upper Canadians at their most patriotic; self-identifying as a defenseless (though hard-working) animal clearly at the mercy of America were it not for the British. Once again, this was on a coin specifically minted for, and dedicated to, patriotism. That is what I mean by humbler goals.

In the years immediately following the Revolution, those who had remained loyal to the British Crown found their homes in the newly birthed republic less than inviting. The War of Independence (and the later 1812 conflict as well) was more of a civil war than an international one. I bring that up because civil strife produces a different psychological impact. A civil war feels differently because it isn't an invasion from beyond, it is a betrayal from within.

Imagine with me for a moment: you and I are neighbours but are on opposite sides of a volatile ideological issue that has turned into war. If I snitched on you to the government and cost you land, money, freedom, or even the lives of some of your loved ones, you will likely retain some hostility towards me. If your side won the war and my side lost, ivt would also be likely that you would use your newfound success to exact revenge on me. I am not saying that you would do that, gentle reader, I am just saying that is exactly what happened to thousands of Loyalists who, in the late 1700s, found themselves on the losing side of a revolution.

These Loyalists, like you did a moment ago, turned their backs on home and walked north to the remaining British lands of Quebec, hoping to find a better life within the Empire they had sacrificed to defend. Although the records are spotty and the numbers are debatable, a conservative estimate is that around 14,000 Loyalists left the former colonies, forcing the British Government to split the French Catholic Quebec into two parts: Upper and Lower Canada. The former would house the English-Speaking, largely Protestant refugees from the States, while the latter would retain a French-Speaking Catholic heritage. This is the start of Ontario and it was peopled with losers from the Revolution just as Quebec was peopled with the French losers from the Plains of Abraham.

So potent is this memory that numerous Canadian cities have statues of the UEL in their downtown cores and numerous churches possess UEL graveyards to commemorate the lives of those who helped create Canada. While Americans enjoy the

Photo taken by Author at Dundurn Castle, Hamilton.

patriotic artwork of George Washington crossing the Delaware to begin the war against the tyrant King George, Canada has artistic representations of beleaguered and exhausted families dragging their meager possessions northward looking anything but dignified or victorious. A true juxtaposition between the two nations if ever there was one.

EARLY BLACK CANADIANS

Included within those UEL was another group all too familiar with the losing side of history: Black freed slaves who desired to flee from America. The numbers and experiences of the Black UEL of Niagara were largely the same. Thanks to the records of St. Mark's Anglican Church in Niagara, we are able to ascertain the names and many of the experiences of the Black UEL who settled on the peninsula.

One such story comes form the 1790s about a free man given the name of Peter Martin. Peter was born into slavery but was stolen from his owner and sold again. He escaped and returned to his original owner, Colonel John Butler of the famous Butler's Rangers. But here is where the tale gets interesting. Under British law, any slave who escaped and sought sanctuary under the Crown, had to be set free. Therefore, Peter was set free but his children had never been stolen so the law didn't extend to them. According to St. Mark's baptism registry from 6 January 1793, Peter's daughter Jane, was baptized and she was listed as "daughter of Martin, Col. Butler's Negro."

The British abolished slavery thanks to the evangelical beliefs of William Wilberforce, a fact that was utilized by numerous colonial Anglican churches throughout the 19th century denominational rivalries to show moral superiority over America. For now, the UEL and the Black UEL provide more examples of those who had lost so much and were attempting to re-build in another land. Sadly, despite the arguments of Anglican clergy, such shared experiences of loss were unable to breed equality between Black and white UEL. Skin colour kept many Black UEL from benefitting in the same ways as their white fellow Loyalists.

Charles Inglis was among the 30,000 UEL who landed in Atlantic Canada rather than Upper Canada. Their arrival cemented the neutrality of Alline's period into a loyalty that had been purchased on the battlefield. The Atlantic UEL, like their Upper Canadian counterparts, had suffered to remain British. Thanks to them, the Maritimes would remain a naval stronghold for the British Empire on the North American continent.

As many as 10% of those who fled to Atlantic Canada were Black as well. The Black UEL helped clear land and build Shelburne as well as starting Birchtown (named in honour of General Samuel Birch of New York, who had issued the certificates allowing them to emigrate). The climate and geography didn't allow for the plantation style of the southern United States and those UEL who had "servants for life" (their polite way of saying slave) often sent their slaves into other warmer climates. While technically free, the treatment of these Loyalists was also anything but equal. As time went by, many built successful lives in Atlantic Canada and men like Inglis baptized many of the Black loyalists and welcomed them into the Anglican fold. However, most were unable to pay the pew fees of the more exclusive churches and so became adherents of the New Light, Baptist, and Methodist churches that were growing throughout the colony, much to the annoyance of Inglis.

Quickly, the social structures of British colonial life ensured that only the wealthiest of Black loyalists could even entertain the notion of entering into white circles of influence. For the vast majority the new life in the old colony created numerous obstacles. Many had issued petitions requesting land and permanent settlement but were coming up against what can only be called institutional racism. However, evangelical philanthropists remained committed to development and the colony's connection to the Empire opened up opportunities not available in America. In 1808, the British Empire established a nation of freed slaves designed to be self-governing. The British government did this, in part, to thank Black subjects who had fought for the Crown in the Revolutionary War. Thus was the nation of Sierra Leone created and the Black UEL of Atlantic Canada were among those invited to apply for relocation there. Colonial authorities, overestimating the freedom the Black UEL felt, estimated 100 colonists might be interested; 1200—nearly half of the Black UEL population—applied.

Those who remained in Atlantic Canada found ways to

build new lives along with, and apart from, their fellow colonists. When Baptist preacher David George brought his message of equality, he did not find a warm welcome within the white community of Shelburne. Concerns grew that such teaching might encourage the servants to jettison their feelings of inferiority and so he was banished to the woods outside of town. George was a freed slave and focused most of his preaching on the motif of freedom that took Alline's similar thinking to an even more personal conclusion. Eventually, he was gifted ¼ acre of land and began his own church in Shelburne that was popular across racial divides. However, when he baptized a white couple, the woman's family became incensed and the remainder of his days George would face obstacles due solely to his skin colour.

In Birchtown, a maimed former slave who went by the name of Moses Wilkinson led a Methodist community and inspired at least 2 Black circuit riders. Anglicans of Brindley Town could claim Joseph Leonard as their preacher. Ultimately, the evangelical and somewhat anti-institutional land created by Alline allowed space for Black loyalists to create their own churches, independent of interference from their white fellow colonists. In the words of Dorrie Phillips, these churches were "the one place they felt autonomous, where they could express their depth of feeling and their hope of salvation. It alone was pure and holy and offered a refuge."[4]

EARLY CANADIAN CHRISTIANITY

The stories of the Black UEL are important and illuminate two important factors for Canadian Christianity. The first is to dispel the myth that Canada was always more progressive in matters of race than America. In one sense that is true as the British Empire outlawed slavery much earlier than the States. In a more accurate sense, the small collection of stories above also demonstrate the substantial obstacles Black people had to—and have to—contend with in Canada.

---

4 Dorrie Phillips, "Early Years of the Black Loyalists." *Loyalists in Nova Scotia*. (Hantsport: Lancelot Press, 1983), 76.

The other reason returns us to my earlier ominous comment about the violent internal conflict within the Canadian story. While there have always been tensions between Black and White Canadians, such tensions have not been as formative to Canada as they have been in America. The more dominant conflict in Canada has always been the English/French divide. The treaties of the 1760s guaranteed French Catholics inherent rights in the British system, but the arrival of the UEL to Quebec throughout the 1780s and beyond put such rights to the test.

The thousands of UEL streaming into Quebec believed the British government owed them compensation and resources for the losses they had experienced due to their loyalty. Chief among such concerns were materials for rebuilding homes, lives, farms, and churches.

Tales of woe and hardship at the hands of Revolutionaries are woven throughout the UEL narrative and some of the most condemning have to do with the treatment of clergy and churches. The Anglican Rev. John Stuart's church was plundered and "turned into a tavern...in ridicule and contempt, a barrel of rum was placed in the reading desk."[5]

History would name Stuart the "Father of the Upper Canada Church" but that only came to be so because of his experience of profound loss. Stuart's journey into Canadian Christian history began when his family, including three small children, eventually found America so unpleasant that they made their way north to Quebec. It took them three weeks but, once they arrived, Stuart also found securing a job problematic. He noted there were only three Anglican parishes present and those that were there had "Pastors...which are Frenchmen." He would take various jobs in order to make ends meet before heading west to a newly forming Loyalist garrison in Cataraqui (near Kingston, ON) in August of 1785. He would provide numerous records of the state of religion throughout the territory in those early days.

---

5 The quotes in this section are all found from sources in William Canniff, *The Settlement of Upper Canada*, (Belleville: Milka Screening, 1971), 260-5.

Pleasantly he would note that the Mohawk Village on the Grand Bend River possessed "700 souls...with an elegant church in the centre; it has a handsome steeple and bell, and is well finished within." More common were his comments about the scarcity of both religion and civilization among the various Mohawks he encountered as well as some UEL settlements. His is only one among numerous stories of Protestant clergy overcoming hardships to make it to British territory and begin the arduous task of re-building churches and communities.

Anglicans, Presbyterians, Baptists, Lutherans, Methodists, Quakers, and a collection of other smaller sects arrived; names like Ogilvie, Stuart, Addison, Langhorn, Wyner, Turner, Holts, Wiem, Schwerderger, Myers, Weant, McDowell, McDonell, Smart, Noxen, Leavens, Hicks, Sand, Lossee, Tuffey, Heck, and Bowman entered into the rolls of newly forming Canadians. I could go on and on about the various UEL names and the places that they founded and part of me wants to do that. However, the more pragmatic part of me recognizes that lists don't make for good reading (I mean, I can't think of too many people who love reading the Book of Numbers) so I will wrap this up by focusing on some of the themes of these various Protestants.

At the risk of over-simplifying the diversity to be found within Protestantism, there are a few themes that can be detected in most of them. First is a desire to be removed from French oversight. Frequently throughout the words of these people is the rejection of a Romish (their word for Catholic) and French government and the demand for a British system of representation.

Next, is the centrality of finding land and structures for the preferred style of worship. The Baptists of Thurlow were jubilant when their small house of worship was finally completed. The chapel completion was a point of pride because it "was mainly built by each member going to the place and working at the building, from time to time." Others, like the Quakers, had less need for formal structures, who preferred being "far removed from the busy haunts of men," and took more time to construct their first Meeting House. In each group, whatever their respective attitudes to sacred space, was a desire to build a community of faith after their own consciences (this is something that we will see again in a future chapter).

However, the most important theme was interpreting the losses each new citizen of Upper Canada had faced. For Anglicans and Presbyterians, loss was framed within the biblical narrative of Israel in which only a small remnant of the faithful were called to rebuild God's chosen nation. They, along with Baptists and the Methodists, pointed to the life of Jesus and reminded their adherents that his "loss" on the cross was actually the moment of salvation. These UEL Protestant clergy preached that the people were not abandoned by God. Rather, they were tasked with a new and holy endeavour by God. The treatment many of the people in the pews had endured at the hands of their former brothers proved that the new United States was a violent, disrespectful, and debauched place. The struggles of their new homeland were to be greeted with thanksgiving and praise because each person hearing such sermons was chosen of the Lord. Despite the losses these Christians had faced, they were asked "if God is for us, who can possibly be against us?"

Such theology reframed loss as a spiritual blessing to be sought after, not avoided, by the faithful. The UEL had received God's blessing, not His wrath; they hadn't been beaten, they had been spared. They had been emancipated from their own hostile Egyptian homeland—a land that abused them for their fidelity. They had been guided through the wilderness (literally) and replanted in the new Canaan. John Stuart is once again useful as he wrote the following to a friend: "How mysterious are the ways of Providence! How short-sighted we are! Some years ago I thought it a great hardship to be banished into the wilderness, and would have imagined myself completely happy, could I have exchanged it for a place in the City of Philadelphia—now the best wish we can form for our dearest friends is to have them removed to us." That, gentle reader, is the power of loser theology.

While America saw their victory over the British as evidence of God's blessing, UEL theology argued the exact opposite. They saw in the formation of the United States just another example of human guile the Bible time and again condemned as fool-hardy and antithetical to the Gospel. The UEL believed their land was a purer land, free from the violence that birthed America. They gave thanks to Providence and laughed at their own inability to see what was right in front of them. They transformed the countless and terrible deprivations, travels, assaults, deaths, fear, and losses they endured into a faith that condemned triumphalism as a false god.

Early Canadian Christians—Catholic and Protestant—were losers, and from that they built an identity that took pride in an industrious faith. A faith that, much like their carpenter Messiah, valued working hard with one's hands. A faith that, like St. Paul, saw beatings, imprisonments, torture, and rejection as indicators of true faith. A faith that was more peaceful, more God-honouring, and closer to the heart of Jesus. A faith that winners like poor America were unable to participate in. Over time, these early UEL ministers and leaders transformed the Revolutionary War into the moment of America's spiritual undoing. They transformed the collections of struggling losers in their folds into the recipients of God's richest blessings. A uniquely Canadian theology was beginning to form and at its heart was a belief in the sacredness of being a loser.

That could be a solid ending to this section, but I don't want to overstate the benevolence in such thinking or argue that Canadian faith was actually more peaceful. Within these teachings lay problematic and violent themes as well. Like the Israelites of old, there was much work for the UEL Protestants to do on behalf of the Kingdom. Like the Promised Land of Moses' time, their new home was also populated by ungodly giants: French Catholics. And like the days of Joshua, many Protestants saw removing these French Catholics as the only way to purify the land for God. This birthed the French and English antagonism that has been a defining trait of Canada and

Canadian Christianity and has caused so much damage to the nation and to countless churches therein.

TO COPE OR TO CONQUER?

Canadian-born historian and Duke Divinity professor Kate Bowler has an amusing way to demonstrate the differences between her homeland and the American nation she now calls home. On her Twitter account she posted the following:

> *One fun example of why Americans privilege a wildly confident and individualistic story about themselves comes from the difference between the American and Canadian constitution.*
>
> *American: life, liberty, pursuit of happiness*
> *Canadian: peace, order and good governance*
>
> *There's a lovely example in a lecture by Robert Fulford about how Americans assume everything must be CONQUERED and not, say, coped with. He writes about a Canadian book by Judylaine Fine called 'Your Guide to Coping with Back Pain.'*
> *When the same book was acquired by an American publisher, it was re-titled 'Conquering Back Pain.' So Robert Fulford concludes:*
>
>> *'[T]here, in a grain of sand, to borrow from William Blake, we can see a world of differing attitudes. Our language reveals how we think, and what we are capable of thinking. Canadians cope. Americans conquer. Canadian readers of that book will assume that back pain will always be with them. Americans will assume that it can be destroyed, annihilated, abolished, conquered. Americans expect life, liberty, happiness, and total freedom from back pain. Canadians can only imagine peace, order, good government, and moderate back pain.'*
>
> *When things get really hard, we must calibrate our expectations to our reality.*[6]

---

6 KatecBowler Twitter account. Post from 9/28/20.

I once saw a sign that read "One day, Canada will take over the world, then you'll all be sorry" and, while meant as a joke, that somewhat gets to my point. We are known for, and take some pride in, an apologetic culture. While Canadians might not be suspicious of control or even dominance, there is an inherent issue with triumphalism. Unlike our neighbours to the south, Canadians do not have a dominant national creation myth and that reality has, in Dr. Bowler's words, calibrated our expectations.

We have no revolution, we have neutrality.

We have no founding fathers; we have loyal losers.

Even though there have always been more Catholics, Protestants have the administrative advantage.

This is a land that seems incapable of overt acts of power. Yet Canadians are also enculturated in American ideologies and definitions of power in very pervasive ways. This is a problem when we cross-pollinate our definitions of success with America's or even Britain's. If we conflate our stories, theologies, and culture with these more obviously victorious nations without seeing inherent differences, we set ourselves up for failure. We don't have the same stories, so we can't have the same definitions either.

This chapter on power has sought to show the origins of Canada as a creation of the modern nation state in relation to the Atlantic triangle of influence. Compared to America and Britain, Canada was the weakest of the three. It had the least amount of people, it was the least developed, its influence was largely as passive recipient rather than proactive agent.

It still had little to call its own in the way of unique culture or thought. However, as I hope you have been seeing, the seeds of the unique expressions of Canadian religious culture were there even if they had yet to bloom. In the next chapter, we will focus more on the internal character of Canada and pay less attention to its relation to the other nations in the triangle. However, as you will come to see, the triangle would never really leave this land that has always retained a connection to both the old and new worlds.

This is a nation built by British and American immigrants, innumerable and unique Indigenous people, French Catholics and English Protestants, Black and White UEL losers. Such a collective possessed humbler and simpler goals because that was all that was available in those early days. If they were quiet, the authorities pretty much left them alone to build a new life in their rugged and isolated world. Many of these people found life better when they simply put their head down and got to work. Since all had experienced humiliating loss, they found comfort in a belief that such loss was integral to a deep and abiding faith.

It would not be until the land began to industrialize that such mentalities would change. What did remain even during those later changes was a detectable attitude of suspicion regarding power. Such sentiments were not necessarily held by those in power, but even they had to contend with the accepted critiques of their fellow Canadians. Even the powerful in Canada acknowledged the suspicions around power and success because, in many ways, it was too triumphalist, and too American. Thus, a Canadian may not know what he or she is but historical precedent dictates that he or she not be American. This is not a land that embraces the conqueror's heart, this is a land that applauds the virtue to be found in coping.

RESOURCES

Nancy Christie. *Transatlantic Subjects: Ideas, Institutions, and Social Experience in Post-Revolutionary British North America.* McGill-Queen's University Press: Montreal and Kingston, 2008.
- A sweeping book that covers the transatlantic nature of early Canadian culture. Christie also introduces the idea that Canadian independence is not a slower moving form of American revolutionary spirit. That is a theme that will be covered in greater depth in the next chapter of this book.

John Ralston Saul. *A Fair Country: Telling Truths About Canada.* Toronto: Penguin, 2008.
- Among the many contributions of this book, Saul argues that Canadian culture came from blending the policies of other nations with the Indigenous influences of this land.

Gordon Stewart & George Rawlyk. A *People Highly Favoured of God: The Nova Scotia Yankees and the American Revolution.* Toronto: University of Toronto, 1972.
- An insightful collection of writings that argue for the importance of religion in forming early political attitudes in Nova Scotia.

Malcom Gladwell. *David and Goliath: Underdogs, Misfits, and the Art of Battling Giants.* New York: Little, Brown & Co., 2013.
- Gladwell's book creatively elaborates on themes, not necessarily the history, of the loser/underdog mentality touched on in this chapter. This Canadian author captures the surprising good news of being overlooked and not considered in a variety of ways. He doesn't cover Canadian history per se but the title of the book should let you know that the famous biblical

story features large in his thesis. It is an inspirational series of ideas that should fill Canadians with hope and maybe even a bit of pride at our overlooked status.

David Borys. *Cool Canadian History.* Podcast. Available anywhere you get your podcasts.

- Billed as a "wild, wacky, weird, wonderful and downright dark stories in Canadian history" this podcast is well-produced, well-researched and insightful. It gives the audience many points to ponder and actively combats numerous false myths about Canada. This podcast also covers topics related to the church frequently and, while critical, is also fair in such treatments.

---

1 IDEA

From inception, Canada possessed a nuanced appreciation of power; our narratives of success have been humbler than both the British and American definitions. Anti-authoritarianism in Canada is not just a product of recent culture, but needs to be understood as an ongoing development of historical ideologies before it can be properly addressed.

CHAPTER 2
RIVALRY
1813 -

Me debunk an american myth?
And take my life in my hands?
— "At The Hundredth Meridian,"
The Tragically Hip

INTRODUCTION

I enjoy the Rev. John Strachan (1778-1867) for the same reason I like any polarizing figure I get to study: because I don't live when he lived. Strachan is arguably the largest religious personality of the pre-Confederation Church of England in Canada. It is not just because he was particularly erudite (which he was) or that he was so influential (which he was) or that he unashamedly placed his nasal protuberance in all sorts of places it didn't really belong (which he did). It isn't even the too-perfect chronological fact that he came to prominence in the War of 1812 (defined incorrectly by many as the start of Canada) and that he died in 1867 (the year of Confederation).

Strachan has given me many chuckles and head-shaking moments with his cruel taunts, perfectly sculpted insults, surprising recommendations, bold lies designed to advance his church, theologically deft sermons, and even surprising humility and compassion; he is a truly complex personality. However, the Upper Canadians who lived during the time of Strachan had a much different experience of the man.

He also provides a bridge to the previous chapter in that the man, influential as he was, also fits into the loser category. This unapologetic Tory lost virtually every battle he engaged in with the Whigs of his day in the areas of education and reform. Those fights were responsible for many of the contentious issues and interdenominational rivalries that dominated 19th-century British North America and form the theme of this chapter.

Strachan perfectly balanced an unapologetic pro-British stance with a rampant and oft-expressed anti-Americanism. Such sentiments may have always been there in some capacity but they came to the forefront of Strachan's rhetoric thanks to the War of 1812. In 1813, Americans had successfully invaded York (present day Toronto) wherein Strachan served as priest of St. James Church.

Soldiers had looted the townspeople, robbed his church, neglected the wounded, and even burnt some buildings in direct defiance of war-time protocols between civilized nations.

Strachan charged that General Dearborn purposefully delayed signing the Orders of Capitulation (a binding legal document that protected those who had surrendered from hostile acts by occupying forces) in due time. Strachan marched into Dearborn's makeshift headquarters and accused the leader of allowing his soldiers just enough time to do maximum damage before signing the documents so that he could claim they respected private property.

Strachan cited biblical law, human decency, and a number of binding legal arguments that were respected in both the United States and Britain regarding war-time behaviour. He concluded his tirade by reminding the leader that Jesus was watching and rhetorically asked what Jesus would think of robbing women and children and neglecting the care of the sick and wounded. The fact that Strachan wasn't thrown in prison at that moment was a minor miracle but, even more incredibly, it appears the invading commander took the clergyman's concerns seriously. Dearborn apologized and curbed such offences for the remainder of the occupation.

Dearborn's actions came too late for Strachan; the gutsy clergyman had already seen the true face of the enemy. The Americans knew how to talk a good game but when push came to shove they revealed themselves to be a treacherous, selfish, and violent race of people bent on their own glory at the expense of their own morality.

These rebels retained only the words, not the character, of the Christian civility they had inherited from their Imperial parents; such Republicans could be given no place in Strachan's beloved British colony. Strachan will return but first we must see how this land was fairing in the years between the American Revolution and the 1812 invasions by those pesky rebels.

Unlike Charles Inglis, Strachan was not a UEL and never lived in the States. Strachan came to the shores of this land from the UK but his lack of personal experience in no way, shape, or form diminished Strachan's profound distaste for any idea or person he deemed too republican in nature. His characterizations and condemnations of what he called "American manners" made him both controversial and uniquely situated to shape a religious setting forever suspicious of the United States.

This is an important detail because a few interesting religious trends were developing between the years 1783-1812. The Revolutionary War created two nations where previously there had only been one. English-speaking Canada was as much a result of the American rebellion as the United States. We discussed the differences between these two lands: one had a story of victory against overwhelming odds and the other was formed by people much more acquainted with the losing side of history. Loosely speaking, the former was able to produce theologies of victory and achievement evidenced by success on the battlefield; the other was forced into humbler beliefs that sanctified struggle.

America was a bold land of intellectual and technical innovation. Their successes inspired other lands to throw off their own traditional structures and chase the democratic dream. On the other side, British North America remained fixated on maintaining ties to the Imperial world. That could be enough to explain the differences between the two lands if that is where the story ended. However, like all real stories, this one proved a lot messier and delivered no satisfying "The End...Fade to black" moment.

Starting a new country is incredibly expensive and some of the victorious American citizenry were either not keen, or not able, to foot the bill. Just a short walk to the north of the United States, these Americans saw another land filled with people building a much more affordable life for themselves. Not only that, these people spoke the same language, had the same religions, and, in some cases, were relations and/or former neighbours.

These Americans began to move north in increasing numbers but, unlike their predecessors, were not driven by their loyalty to the Crown as much as they were by cheap land and much lower taxes. In short, they were opportunists. These incorrectly labelled "Late Loyalists" began to stream into Upper Canada through the last decade of the 18th century and the first decade of the 19th. The arrival of these former republicans was greeted with mixed feelings by the UEL communities. These communities were just beginning to put the hardships of the Revolution behind them and rebuild their lives.

By the spring of 1812, the population of Upper Canada had exploded from the original 14,000 to approximately 91,000 people. Almost all of these newcomers were American-born and raised, and their loyalty to the Crown was suspect at best. Their questionable motivations and the meteoric growth of the American Republic inspired most of the tensions that made up the Canadian religious landscape in the years before Confederation.

In your brief introduction to the man, think about how concerning this statistic would be for Strachan and others who thought like him. As churches fought each other for control of the colony, they impacted everything from education to immigration, industry to policy, politics, culture, and theology.

Strachan's anti-American stance became a matter of public attention in 1825 after the death of the Anglican Bishop in Quebec, Jacob Mountain (1749-1825). Strachan was tasked with the funeral sermon and in it he blamed Mountain's lackluster record on the pervasiveness of both Catholic and Methodist influences. Strachan preached that these rival spiritual claimants undermined the Bishop's best efforts at evangelization and organization.

Catholicism has frequently been viewed as a juggernaut by Protestants and the amount of French Catholics in Quebec only added to that fear. This book will detail the numerous ways in which Catholics and the French were the frequent bane to all Protestant endeavours so, for now, it is more beneficial to talk about Strachan's comments regarding Methodists.

To the Anglicans, Methodists were like comets that brought temporary flashes of spiritual warmth but left the recipients colder when the riders inevitably moved on to the next village or farm. They were accused of being overly emotional, theologically illiterate, uneducated showmen, and deceivers of the most pernicious order. The newly forming loyal nation needed to rid the land of such scourges who were using their religious mannerisms to sow within the colonists' minds seeds of dissension and disloyalty.

If the people of Canada continued to entertain these mendicant travelers, they would be flirting with disaster. Strachan pulled zero punches in the sermon that was printed and distributed throughout the realm. Needless to say, the Methodists who read it were both enraged and concerned. They saw in this sermon both the dismissal of their beliefs, and an attempt to oust them from any public sphere of influence. They were right—that is exactly what Strachan was trying to do.

The Methodists needed a champion to offer a political and theological corrective to the influential Strachan. That man turned out to be the equally controversial Egerton Ryerson (1803-1882). Thanks to that 1825 sermon and the rebuttals of Ryerson that were also printed and disseminated throughout the land, the battle for the soul of the colony had begun.

RIVALRY

In this chapter we are going to look at the various ways in which Protestants and Catholics fought for religious supremacy in the young British colony. The narrative of loss that became popular in the 1780s and 90s had the potential to align each of these different factions into a shared story. I say potentially because, as the 19th century dawned, the theme of loss expanded to make room for the modest success the colony was enjoying. The growth of farms, villages, and even a couple small cities proved that God had not abandoned His loyal colonists. Life was tough and the land was still largely untouched but the ability to survive and grow in such a rugged world became another source of pride. A pride that was pricked when the aforementioned later American immigrants continued to show up and reap the benefits of the UEL's earlier labours. A pride that sowed dissension between denominations.

Missionary efforts had brought substantial amounts of First Nations people into the Christian faith. Notable among such efforts were the Moravians, Anglicans, and Catholics. Thanks to them, even the spectre of the fearful Savage (their words) was being mitigated. Communities like Moraviantown or Grand River, near an established Mohawk Mission, had grown increasingly comfortable and conversant with this nation's first inhabitants. The First Nations proved incredibly helpful to Settlers in the realms of survival and most missionary journals of the time admit relying heavily on Indigenous guides to travel safely throughout the rugged land.

Since the early 1500s, French Catholics had been working among numerous Indigenous communities and many of them were familiar with White Settlers and Christianity. The Metis were an established people in the Western lands at this point and numerous Inuit people had been dealing with Hudson Bay employees and Catholic missionaries for generations. Many areas had large collections of Indigenous Christians that were another source of pride for whichever denomination claimed them (more on that later in the book). Although fears of Indigenous violence remained a perpetual threat for colonists, this was based on rhetoric and imagination that served a variety of agendas but had little bearing in reality. History proves what most readers of the 21st century already know: when it came to violence between First Nations and Settlers, the former were almost always the victims, not the perpetrators.

Despite being a source of pride for denominations like the Anglicans, Indigenous followers were not as valuable to church growth as were the White Settlers. The kinds of rivalries that were destined to shape the land pitted missionary agencies and churches against each other in a race for colonial adherents. Before we look at some of those tensions and rivalries, let's take a quick overview of the various denominations, locations, statistics, and tensions within Canadian Christianity at that time. [1]

Catholic: predominantly focused on the French of Quebec. However, they also had a substantial presence in the Atlantic regions. Scottish highlanders and Irish Catholics were increasing English-speaking Catholicism as well in Upper Canada. Catholic missionaries were also very active in the West (we'll look at that more in the next chapter). Supplied by parishioners and connected to the Vatican, they also received support from England due to their legal status in British North America. Easily the largest and most stable of all churches at that time. By 1901, when Canada's entire population was 4,671,815 Roman Catholics had a membership of 2,229,600; just shy of half of the entire population of the land.

Church of England (Anglican): The Established Church of British North America. This meant they possessed the Clergy Reserves (more on that later) and were supported by taxes and government funds along with their parishioners. This was the church of the elite and influential as well as large collections of First Nations. They had the most money and potential to be the dominant form of Protestantism but were unable to meet the demands of the rural communities due to lack of staff. They also tended to view other denominations as competition. The majority of Protestants in Quebec were Anglican. By the end of this contentious century, they claimed the loyalty of 680,620 inhabitants, placing them third in Canadian Protestantism's "big four".

---

1 The statistics come from 1901 census data. While later than the time period covered in this chapter, I have chosen this year for a few reasons: 1) it defends my closer examination of Protestantism's "big four" of Anglicans, Presbyterians, Baptists, and Methodists because, as you'll see, they were clearly the largest Protestant denominations during the 19th century; 2) the statistics were more reliable by this time. Other statistics will be used in this chapter but I really wanted you to see a comprehensive and reliable collection of data; 3) the multiplicity of religious persuasions and the clear numerical superiority of certain denominations in Canada by 1901 strengthens my argument about rivalries and the problems certain policies created for most Christian denominations.

Presbyterians: As the official Church of Scotland, they also had Establishment status but didn't reap anywhere near the benefits that the Anglicans did. They received supplies from their own missionary agencies and family connections back in Scotland. They were also supplied from America and formed their first presbytery with American help. They fought with the Catholics over the faith of the highlanders, the Anglicans over establishment status, the Methodists over their theology, and each other over most everything else. Their adherents mostly came from smaller territories connected to Scottish regiments from the Revolutionary War and other Scottish immigrant communities throughout the Canadas and Atlantic territories. In the early 19th century, they were just shy of the Anglicans in numbers as it pertained to Lower Canada. By the beginning of the 20th century, they had surpassed the Anglicans and recorded 842,442 active members.

Wesleyan Methodists: Focused mostly in Atlantic regions with some influence in Lower Canada. They were connected to England (hence the name) and fought mostly with other Methodists. Not a large collection but the most acceptable form of evangelicalism as far as the Anglicans and Presbyterians were concerned.

Episcopal (American) Methodists: This was easily the most dominant form of evangelicalism in Upper Canada. They had ceded the Atlantic lands to the Wesleyans in 1799 and focused on the American farmers in the rural parts of Upper and Lower Canada. They were supported by American missionary agencies and were very popular with the rural communities. Such popularity, coupled with their connections to America, made the Established Churches fear them the most.

When the various branches of Methodism combined to form a united denomination (somewhat...a topic we'll explore in this chapter), they were easily the largest collection of Canadian

Protestants, coming in at a whopping 916,886 members.

Baptists: Smallest of the "big four" churches, like the Episcopal Methodists, they were evangelical and were supplied by American agencies and faced similar condemnations. However, since they were not as big in Upper Canada, they didn't receive as much attention. They were very numerous in the Atlantic regions and were well entrenched thanks to events like the Great Awakening. It is worth noting that they were only around 3% of the population in the Canadas but in Atlantic Canada they were consistently north of 25%. By the end of the century they continued to grow but maintained their status as the smallest of the "big four" at 292,189.

Lutherans: Similar to other insular groups, they stayed within their German linguistic spheres and their work ethic, along with their lack of influence over the English-speaking people, made them easy enough to ignore. They were also used to help populate the West (something we'll talk about next chapter). Lutherans were not quite big enough to be in the top four, but they were definitely the biggest of the smaller denominations at 92,524 across Canada.

Quakers, Mennonites, Children of Peace: Very insular and either liked or ignored, for the most part, by the other groups. Since they stuck to their respective communities, had refused to fight in the Revolutionary War (due to their pacifism), and were good farmers, they were granted some leniency. Mennonites were listed at 31,797; Quakers at 4,100.

Moravians: Like the Methodists, they were evangelical and missionary-minded. However, they focused their missionary work on the Indigenous people and built Moraviantown in the Thames Valley. Many left after the town was burned by American soldiers in the War of 1812 but the mission remained to a lesser degree. They were also supplied by American sending agencies but their focus on Indigenous people did not make them a threat. They were not listed by 1901.

Rounding out the other smaller churches were the Congregationalists (a group we're going to look at more a little later) with 28,293; Disciples of Christ at 14,900; Salvation Army at 10,308; and the Hornerites were slowly bringing the Holiness movement to Canada with 2775 members. Very interesting to note was that, by 1901, there were 16,401 registered Jewish Canadians; 15,360 Greek Orthodox; 10,407 Buddhists; 5115 Confucianists; 6891 Mormons; and 47 Muslims (referred to as Mohammedans) in the census.

Most interesting to the topic of secularization are the following groups and their numbers: there were 3613 Agnostics (referred to also as Free Thinkers, Infidels, Sceptics, and Secularists); 4810 listed no religion; 616 Spiritualists; 15,000 Pagans (to be honest, not exactly sure what that means); and 43,222 listed as Unspecified. While individually small, that collection of non-traditional religious adherents comprised 67,261 Canadians; making them the next largest religious group after the Lutherans.

DENOMINATION	SIZE IN 1901
Catholics	2,229,600
Anglicans	680,620
Presbyterians	842,442
Methodists	916,886
Baptists	292,189
Lutherans	92,524
Mennonites	31,797
Quakers	4100
Congregationalists	28,293
Disciples of Christ	14,900
Salvation Army	10,308
Hornerites	2775

DENOMINATION	SIZE IN 1901
Jewish	16,401
Greek Orthodox	15,360
Buddhists	10,407
Confucianists	5115
Mormons	6891
Muslim	47
Agnostics (Free Thinkers, Infidels, Sceptics, and Secularists)	3613
No Religion	**4810**
Pagans	**15,000**
Unspecified	**43,222**
Spiritualists	**616**
Total of this last grouping	**67,261**

While cooperation has always been necessary within Canada due largely to the power and length of winter, rivalry must also be considered when we talk about the internal dynamics of Canadian Christianity. While this is a more internal look than the previous chapter, I don't think it will be hard for even a casual reader to see the ongoing influence of the Atlantic triangle.

In this chapter we are going to look at the following:

1. Problematic geography

2. The Evangelical invasion

3. Canada's ongoing issues with revivalism

4. The fight for education in Canada

5. The growth of loyalty as a defining trait of a true Canadian

6. How the churches handled secularization that had numbers almost as high as today

7. Canada's struggle to create an "other"

8. 19th century secularization

PROBLEMATIC GEOGRAPHY

If you have ever gone camping in the natural parks of this land, then you know the awe-inspiring views that can greet you.

Mountains as high as the heavens, lakes deep and blue and clear, trees that stretch on seemingly forever, fresh air, and bountiful wildlife to admire. However, such wonders can be seen as wonders thanks to electricity, heat, cars, water, groceries, and Wi-Fi (apologies to the campers who view what I just wrote as blasphemy). It is quite another thing to be at the mercy of those wonders, as Susanna Moodie (1803-1885) noted frequently and scathingly in her memoirs of that time.[2] Calling Upper Canada an isolating prison of massive trees, she lamented her uncultivated home for possessing too few safe roads, too many vicious animals and people, and a shocking lack of anything even remotely resembling civilization. In short, Moodie was not exactly a frontrunner for the tourism board of young Canada.

Moodie was not wrong, nor was she the only one to note the sometimes crushing beauty of her new home. The land was simply too large, remote, disconnected, underpopulated, and underfunded to have many established churches. When later American immigrants began arriving they brought with them resources, finances, population growth and, thanks to their industry, cultivation as well. However, they also brought American-style religion with them and ushered in an age of ecclesiastical tensions that had not existed previously.

As already stated Catholic, Anglican, and Presbyterian Churches had expansive missionary programs, but tended to build their churches mostly in cities or on Indigenous land. Attending city churches was not realistic for the vast majority of people who lived in the densely wooded lands far removed from any sort of metropolis (though some did attend various Indigenous chapels).

Strachan in York and Robert Addison (1754-1829) on the Niagara Peninsula were heroic in their efforts to ride far and wide to bring the Gospel to the farmers in their communities. The reality was they did not have enough money or people to

---

2 Susannah Moodie, *Roughing it in the Bush or Forest Life in Canada*, (London: T.N. Foulis), 1913.

adequately remedy the isolation most of these early Canadians felt. The Anglican and Presbyterian approach to church focused on sober, academic, and honest reflection on the logical and moral teachings of the Bible. Their Establishment status gave them a mission to disseminate salvation as well as decent (in other words, European) social values needed to insure God's ongoing blessing.

The church—these denominations argued—was a vital socio-spiritual foundation upon which the structures of civilized society were to be built. The church was responsible for biblical teaching, moral guidance, proper marriages, sacred funerals, and educating the masses on their responsibility to God, each other, and the King. They were ideologically and structurally connected to the Empire they believed was blessed by God, and from the royal coffers they drew substantial monetary blessings. However, that also meant that it took time for supplies, preachers, and money to cross the Atlantic. This reality slowed the ability of these churches to serve the needs of their people in real time.

THE EVANGELICAL INVASION

In contrast, the missionary societies of evangelicals like the Baptists and Methodists were housed much closer in America. While they had less money or political clout, they were able to send riders and supplies with greater frequency and much less paperwork. The ecclesiology of these more evangelical groups was influenced by John Wesley's famous maxim "the whole world is my parish" so they focused less on building churches and more on ministering to people. If you will excuse the pun, these evangelicals brought the mountain to Mohammed.

The tales that come from this time are testimonies to fortitude and faithfulness. Itinerant missionaries from places like the Genesee district in upstate New York travailed all sorts of inhospitable terrain and legitimate dangers to bring Jesus' good news to these isolated farmers. Methodists and Baptists were, to borrow a phrase from our present day, skilled and efficient networkers. They learned where the neglected lived and simply sent missionaries to serve the people in the gaps. Such relational networks were not represented in the elite halls of power during this time. However, these missionaries were instrumental to the formation of communal identities, and that would serve their denominational goals in the generations that followed.

The clergy of the Established Churches, with their black robes, powerful voices, rational arguments, authority to marry, bury, and baptize seemed to possess a power akin to God the Father himself. Naturally, there was reverence and awe but there was also disconnection and distance (both physically and socially).

The Methodists, on the other hand, were more like Jesus with their colloquial language, willingness to live among the people, spiritual enthusiasm, and visible sacrifices to ensure that all people—regardless of status or importance—heard the gospel message. If we hold to a stereotypical—though theologically incorrect—view of God the Father as the bearded judge on the throne and Jesus as the forgiving, self-sacrificing, and loving champion of humanity, then you understand how people held respect for the former and a more affectionate view for the latter. While these examples are specific to Christianity, in such tensions we also see the Canadian penchant for revering Old World austerity while responding to New World ingenuity.

CANADA'S ONGOING ISSUES WITH REVIVALISM

But the real problems began in the picturesque lakeside community of Hay Bay in 1805. Colonial authorities and Anglican clergy grew very concerned when over 2000 of their rural colonists—the same people who made no effort to attend Sunday services—showed up to learn about personal salvation from (gasp) American Methodist missionaries. Such revivals were famously uncouth, filled with emotional outbursts as men and women together (gasp again) became convicted of personal sin and then became ecstatic when they learned of Jesus' sacrificial death on their behalf.

These people would wail and cry and throw themselves on

the ground in spiritual agony; then they would dance and sing and laugh as the burden of damnation was lifted from them. These temporary camp towns would be erected with stages for various preachers and would often last the better part of a week, if not longer. They would feature music, food, and entertainment in an environment more like an outdoor festival, or country fair, than a respectable indoor church service. While spiritually rewarding, it was also a lot of good fun, especially if you spent most of your time chopping wood and trying to grow food in the cold of British North America.

Good fun, that is, unless you were a member of the more British churches who saw such displays as emotional dribble at best and outwardly seditious at worst. The aforementioned Hay Bay Revival of 1805 not only attracted bored farmers and the genuinely pious but also spies who believed American Episcopal Methodist missionaries were couching "Americanism" in religious language. All the emphasis on personal responsibility and the accusations that state religion was more Pharisaical than Christian only further cemented the fear that enthusiasts were a threat to the loyalty of the colony.

While some found it difficult to admit in those early days, others saw the writing on the wall: the republic to the south was growing stronger. As detailed in the previous chapter, the UEL had a complex relationship to power, a relationship exasperated by a fear that the Empire had only a tenuous hold on the colony. Adding to such concerns was the clear fact, evidenced at Hay Bay, that few people in either country cared about the Revolutionary conflict or the border that conflict created.

Even the second Anglo-American War of 1812 did little to dampen warm international relations between the citizenry. Most people at the time had little idea what the war had been about in the first place (Canadian citizens standing up against American forces was a myth of later generations). In fact, American missionaries were eagerly invited back to their former territories (which they called circuits) literally within days of the war's end. The porous nature of the Canadian/American border became a real problem for the churches with stronger connections to Britain. They fought against a growing American influence over colonial society and theology.

While such concerns were obviously coloured by jealousy, the Established Churches had some legitimate grievances that were not totally unfounded. The American focus on individualism, for one example, brought with it the potential to undermine the institutions of the Imperial world. The very institutions the UEL had fought and suffered to defend, and the very institutions that supported the Established Churches. As the memory of the Revolution faded, and as each new American immigrant—a person with no discernible record of Imperial loyalty—entered into the colony, these fears moved closer to becoming an inevitable reality. The Episcopal Methodists were not missionaries; they were seen to be Republican wolves in clerical sheep's clothing.

This second wave of Americans substantially outnumbered the UEL, and their brand of faith could steal the souls of the colonists away from the blessings of God reserved for loyal British subjects. At the exact moment American farmers were writhing in spiritual ecstasy upon the British soil of Upper Canada, the mother country was fighting for her life against Napoleon. The "Petite Emperor" was a devastating and terrifying threat, but he was also an obvious one. A subtler threat was facing the colonists: Methodist teaching, masquerading as Christianity, would seduce loyal colonists and transform them into selfish, vainglorious, and violent republicans.

The secularism of the early 19th century was understood by men like Strachan as a competing worldview that, if followed, would infect the colony and destroy their God-honouring culture. Would the peace, order, and good government that underpinned the blessed British Empire be usurped by these American Methodists' theology of life, liberty, and the pursuit of happiness?

Hay Bay was not the first or the last revival to take place in Canada, but it is an important one because it demonstrates how such revivals were viewed by some influential people. Although Methodism could claim more adherents than Anglicanism, the Church of England had more power. Unable to force change (because that is how power has tended to work here), the Established Churches had to be creative in the safeguards they created to protect the land. One of the most enduring safeguards they set up was in the realm of language.

In this realm, our buddy John Strachan was a master. Using his substantial political clout as a member of the Family Compact—a small collection of powerful politicians and legislators who shaped many of Upper Canada's earliest policies—he helped make the term "loyalty" preeminent in the early 19th century religious lexicon. Like all words, it is not just the word itself that matters but the definition given to the word that grants us insight into the culture of the time. Make no mistake, Strachan and his influential friends sculpted their definition of loyalty intentionally and with such precision that it successfully undermined the Methodists and forced them to make some drastic changes.

If they desired to remain an active force of faith in early Canada, Methodist leaders soon realized they were going to have to align with the more Established definitions of such terms. Quickly they realized that one of the first things that needed to go was the camp-style revival. And that, gentle reader, is one of the first reasons why revivalism has not been the key to church growth in Canada for the past 200 years.

THE FIGHT FOR EDUCATION IN CANADA

To really hammer home this point, I would like to tell you a story of education reform that took place in the House of Commons in Upper Canada in the year 1828. Riveted? Thought so.

While the history of policy is rarely a crowd-pleaser, the events of that year matter more than you might think. It begins with an historic first: 1828 was the first time the rural populace I just mentioned actually made it to the halls of power. These Reformers finally held a majority in the House and they were poised to make some changes they thought were well overdue.

The Family Compact—including our buddy Strachan—had been shaping policies and politics for several years in ways that best suited them. Change was in the air as the masses were increasingly vexed by policies that were clearly for the advantage of a wealthy minority. One issue in particular struck a chord in the chambers: building an institution of formal education. If Upper Canada was ever going to become truly civilized, the young colonials who called it home needed to be learned in the realms of law, medicine, literature, politics, and theology. On this, no one disagreed.

Round one of the fight came after John Strachan made the following appeal to King George: the royal charter for this inaugural school must ensure that the faculty be members or clergy of the Church of England. Citing specious statistics, he argued that because education formed the minds of the young, no Methodist should be allowed access to such a resource. If they did get influence over the hallowed halls of the academy, British North America would go Republican within a generation.

He stated the vast majority of colonists held warm sentiments towards Establishment (the British policy of having one church as the official church of the land) and if the Crown increased Anglican budgets to hire and build then the vast majority of Upper Canadians would gladly desert Methodism and join the Church of England. However, Strachan argued, if the realm of higher education allowed Methodist instructors then their American sentiments and beliefs would undermine the Crown and create a generation of rebels.

Strachan pointed to the recent War of 1812 to demonstrate just how dangerous America could be as it continued to set its dastardly sights on the northern jewel of the British crown. After all, Strachan had seen the Americans in action in that war and knew that their words concealed their true desires to pillage; and the minds of young colonists were inestimably more valuable than a few burnt buildings. The King was warned that while Methodism was an acceptable version of the faith in

England, the American brand created disloyalty.

"Nothing could be further from the truth!" was the sentiment of the 1828 House of Commons. People chose to be Methodists or Baptists out of personal conviction, not a lack of options. There was no animosity towards the Established Church, but neither was there any sense that Methodism was a less-desirable consolation church. Such anti-Methodist beliefs were laughable but what was decidedly not funny was the charge that Methodism created disloyal subjects.

One Member of the House raised his hand to speak to this. Point of fact, he raised his only hand because the other one had been blown off in the aforementioned 1812 conflict. And for which side had this Methodist fought? You guessed it: The British. "You call my loyalty into question? Me? The man who lost a limb fighting for this land!"

The House of Commons created their own arguments and statistics to counter Strachan's and, on every point, were able to offer up more cogent logic and better statistics from a wider variety of people. Their report showed, almost irrefutably, that Methodists and Baptists were just as loyal and that denominational loyalty did not threaten Imperial loyalty. The War of 1812 was 13 years in the past by the time of the Report, and if any of their number held seditious beliefs, they would have been discovered by then. Their arguments were solid, their research more ethical and, as I wrote a moment ago, their logic was almost irrefutable. But it is the "almost" in that previous sentence that we must focus upon. When the House of Commons put together a counter proposal for the King, they ended up authoring a document that could not have proved Strachan's point better if he had penned the thing himself.

Showing story after story of American-born Methodist loyalty to the crown, the 1828 "House of Commons Report on the State of Religion in the Canadas" argued that the King should ignore Strachan's recommendation about the Established Church and, instead, grant his subjects freedom of religious conscience. Were the King to fund all churches and not just the

Church of England, he would find himself the beloved ruler of the most loyal subjects in the entirety of his Empire.

They cautioned against forcing establishment upon the people, gently suggesting such a policy forced Upper Canadians to choose between their God and their King. Even though everyone agreed Establishment was one of the pillars of British civilization, the argument was put forward that British North Americans preferred a policy of multi-denominational inclusion. A controversial argument, sure, but not over the top given that allowances were made for Methodists and other Dissenting groups throughout the entirety of the Empire.

The problem occurred when the House Report offered a counter proposal that better represented the realities of their colonial experience: dissolve Church Establishment and institute ecumenism. Thus, the young could be educated, their parents' spiritual convictions upheld, and everyone in the colony would increase in education and loyalty to their benevolent, wise, and Christian King. This was the Reformers' take on the term loyalty and, unfortunately for them, they grossly misinterpreted the ramifications of that word.

For the Family Compact, loyalty was about creating a wee Britain in the colony and Establishment was necessary for such a thing to occur. It didn't matter that their proposal made almost no sense in their colonial reality. These men had mastered imperial vocabulary and knew what to say and to whom. The Reformers thought they understood the vocabulary but they failed to take into account the differences that exist between the heart of the empire (London) and the Reformers' place in the wings. They were honouring the spirit of the law, they really were, but the colonial counsellors an entire ocean away were more concerned about the letter of the law.

As balanced as the prospective plan sounded to the Reformers, to the King's counsellors it sounded like the Federalist argument for the separation of church and state. In other words, it sounded very American, the very thing Strachan warned would happen. For all their research, the Reformers failed to realize that they were perfectly demonstrating how pervasive American thinking could be and how it could infect the colonies.

To the Imperial authorities, these colonists—in the interest of loyalty no less—desired to overturn a foundational British institution in favour of a clearly American idea. While arguing that American sentiments posed no threat to the demonstrably loyal inhabitants of Upper Canada, they had unwittingly made Strachan's point for him. Thus, the charter for King's College—the first institution of higher learning in Upper Canada—permitted only Church of England faculty, by order of the King.

HOW THE 19TH CENTURY CHURCH REVERSED SECULARIZATION OF ITS TIME

There's a running joke within historians of Canadian religion: in the 1840s there were three pubs on the corner of every town, by the 1870s there were three churches (I didn't say it was a good joke). From a statistical point of view, census data from the 1840s lists 16.7% of Upper Canadians as having "No Creed," their way of saying that they didn't belong to a church. Think about that number for a moment, it is not far off from present-day Canada's census data which has approximately 24% of Canadians saying something similar.

And this is in the 19th century, before Darwin's *Origin of the Species*, German higher criticism of the Bible, scientific advancements, globalization, the internet, multiculturalism, or any of the other myriad of influences that vexed 20th and 21st century Canadian Christianity. By the census of 1871 that number had dropped to just over 1%. This means that Canadian churches faced a religious culture similar to the one of today and successfully reversed the tide. How did they do that? There are four reasons:

REASON 1: THE END OF ESTABLISHMENT

One of the numerous perks that came with being the Established Church meant that the Church of England had sole possession of the Clergy Reserves. The Reserves meant that 1/7 of all the land in the colony was dedicated to the church. On this land Anglicans could build their churches and from this land they could gather rents from the people they allowed to live there. A seventh of all land created income for the church and this was another reason that Strachan's request for more money was greeted by scoffs from the Reformers of the 1820s and beyond. How much more did they need to prove that their problem wasn't a lack of capital?

The Reserves issue was finally settled in the 1850s largely due to the increased awareness that some of the old models (Establishment for example) were simply not working in the new world. Old conservative institutions needed to be re-examined in light of global political changes (sound familiar?). The Presbyterians had successfully lobbied to have access to the Reserves because they were the Established Church of Scotland. Since Canada had plenty of Scots, their church had as much right to the Reserves as the English Church. The Catholics also had some allowances as they were the (unofficial) Established Church of Lower Canada. But what of those pesky and problematic Methodists?

The problem for the more evangelical churches was that there were simply too many of them and their differences with each other prevented them from being identified as one cogent denomination. Since we have spoken so much about it, let's return to the War of 1812 for a moment. In the years after the war, rival versions of Methodism vied for adherents. The American-based Episcopal Methodists lost scores of members in both Canadas during the war as their missionaries were prevented from crossing the border. In the interim, Henry Ryan had single-handedly done his absolute best to stem the tide, but geography and resources proved obstacles too daunting to defeat.

During that time, Wesleyan Methodists from Britain moved ever westward from their strongholds in Atlantic Canada to offer a more Anglo-friendly version of the evangelical faith. However, as noted earlier, the war did little to cool international relations after 1815 so the Wesleyans and Episcopals found themselves fighting each other over spiritual territory. In a somewhat ironic twist, the American Episcopals employed the language of invasion, accusing the British Wesleyans of invading and occupying their land. The irony that the Episcopal homeland had literally invaded the disputed territory with an actual army appears to have been lost on them.

Henry Ryan felt slighted by both sides as the Wesleyans accused him of being a traitorous American (he was Irish) and his own Episcopals overlooked his Herculean efforts on the denomination's behalf. He eventually formed his own group— the Ryanites—and thus there were three versions of the same branch of evangelicals claiming to be the Methodist voice for the Canadas. Strachan shocked absolutely no one when he interceded on behalf of the Wesleyans in the hope that if he had to contend with evangelistic enthusiasm, he would rather it be of the British persuasion.

Eventually, an uneasy truce was declared that saw more Wesleyans in Lower Canada and, much to Strachan's chagrin, Upper Canada left to the Episcopals (Upper Canadians were mostly Americans anyway). Ryan was summarily dismissed by both groups. This is just one example of the many (and I really do mean many, I didn't even get into the whole early push for a Canadian Methodist Church) manifestations of Methodism that would ebb and flow throughout the 19th century. Added to that was the Baptist realization that they must also begin to grow more Upper Canadian ministers and so, after 1820, they increasingly cut ties with their American agencies.

As the idea of disbanding Establishment and selling off the Reserves grew in the minds of the colonial authorities, it was incumbent upon the Methodists to put aside their feuds if they hoped to gain any of the funds. And this they eventually did, for a while anyway. The House of Commons reforms from 1828 finally gained traction after only a short 12 years.

In 1850, the officially titled Anti-State Church Association originated and held its inaugural meeting at Knox Church in Toronto. One year later, the Baptists also held their own conference, presenting an argument that Clergy Reserves were "at variance with Christianity as revealed in the Bible." John Strachan, not to be outdone, held a counter conference and the Wesleyans, though seeing the political benefit of courting Strachan, eventually sided with those who opposed Establishment.

The Reserves were not the only reversal in the wind. In 1849, the Baldwin University Act—a direct rejection of King's College sectarian system—was passed. Education was no longer the sole property of the Church of England and the wee Britain the Family Compact had been building was beginning to disintegrate. The ongoing feuds and rivalries between the various faith groups created some interesting dynamics. The Church of England had the power, money, and influence but not the numbers or support of the masses. The Roman Catholics were the largest expression of Christianity, growing beyond their French roots as Catholic Irish, Scottish, and German immigrants arrived. This too brought increased rivalry as the Presbyterians, for one example, fought to win their fellow Gaels away from Rome.

For all the policies of inclusion, Catholics were not likely to go very far politically in Canada's Protestant system. The Presbyterians had so many splits and rivalries brought over from the Old World and originating in the New, that neither the Atlantic territories nor the Canadas could find a unified voice for this, technically, Established Church. I would add more to that statement but I fear that—like the Methodist fights with each other—even a cursory examination of internal Presbyterian rivalries and sects will add only confusion; suffice it to say, they were not a unified front.

However, with the exception of Strachan's Church of England, the sentiments of these fractured and warring groups (Catholics included) were definitively anti-Establishment and pro-Empire. Strachan's argument that Establishment curbed disloyalty had proven to be false. More politicians were coming to see that evangelical belief based on personal conscience not only provided a sincere form of Christianity but also seemed to create very respectable citizens as well. These groups opposed Establishment but they also opposed churches receiving any funds from the government for fear that corruption and pandering would ensue. An 1844 report from the Free Church of Scotland stated "it would be deeply injurious to [accept] any grant of public money from the government" because then the church would bow to the state and the voluntary nature of faith would be inextricably compromised.

REASON 2: WEALTHIER CHURCHES

By 1854, the Reserves were no more. They were sold for an amount just north of 380,000 pounds. Those funds were doled out and 65% went to the Church of England; 28% to the Church of Scotland (not the Free Church or numerous other Presbyterian groups); 5% went to the Roman Catholics; and about 2.5% went to the newly united Methodists, who put aside their theological and polity disagreements long enough to form a denomination eligible for a substantial amount of money and acceptance.

What the dissolution of the Reserves meant was that Upper Canada was officially sanctioned as a land of religious diversity. As the 19th century entered its second half, some churches had succeeded in putting away earlier schisms but, for the most part, the motivation seemed to be less ecumenical and more about financial gain and/or teaming up against shared ecclesiastical enemies. Rivalries were still a dominant motif of the Canadian religious landscape. Such battles prevented many churches from reaching their intended goals of successfully serving the still largely disparate colonists. Society was not benefitting as these various groups fought each other to the neglect of their role as agents of social cohesion.

The 19th century was one of change as the modern age was maturing and casting off the ill-fitting clothes of the previous epoch. The colonial government rewarded a few select churches who could move beyond rivalry and invited them into a new world where, theoretically, the playing field was a little more level. For the first time since they entered Upper Canada in 1799, the Methodists had a financially independent Upper Canadian based mission from which they could begin the serious work of evangelizing the land and becoming a respected institution.

But that respectability came at the price we talked about a little before. The Canadian Methodists minimized the camp revival that was a cornerstone of their ancestors' ecclesiology. If all Strachan wanted to do was end revival meetings, then he did so with shocking success. These newly minted Methodists were church builders and, taking a cue from their 1825 champion Egerton Ryerson, were about to become powerful policy makers as well. In the 1850s, four different Christian groups had the blessing of the government and some deep pockets to evangelize and build, but would the people accept them?

REASON 3: THE CHURCH AS SYMBOL OF CIVILIZATION

Yes, they did, of course they did. And that sets up an important theme within Canadian Christianity that has continued to be true for numerous subsequent generations: church adherence grew because of a perceived societal need more than successful evangelization. Churches were not just houses of faith but also signs of increased civilization. While the land was still largely agrarian, cities like Toronto, Montreal, and Kingston were growing in number and size as immigrants from America and the heart of the Empire continued to arrive. These immigrants longed for the comforts of home in their new land.

A familiar church was an integral part of that comfort. With newly loosened purse strings, building programs became all the rage. Gothic Cathedrals began to be erected as even the Methodists moved from their camp-meeting, mobile style to embrace a more established ecclesiology of sacred space. A profusion of spires began to dot city skylines, loyalty was fading as a concern, and the need for social respectability was rising.

Marriage and family law also changed. Until 1831 the Church of England and the Catholic Church were the only denominations legally able to marry colonists. This meant many early Canadians were living in sin (to borrow from our vernacular) because they didn't want to switch their theology to suit a law they didn't support. The legitimacy of such laws didn't translate into the isolated world of most Upper Canadians; so, as usual, they simply ignored them and went about their lives and raised their families.

It took a while but, as the century continued on in a more reformist tone, marriage, baptism, and funerals also became open to more denominations. The major milestones of life from the cradle to the grave were now within the sphere of almost every version of Canadian Christianity. Churches were cultural touchstones and while the Church of England still tended to have the more elite and wealthy adherents, influential politicians were making strong cases for Methodist respectability in the realms of education and culture.

The desire for civility was not only about creature comforts or quasi-national respectability but also about competing against America (of course). As Strachan frequently commented, romanticizing the American experiment dangerously overlooked the darkness he believed lay at the heart of that rebellious nation.

His argument gained new impetus as the 1860s birthed the cataclysmic American Civil War that plunged the land into violent—and very public—chaos. America was once again revealed to be a violent nation in love with bloodshed. The fact that the British Empire had officially outlawed slavery almost six decades earlier only crystallized Canadian moral outrage with their neighbours. Canadian sermons and published responses to the American Civil War was another display of our true pastime that supersedes even the love of hockey: Canadians truly enjoy looking down our noses at America and claiming the moral high ground.

A source of pride is that the Canadian Churches, almost universally, supported the North in the Civil War (spoiler, there were Canadian Christians who supported the south as well). It should be noted that the reasons behind such support had more to do with geographical proximity and favourable governmental policies than any moral outrage regarding slavery (this would be a trope of later generations). The hypocrisy of Canadian moralizing during this time will be revealed in the second last chapter of this book as we look at the residential school tragedies. For the time being, it is important to note that many saw the Civil War as further proof of America's moral degradation and one more reason to strengthen Canada.

While the churches were still largely silent during the 1860s about the Christian character of the nation (they will find their voices in the next chapter) they had plenty to say about American debauchery. Historians of the 19th century tended to view the development of humanity as a climb out of savagery into civilization and the church had a key role to play in articulating such growth. Thus, the European settlers of Canada desired a church that could teach civilized values and combat personal vice. However, in keeping with our theme of rivalry, there were also plenty of sermons which assured adherents their version of the faith was the correct one. While less flashy, their nation was superior in character to the home of their fellow believers south of the border.

REASON 4: IMMIGRATION AND CHURCH GROWTH

Which brings us to the final point we can learn from 19th century Canadian Christianity: it grew thanks to immigration. Immigrants, irrespective of denomination, brought their faith to the New World and believed church was essential to survive the risky venture all immigrants experience. The fact that many were farmers only increased their desire to please the God of the harvest and so Christian numbers rose along with the immigrant population. While the professions have changed, statistically the same proves true today.

However, Canada's reputation for being a cold and foreboding land ensured that it was perpetually a distant second

The Emigrants' Welcome to Canada. Date and Author Unknown.
Print housed in the Canadian National Archives: Peter Winkworth Canadiana Collection.
Accession number: e002511221

to the more appealing life promised by America. The cartoon printed on the next page is one example of satirists mocking the British appeals for emigrants to populate the colony across the Atlantic. Sure, there was land, but it was under miles of tundra; sure, there were apartments but they were bear-filled caves; sure there were resources as long as you had the patience to grow it all in the snow; so the comic strip goes. As the goose at the top sardonically questions the new immigrant about who the *real* goose is, the reader is left to wonder why anyone would choose to live in British North America?

This harmed Canada as more accomplished students, professionals, entrepreneurs, and the like tended to emigrate to America, believing Canada to be a consolation prize. This is not what I think of these 19th century immigrants, I am merely noting such ideas about Canada were circulating during this time. Such sentiments fed into the already humble beliefs early Canadians had about their home and strengthened, in the words of this book, their loser theology.

New immigrants also brought cultural strife, even though many of them at this point were from desirable locations. British soldiers from the Napoleonic wars, Protestant Irish, Scots with money and influence, and German farmers overtook Americans as the dominant percentage of new British colonists. Despite this, similar tensions were created as occurred in the early 19th century. They, like most immigrants, had little vested interest in the foundational stories of the colonists who were already there. Like the second wave of American immigrants from the earlier generation, these new people brought with them new ideas that challenged elements of accepted colonial culture.

You would think being raised in the heart of the Empire made these immigrants' inclusion into early Canadian society easier. That turned out to be disappointingly untrue. Apparently Strachan's Wee Britain had diverged in some key areas from actual Britain and his Anglophile stance took some real hits during this time. His ideal of what Britain stood for met the harsh reality of what actual British immigrants believed. Chief among his concerns was the disgusting admiration many of these new colonists had for America.

The United States was romanticized around the world as a wild and adventurous place where anyone could become anything. Even in London (perish the thought), the Republic was a subject of curiosity and delight, much to the chagrin of Strachan. When that adoration came to British North America it triggered a reaction through pulpit and press as the older immigrants did their best to bring these new people into line and educate them about the real America. To do this they returned to a familiar weapon from an earlier arsenal: loyalty.

One thing all colonists had to agree on was that they were to remain loyal, but defining that term once again brought plenty of trouble. For Strachan and the Family Compact, it meant policies that helped them advance their version of Britain. For the Methodists in the House, it meant creating a land with religious freedom. For the growing collection of Protestant Irish, loyalty meant never working with Catholics, even though Catholics had proven their loyalty in the 1812 conflict; a conflict the Protestant Irish had likely never heard about.

The collision of immigrant and Canadian worldviews about

America, loyalty, and a host of other issues sparked a myriad of other rivalries. Despite this (or because of this) the immigrants who braved the Canadian nation also brought a tremendous amount of growth to a variety of churches. A more important lesson we can learn from the impressive reversal of numbers by the 1870s is that the churches were the recipients, rather than the architects, of such changes.[3]

Sure, the churches ran programs and evangelized people but the ongoing quibbling and rivalries had weakened every single form of Christianity in the land. The Catholic Church alone seemed immune to such struggles but cracks were beginning to show even within that monolithic structure. Quebecers struggled with adherence to their present home, their relationships to France and Rome, and the political and theological issues that were making their way across the Atlantic. English-speaking Catholics and French-speaking Protestants also created internal tensions that were about to erupt at the dawn of the next century.

CANADA'S STRUGGLE TO DEFINE AN "OTHER"

I remember reading a British editorial written during the Napoleonic War in which the author wrote of the atheistic, superstitious, violent, unsanitary, sexually promiscuous, drunken and largely illiterate French population. As an historian, what does this tell me about French culture at that time? Nothing. But it tells me plenty about English sensibilities. It tells me that this author values religion (Protestant most

---

3 In 1842 census enumerators recorded 16.7% of the population as having no religious preference or as professing no religious creed, and contemporary testimonies agreed that the proportion of uncommitted upper Canadians had been greater in earlier years. By 1871 only 1.2% were so recorded. The gradual maturing of the province, which stimulated in its inhabitants a desire for the amenities of civilized living and made available greater resources for securing them, was a major factor in bringing about this change...Most influential, however, was the missionary awakening that stirred English speaking countries around the turn of the 19th century, and lead to the militant evangelism of saddlebag preachers, the involvement in proliferating missionary societies, and the rising level of piety among success of waves of immigrants. John Webster Grant, *A Profusion of Spires: Religion in Nineteenth-Century Ontario*, (Toronto: University of Toronto), 222.

likely), cleanliness, sexual conservatism, education and so on. If this was a particularly popular editorial, then it is fair to say that many of the English readers shared such beliefs. This helps me understand the culture and norms of that time and place. This is what we call the construction of the Other and it can be very helpful on both macro and micro scales.

While England had France as a convenient national foil for much of its existence in the imperial age, British North America couldn't say the same. After all, the largest population of colonials had French roots, spoke French, and retained their Catholic beliefs. Not only that but these elements of their culture were protected under the constitution of the Protestant British Empire. To fight against them would be to fight against the Empire. On top of that, those French Catholics had fought in two decisive battles in the War of 1812 and likely saved Upper and Lower Canada for the Crown. French Catholics fought to maintain their lives as subjects of the British Protestant King; hardly an effective Other. Again, it needs to be noted that English-French rivalries in Canada have always been very contentious and violent, but that is an internal tension. The French are one of the founding people groups of modern Canada and, as such, can't be an external Other like they were across the pond.

But I did just mention the War of 1812 so clearly America would be to Canada what France was to England. Except, of course, roughly eighty percent of the people in Upper Canada were American. As already mentioned, even the invasion did little to dampen the connection for the colonists, many of whom were more than happy to welcome Americans back into their lives for commercial and personal reasons. So, America was not a compelling Other either.

Canada had no clear and forthcoming national Other from which to derive identity. Instead it had a series of internal Others that were more regional—or theological—in nature. Leaders like Strachan employed language to make the Episcopal Methodists into ideological Others but Canadian history shows that such rhetorical Others lacked the impact provided by national foes.

Sure, large regions of Upper Canada and Protestant sections of the Atlantic provinces were comfortable bad-mouthing and condemning the French. However, those attitudes clearly didn't catch on in Quebec or the Catholic sections of the Atlantic Provinces. They only entrenched enmity between English and French Canadians. In Quebec, clergy condemned America as responsible for the destruction wrought by the French Revolution. However, numerous new immigrants looked on America with fondness and it was a favourite vacation spot for those who could afford to travel. This is important to remember for two reasons: the first is that the lack of a national Other once again offers us an explanation as to why Canadians have an identity crisis.

The second reason Canada's lack of an Other is important has to do with the impact over Canadian Christianity. The lack of a unifying external enemy focused many clergy inward toward concrete ecclesiastical rivals. So seriously was this taken that any Anglican clergyman who even thought of learning from the Methodists risked being ostracized. Interdenominational dialogue between these two groups was strained as even the suspicion of being an Anglican "enthusiastic" could have serious ramifications for future employment within the church.

The love affair newer Canadians had with America waned as the century moved on. The Civil War played a large role in the souring of earlier adoration. But the number of sermons critical of the States that were preached, printed, and circulated throughout the land helped as well. Such sermons showed that America failed to create decent, peaceful, and socially-minded people. The Republicans were drunk on their perceived freedom and, like all drunks, were given over to flowery words and dark deeds.

These messages denigrated American-style politics as a whirlwind of lies more at home in a debased theatre than civilized government. They labeled the various American wars of extermination with First Nations as diabolical (these Canadians were clearly not listening to Jesus' "take the log out of your own eye before pointing out the sliver in another's" lesson about hypocrisy, but we'll return to that later in the book). They juxtaposed Britain's earlier, peaceful abolition of slavery against America's much later and bloodier journey to emancipation. As a surgeon amputates a gangrenous limb to save a person's life, so too had God amputated America from the British in order to save the sanctity of His chosen Empire. The loser theology of the late 18th century was finding a new and appreciative audience once again.

I hope you hear the echo of previous UEL sermons that interpreted the loss in the Revolutionary War as a gift from God. Such theology was not a consolatory teaching; it was a sacred element of colonial life that needed to be seen as underpinning all that made the land great. Colonists would be courting disaster if they turned their backs on King and Constitution in favour of Republicanism.

The problem is that such teaching created, at best, an ideological Other. The American nation couldn't be a true Other because too many Canadians enjoyed it as a commercial partner and as a friendly neighbour. However, American theology (what some clergy called "sentiments" or "manners") was something else entirely. I hope you are a little confused by this because so too were many of the Canadians back then. Despite the influence Methodism enjoyed, they really did have to alter their polity to suit their Canadian spiritual climate. The Anglican suspicion around revivalism and their condemnation of American theology forced Methodists to abandon what, earlier on, defined them as a denomination.

Canadian Methodists were on a new path that was unique and separate from their co-religionists in America. If they were going to succeed in Canada, they were going to have to find different solutions than America. Thus the building programs and removal of revivalism that would define later 19th century Canada's evangelical giant (moves that invited criticisms as we will see in a later chapter).

Loyalty was still a dominant theme but it was losing

its earlier impact, while respectability was becoming more the watchword of that time. The bad behaviour of America embarrassed Canadian Methodism and so they also became increasingly critical of their denomination's original homeland. The Canadian context as a land with legislated religious diversity coupled with the lack of a definitive national foil heightened ideological and theological rivals; and that is where the confusion came in. Human enemies are easy to spot (theoretically); intellectual enemies can be much less so.

19TH CENTURY SECULARIZATION

The point we should take away from all of this is that, from the Anglican perspective, the Methodist threat was seen as similar to the secularization threats of today. This was a collection of rival, exciting, and undermining ideas that were finding an increasing audience amongst Canadians. Adherence to such evangelical beliefs increased church attendance—a noticeable difference from today's concerns—but that also increased the weakening of established Christian ideals.

For the Methodists of the 1850s and beyond, giving up certain foundational attributes in order to remain relevant also created internal conflict, more than a few splits within the denomination, and concerns about church integrity similar to today. From our perspective, such tensions might seem silly and miniscule when compared to the so-called secularization of today. However, for the people of the time, these contests were nothing less than a battle for the souls of all Canadians.

Despite numerical growth and somewhat increasing unity, 19th century Canadian Christianity was fractured, contentious, and left many Canadians feeling left out in the cold. The dominant worldview was still steeped in traditional Christian views but the latter half of the 1800s would bring cataclysmic changes to many of those teachings. Inter and inner denominational squabbles seemed all-consuming to the clerics involved but, to the vast majority of the colonists, all they saw was the lack of care they were receiving. Once again, not so distant from today's Canadian religious world.

While denominational loyalty was somewhat abiding, we do have numerous records of people switching churches for reasons of romance, business, socializing, convenience, and better care. Only that last item on the list had anything to do with actual church activity. What can be taken from this is that Canadians have always been willing to entertain the notion of church hopping if one group can care for their daily needs better.

By the 1870s this trend was turning as more people were coming to the land and church choices were seen to be a necessary sign of civility and a source of pride. Increased industrialization meant that earlier material assistance was less of a concern for the newly arrived. Therefore, by and large, denominational loyalties tended to be pretty stable and unchanging from that time of building.

What should be noted from this period is that the churches could take little credit for growth or even financial stability as these were not the result of effective evangelization or revival. Rather, they came from government policies and a societal belief that visible churches were indicative of decent society. The same argument could be made for the increase of schools, theatres, hotels, and banks at that time as well.

The land was increasing in industry and commerce but there were concerning rumours coming from across the Atlantic. Rumours of new intellectual streams that were challenging Christian truth claims and the increasing popularity of American political ideologies were literally toppling former nation states. If Canada was going to keep up it needed to adapt, and if Canada was going to adapt in good ways, it needed churches to step up and insert their influence. Little did the leaders of the later 19th century realize just how dramatically their world was about to change.

RESOURCES

John Webster Grant. *A Profusion of Spires: Religion in Nineteenth-Century Ontario*. Toronto: University of Toronto, 1988.

- Grant shows the ideologies and culture behind the building programs discussed in this chapter.

John S. Moir. *The Church in the British Era: from the British Conquest to Confederation*. Toronto: McGraw-Hill Ryerson, 1972.

- This is part two in a three-part series that looks at Canadian Christianity during the French Era as well as the later developments of the church in the Canadian Era. Many of the issues discussed in this chapter are also discussed in Moir's book.

Scott McLaren. *Pulpit, Press and Politics: Methodists and the Market for Books in Upper Canada*. Toronto: University of Toronto, 2019.

- This work details the influence Methodists had thanks to the centrality of literature in their missionary work. Tracking book culture, this work shows the tumultuous world of early Upper Canadian religious climate.

Todd Webb. *Transatlantic Methodists: British Wesleyanism and the Formation of an Evangelical Culture in Nineteenth-Century Ontario and Quebec*. Montreal and Kingston: McGill-Queen's University Press, 2013.

- Todd Webb delves into the divisions of Methodism both in Canada and across the pond that this chapter only touched upon. While Wesleyan Methodists in Britain played a key role in determining the identities of their colonial counterparts, Methodists in Ontario and Quebec helped to trigger the largest division in British Wesleyan history. This book shows definitively that Methodists on both sides of the Atlantic shaped— and were shaped by—the larger British world in which they lived.

J.L.H. Henderson (ed). *John Strachan Documents and Opinions.* McClelland & Stewart: Toronto, 1969.

- This collection of writings from and about John Strachan details his thoughts about, and influence over, Canadian religion, culture, and politics throughout his tumultuous life. This larger-than-life character can be better understood through his own words and the balanced treatment he receives from Henderson.

---

1 IDEA

While still culturally significant, denominational rivalry weakened the ability of churches to meet the needs of Canadians. As a consequence, substantial times of church growth during this period are due to cultural desires and investments, not successful church evangelization.

CHAPTER 3
INFLUENCE
1867 -

Interesting and sophisticated
Refusing to be celebrated
It's a monumental big screen kiss
It's so deep it's meaningless
— "So Hard Done By,"
The Tragically Hip

INTRODUCTION

Neville Trueman lived up to his name. He was a "true man" who displayed, on numerous occasions, bravery and character second to none. As a Methodist missionary in the early 19th century, his dedication to the people of Upper Canada was a thing of legend. He fought for the British in the War of 1812, one of those loyal Methodists who risked life and limb for his adopted land in war and peace. He believed in the power of revivals and his life was one dedicated to preaching the gospel at all times, whether in word or in deed. If Neville Trueman saw the vapid weakness and political pandering that came to define his beloved Methodist denomination by the end of the 19th century, he would have spun in his grave. Fortunately for Neville Trueman, he never actually died.

Louis Riel also rejected the vision of Canada coming to fruition in the late 19th century. Unlike Trueman, Riel's experience was not that Canada was losing its earlier ruggedness, but that it was a tyrannical force being thrust upon him and his fellow Metis. Riel was Catholic and so this is a Catholic story almost as much as it is a Metis one. I don't say that to take away from his Metis status but to show that his Catholic theology also enraged the Canadian leaders in Ontario. His legitimate grievances found no sympathy from the Protestants of his time. He would even strain Catholic support when he began to view himself increasingly as a prophet for his people (you can see why I wanted to include this guy). He was a descendant of Indigenous people who, in the 17th century, had blended with the French and incorporated aspects of European religion, commerce, and language into their own culture. Thanks to industrialization, these centuries-old alliances were being threatened. While Metis and others were allowed to stay, they could do so on Canada's terms only, terms that intentionally devalued First Nations as well as Catholics. Even though these people had lived in this land thousands of years before any Protestant, their future in this new Canada was uncertain.

Rev. James Bainton stepped into the pulpit of his

Congregational Church in Victoria B.C. to address an issue of pressing importance. Canada was involved in its first international war, fighting on the side of England against the Dutch Boers in South Africa (1899-1902). While Congregationalists were pacifist in their make up, some influential members of his flock were challenging their minister's belief that war is a failure to live like Christ. Bainton had taught about the horrors of war and had the audacity to pray for everyone involved in the conflict. Such teachings and prayers caused anger within a faction of "super patriots" who believed this English-born and respected preacher was breeding treason. The toll this church conflict took on his family proved more than the minister was willing to endure. He moved his entire family to the United States for the remainder of his career. That's right, this English man found rebellious Americans more palatable than his congregants of British Columbia. Was it just his views on the war? I argue that his British sensibilities are more to blame.

I bring these three men to your attention because their stories have a lot in common that we need to unpack as we look at the influence the churches were exerting over Canada. All three men saw the landscape of Canada changing and all three men had concerns about those changes. All three men believed that their faith communities were being swept up in an increasing sense of Canadian nationalism. All three saw Canada growing and understood that the church needed to speak into that growth. Finally, all three men offer us insights into some of the dominant trends that would compose Canadian Christendom.

INFLUENCE

As we look at the current state of Christianity in Canada, we need to have a more accurate narrative of what we are actually talking about. Before we can lament the passing of Christendom, we must understand the nature of what it is we are being called to lament. For the record, the passing of Canadian Christendom actually makes a lot of sense to me. But before we can really talk about what the passing of Canadian Christendom means, we must spend some time talking about what it actually was. With that in mind, this chapter will explain the following:

1. James Bainton
2. Canadian Christendom as explained by a postage stamp
3. Racial policies that shaped Canada
4. The myth of the cold-loving Canadian
5. Uniting churches for Canada
6. Neville Trueman
7. Catholic superiority in missions
8. Louis Riel

Before returning to the three stories we must understand the context of late 19th and early 20th century Canada. It makes sense to begin in 1867 because in that year Ontario, Quebec, New Brunswick, and Nova Scotia joined together into a confederation of provinces. The nation of Canada would be officially born on 1 July 1867, and the churches' response to Confederation was as profound as it was unanimous: nothing, they said nothing.[1] To be

---

1   "The Union of the Provinces of Canada, Nova Scotia and New Brunswick, under the new Constitution, takes effect today. We heartily congratulate our readers on the event, and fervently pray that all the blessings anticipated from the measure, by its promoters, may be fully realized. So far as the people of Upper Canada are concerned, the inauguration of the new Constitution may well be heartily rejoiced over as the brightest day in their calendar. The Constitution of 1867 will be famous in the historical annals of Upper Canada, not only because it brought two flourishing Maritime States into alliance with the Canadas, and opened up new markets for our products, and a direct railway route to the Atlantic through British territory, but because it relieved the inhabitants of Western Canada from a system of injustice and demoralization under which they had suffered for a long series of years. The unanimity and cordiality with which all sections of the people of Canada accept the new Constitution, gives the happiest omen of its successful operation. And, assuredly, if the people of the United Provinces are true to themselves and exercise a persistent and careful control over all public proceedings, there is not a shadow of doubt as to success. The only danger that threatens us is, lest the same men who have so long misgoverned us, should continue to misgovern us still, and the same reckless prodigality exhibited in past years should be continued in the future; but this we do not fear. We firmly believe, that from this day, Canada enters on a new and happier career, and that a time of great prosperity and advancement is before us." – The Globe Monday, July 1, 1867, vol. 24, no. 156, supplement, p. 4, col. 1. "Apathy is a word chosen often to describe the attitude of the Protestant churches to the proposal that the British North American provinces form the nation of Canada." Phyllis Airhart, "Ordering a New Nation and Re-Ordering Protestantism: 1867-1914," In *The Canadian Protestant Experience:1760-1990*, Edited by George Rawlyk, 91-138. (Montreal & Kington: McGill Queen's University Press, 1990), 98.

fair, Confederation was largely the invention of politicians and those with a vested interest in a railroad and held little interest for clergy. It would take some years but, eventually, the churches began to see what was happening and they ended their silence and got down to the serious business of building a nation. This chapter will look at what kind of nation they were looking to build.

Some believe that Confederation was a slower moving, and politer, version of the 18th century American Revolution. It is wrong to think that Confederation was Canada's Declaration of Independence. I hope previous chapters have shown that *British North America* was always unique amongst imperial holdings and Confederation didn't signal the end of such loyalty. Canada's famous (and infamous) first Prime Minister, John A. Macdonald put this strange dynamic succinctly when he said that he was "born a British subject" and would "die a British subject."[2] Therein lies a truer understanding of Canadian desires that can't be overlooked. Confederation was not a slower moving form of Republicanism, it was a desire for home rule in order to bring swift and desired benefits to loyal subjects. Such subjects identified with the shifting political realities of the time but didn't cast off their imperial identities.

Ordering this new nation, as Phyllis Airhart notes, meant that Protestant leaders intentionally "re-ordered" to align this newly forming Canada with both God and Protestantism. Although acting in his role as a politician, it was his Methodist beliefs that inspired Leonard Tilley of New Brunswick to label Canada a "Dominion." Different names were being kicked around during the 1860s but nothing seemed to fit. The Kingdom of Canada was given serious consideration but was ultimately deemed too "pretentious and potentially offensive to Americans" (there's that humble loser theology again), so the search for Canada's

---

2 Granted the context of this statement was in an election against Wilfred Laurier whose economic policy with America was twisted by Macdonald to make it seem that, if the Liberal party got into power, Canada would be annexed by the States. Macdonald's success revealed the ongoing fear of many Canadians that America, as well as being our greatest ally, was Canada's largest threat as well.

official moniker continued.[3] Looking to the Psalms early one morning, Tilley read that God would have "dominion from sea to sea" and could think of no greater title/mission statement.[4] It was absolutely perfect for a God-honouring land such as Canada on the eve of Confederation and expanding coast to coast with a new railroad.

It would be the word Dominion, not Confederation, that lit the fire under the Protestants and inspired in them a vision for what this new nation should be. The fragmented religious ethos of previous generations was fading and a more unified Canadian church focused on voluntarism, reform, and personal conscience grew. Don't forget that by the 1870s, Canada was the land of three churches on every street corner (not literally) so the influence these churches held was substantial.

Airhart reminds us the "secularization of the clergy reserves" meant new money and influence was available for any denomination that could get its act together.[5] I don't want to move past the fact that Airhart chose the word secularization. This is important to note because, from the vantage point of Anglicans and Presbyterians, the government's decision to dissolve the Clergy Reserves was secularization. It was shifting the character of a time-honoured religious institution in order to better fit the parameters of culture.

While we may be tempted to think of secularization in this age as the disintegration of the church in favour of secular, or non-religious, values, I want you to see this was the argument of mainline clergy in the mid 19th century as well. You might not think that land sharing is anything like the issues of today but I would caution you against such a belief. We must see this was

---

3 Ian Rayburn, *Naming Canada: Stories About Place Names from Canadian Geographic*, (Toronto: University of Toronto, 1994), 16. Rayburn would go on to report "Queen Victoria did not like [Kingdom of Canada]" once again displaying the Atlantic Triangle. Rayburn, Naming, 16.

4 Psalm 72:8

5 Airhart. "Ordering," 99. In this article she also notes that the Presbyterians united by 1875, the Methodists were more unified by 1884 and the Baptists had formed an Ontario and Quebec convention by 1888.

a monumental shift in the religious understandings of the day. The church underpinned social morality (similar arguments are made today), and Establishment as well as the Clergy Reserves were the government's way of acknowledging such beliefs. To remove both from the landscape of Canada looked very much like the dissolution of religious faith, even though it was meant to achieve the exact opposite.

Such decisions intentionally weakened certain churches' influence in order to free the people to explore new options. One fun result is that while Methodist influence was largely responsible for these changes, it would be the Methodists themselves who would help bring establishment back into the mix. Granted, the intent and temperament had profoundly changed but nevertheless Methodists, Presbyterians and even Anglicans began serious conversations about joining forces and creating a united church for Canada. This established church would not be the divisive one of the early 19th century but would be a church for Canada, by Canada, and across Canada. By bringing these previously rival denominations into one fold, the railroad (completed in 1885) was truly unifying this land into a Dominion from sea to sea.

JAMES BAINTON

Congregationalism, a group destined to join in on those unity talks, provides a good case study for the desires of Protestants in those early Dominion days. Like most other evangelical groups, the first Congregationalists were sent by American missionary agencies. Unfortunately for them, their initial foray into British territory came in 1837; just in time for the entire denomination to be caught up in the famous rebellions of that year. Almost from inception, the loyalty of this small group of anti-Establishment, American-based missionaries was questioned. Given the nature of our last chapter, you know how damaging such accusations could be. Even as those charges waned as the years went by, the denomination never really recovered.

The irony is that, if ever there was a denomination set up to succeed in Canada, Congregationalism was the one. Despite their American connection, they were British in origin and this made them somewhat more palatable to the churches with stronger transatlantic connections. They formed as a direct rejection of Church Establishment, placing them also in the camp with other evangelical denominations. Like the Wesleyan Methodists, they embodied British sensibilities but with an entrepreneurial drive, determination, and evangelicalism that aligned them with their chosen home of British North America. Their ecclesiastical model was small, self-contained and self-governing churches joined with other like-minded churches in mutually beneficial relationships; another good fit with the burgeoning British North American culture. They created driven missionaries and valued education above almost all else and this set them up, both theologically and practically, to speak into the fragmented domain they entered. And yet they never did achieve much and their entrance into union talks came more from desperation than ecumenism. What happened and what can we learn from this group?

Congregationalist leadership quickly realized that, in order to best achieve their ministry goals, they needed to change their missionary base from America to England. Such a geographical change, while necessary in order to avoid charges of disloyalty, prevented them from ever blossoming to cultural significance. Congregationalists fell victim to the same economic and supply problems as other transatlantic churches. The end of the 19th century saw them still dependent on funds and leadership from London.

In the competitive landscape of the Canadian Dominion, they were unable to pass the one test every denomination needed to pass if it hoped to remain culturally influential: the ability to successfully plant sustainable churches in the west. Churches that failed to do this risked increasing irrelevance in former strongholds like Upper Canada (then known as Canada West). It would not be until near the dawning of the 20th century that Congregationalists would receive sufficient resources and ministers to finally advance into western territories. That is what brought Rev. James Bainton (1867-1942) from England to the shores of Canada, and the railway brought him and his family across the Dominion to the west coast city of Victoria.

Not long after that, Bainton would become embroiled in the scandal that would end his brief time in Canada and bring his family into the welcoming fold of American Congregationalism. So pervasive was this disappointment that his son, famed historian Roland Bainton, would write about the impact on his parents many years later. To be clear, Bainton Senior's views were kind, balanced, biblical, and simply lamented war as a failure of Christ-like attitudes to win the day. Such beliefs espoused during war time were seen by some in that small church as seditious. I tell you this story because it illustrates Protestantism's role in developing Canadian patriotism.

Canadian churches were almost unanimous in their support of the war effort and those, like Bainton, who were critical were so few in number, and spoke so infrequently on the topic, you would be forgiven if you didn't notice them at all. What Bainton stumbled into was a disturbing trend among religious leaders of that time to see war as another proof that Canada had come into its own. That attitude would come back to bite Canadian Christianity after World War I (we will look at that in the next chapter) but, during the South African Boer War, it was still very much en vogue. Bainton missed a crucial element of Dominion patriotism due in large part to his English origin. Ironic to say the least, given Canada's ongoing connection to the Empire, but also instructive for us because in the Bainton account we see an example of the complex relationship post-Confederation Canada had to Mother England.

The Discovery of Islands by J.G.A. Pocock sheds light on such complexities. In this influential work on the British Empire, Pocock advanced a theory he referred to as the "metropolis and periphery" dichotomy. He argued that the closer you are to the heart of power (metropolis) the more freedom your loyalty affords you. In other words, inhabitants of London can challenge and ridicule the Empire without their loyalty being questioned. In some cases, such ridicule was deemed necessary, if not always desirable.

However, the farther you move from the metropolis towards the periphery, the more those rules change. Loyal colonists on the wings of an empire encounter struggles to maintain their allegiance that those closer to the heart don't understand. Therefore, challenging Imperial ideologies has more disruptive potential on the periphery than it ever could in the more stable metropolis.

As it pertains to our story, James Bainton was raised in a metropolis able to look more critically at itself (especially given that Congregationalism was born out of critiquing the Church of England). Because of this he took a more critical stance about Canada's role in the war. He didn't take into account that British Columbia was on the periphery of both the global empire as well as the nation of Canada. British Columbia was on the farthest and most isolated periphery of an already peripheral colony. While the railroad had connected British Columbia with other provinces, the Rocky Mountains and its profound distance from centers of control like Ottawa or Toronto, only increased the isolation many felt. In the province that literally contained the word British in its name, connection to the empire was of paramount importance; especially during wartime.

Thus, Bainton's reflections about Jesus' love of peace were not received as Gospel but as disloyalty. I offer you this story not as a condemnation of that church or Bainton, but as a reminder of the ways in which culture colours all interpretations of the Bible. All of the faith groups contained in this book placed the Bible at the forefront of their teaching. That is the one and only thing they all have in common. What alters from church to church is how they framed biblical stories and interpreted them in light of the circumstances in which they lived. Bainton interpreted Jesus' teachings well, he just didn't interpret them well for his time and place. I'll leave you to dwell on that.

CANADIAN CHRISTENDOM

My earlier argument about Canada's lack of a unifying national origin story still holds, but the term Dominion was beginning to fill that vacuum. It was a biblical symbol around which Protestants could gather as they debated what Canada was going to become. If they desired to live up to the name, they needed to understand how best to bring the Kingdom of God to this part of the earth. However, such grandiose theological aspirations were only possible thanks to the advent of the railroad; a tool that brought commerce from coast to coast as well as a growing national cohesion.

Dominion brought the churches to life and they in turn helped to create the spiritual underpinning for many of Canada's new nationalistic goals. Many of their ideas found favour with the masses but these ideas were built largely on earlier issues and interpretive themes from those earlier days remained, albeit modified to fit the new context. Loyalty was no longer a watchword but America remained a perpetual threat, especially in the race for the west. While some denominations mended old wounds and began to talk of national goals, many of these unions proved unstable and problematic. The fragmented religious ethos changed but didn't disappear and new cracks began to develop. However, gentle reader, the most important element of this chapter is that you and I can finally start talking about Canadian Christendom as an actual cultural entity.

S.D Clark, and other historians, argue that Canadian Protestants are chief among their western counterparts in the realm of influence. It has been skillfully argued that 19th century Canada was more Christian than even our more religiously vocal neighbours to the south. There are numerous stories I could tell about church influence over the new nation of Canada but, instead, I would rather show you this postage stamp:

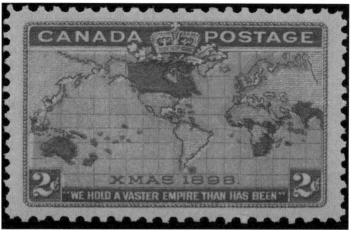

Image from wikimedia.com. For more on this stamp see postagestampguide.com

Need I write more? I thought not. Case closed, head to the next chapter.

Then again, for those of you who so desire, perhaps I can provide some context.

The date is the first thing I want you to see as I attempt to make my point. Confederation was 31 years in the past when this stamp was issued. Although they didn't know it, the people of that time were in the final days of Queen Victoria's reign. The brilliant and, until Queen Elizabeth II, longest-reigning monarch had done more than any of her predecessors to grow the might of the British Empire. If ever there was a season of Imperial patriotism, this was it.

As we have already briefly touched on, the British Empire was fighting in South Africa against the Dutch Boers. While receiving less historical attention than World War I, the prayers, sermons, and rationales utilized by various Canadians churches from 1914-1918 were first used during the Boer conflict.[6]

This was also a time of growing Canadian pride as the Bainton situation highlighted. For the first time in Canadian history, homegrown troops were being sent overseas to support a British cause rather than the other way around. This was a

---

6 For more on this see Gordon L. Heath, *A War with a Silver Lining*, (Montreal & Kingston: McGill-Queen's University Press), 2009.

momentous step as the young cub of Canada was rushing in to defend the mother lion of England, and this ideology was echoed by Protestant clergy.

The love of Victoria, the financial blessings her reign had brought, the philosophical, technological, and medical advances she had overseen (more on that in the next chapter), and the fact that Canada had grown strong enough to aid England's South African enterprise solidified, for Canadians anyway, that the nation was truly a global presence. The churches took pride in that and sermonized on such motifs and printed numerous reflections in denominational literature that were speeding around the land as fast as the locomotive could carry them.

The churches' foray into nation building was going well and the sense as the 19th century was closing was that Christian faith was firmly planted in the Dominion. The west was being reached for Christ and, as we will explore later in this chapter, frontier histories began to emerge. These fanciful stories heralded many denominations back to the earlier days of their respective churches with hagiographic and morality themes designed to inspire and correct. Catholics created inspirational characters who saved the faith and language from tyrannical British rule. Evangelical denominations recounted the exploits of their pioneer ancestors. Such stories reveal that the nation was feeling old enough to actually possess a bygone yesteryear to which they could harken. Slowly, Canada was becoming its own metropolis and was relying less on its identity as a periphery in the British Empire.

Building on that is the location of Canada on the map. You will no doubt notice it's centrality, which makes sense given the stamp was designed in Canada. That is not simply a stylistic choice but also reveals a theological belief prevalent in almost all of the Protestant churches at that time. There was a belief Canada held a special place in God's plan for this world based almost entirely on geography. This theology argued the climate and global positioning of Canada made it a necessary feature of God's eschatological plans.

As the stamp clearly states: "we hold a vaster empire than has been," a true statement even if a touch boastful. The red places located all over the stamp indicate the holdings of the British Empire and, as you can plainly see, the claim of vastness was accurate. Please note the "we" which indicates that while Canada's identity was shifting, it still contained connection to the British Empire.

However, the "we" also shows that Canada was an active agent in the advancement of that Empire and not merely a passive recipient of it. There was a pride in being part of an Empire over which the sun never set, and the small physical size of England only amplified the nation's stunning influence across the globe. Granted that maritime supremacy greatly aided British conquests but, from a more theological perspective, what Britain accomplished was due to a Providential plan.

That is nothing new as most forms of visible and material success tend to be viewed as God's definitive blessing and explicit support. As it pertained to the British Empire, Matthew 28 also factored into the equation. In the last moments before his departure, Jesus left his followers with a great commission to go out into the world and teach everyone his lessons and baptize them into the Christian fellowship. Once every tribe and tongue had heard the name of Jesus then a very particular event would finally be allowed to take place: the return of Christ and the end of the world. Britain's mission to civilize and Christianize the world was not merely material or political, it was eschatological as well. The land that literally included the church as part of its government had a missiological motivation for world domination. The Empire had a Christian duty to evangelize the world and stop anyone that tried to stop them.

The Dominion of Canada had a distinct role in such cosmic plans that included, but was not limited to, supplying soldiers. Canada was located in the middle of the globe (not that such a thing exists on a globe but you know what I mean) so travelers from around the empire would inevitably find their way to the chilly shores of either Victoria or Halifax. Canada had been a nation with a strong transatlantic connection that had been incredibly formative. However, with the completion of the railroad, Canada could now also enjoy a transpacific relationship as well.

Once in either of those prominent naval ports, visitors or immigrants could continue their travels in relative ease, comfort, safety, and speed via the impressive railway that united God's Dominion from sea to sea. It was up to Canada, an integral part of the vastest empire in human history, to maintain Christian character across the entirety of the land. If a person stopped in Vancouver, Calgary, Red River, Ottawa, Montreal, or Moncton he or she would be setting foot on soil consecrated to God. Canada was called to display the integrity instilled in it by God's chosen Empire to help bring about the glorious Day of the Lord.

This was not to say that Canada was blindly imperialistic (although it was from time to time) because the Dominion's understanding of Imperial connection was altering in the post-Confederation days. When Irish Fenians invaded Fort Erie in 1866, some religious presses wondered where the British Empire had been. Since the attack was motivated by England's occupation of Ireland, Baptists and Methodists alike questioned the wisdom of an ongoing relationship with such a distant and violent Empire. Canadians were well aware of the violence that Britain had unleashed on places like Ireland and India (though that second one didn't concern them as much as we'll see in the next part of this chapter) but this was not enough to dislodge Canadian Protestants from their Protestant monarch. Such things were merely lamentable realities of creating an Empire in a fallen world.

But that truth opened up a role for Canada. The blood-stained hands belonged to England; Canada was blameless on the world's stage. Canada, in essence, had the best of both worlds. Canadians enjoyed the comforts and advances that Victoria had brought to her subjects without the dark reputation that accompanied such achievements. Canada was free to teach and guide its inhabitants about the blessings of British civilization without receiving the chastisements that England so frequently received. Canada was to be a land of peace and civility and fidelity and compassion. Canada would take up the mantle of leadership and Christian mission around the globe and, of course, attend to the poor godless inhabitants within her own realm. But the question remained: if Canada was supposed to be a flagship Christian nation, what was that Christianity to look like?

According to many of the denominations, the best version of Christianity was Protestant, masculine, and Anglo-Saxon.[7]

RACIAL POLICIES THAT SHAPED CANADA

The proliferation of Orange Orders and the increase of blatantly pro-Protestant teaching during the latter half of the 19th century bears witness to such themes.[8] Catholics, women, and most non Anglo-Saxon ethnicities were dismissed outright when they were considered at all. Writing in 1922, W.G. Smith sought to explain the "problem" of immigration when building a united Canadian identity. He tackled immigration from numerous corners of the globe and noted that immigrants from certain nations were more welcome than others. The main criteria? Ethnicity.

Social Darwinism neatly and scientifically supported this Anglo-Saxon, Protestant dream although few churchmen of the time would have found such a comparison flattering (more on that in the next chapter). In essence, white races were seen as superior to other darker races, and on the very top of the

---

7 "The Dominion of Canada was to become an English-speaking Dominion of the Lord where Catholics and French Canadians were to be kept in their assigned roles." Robert Choquette, *Canada's Religions*, (Ottawa: University of Ottawa, 2004), 232.

8 Orange Orders were Protestant organizations, begun in Northern Ireland, to celebrate all things Protestant and to aid Protestant immigrants around the world. The Orange Order in British North America was officially inaugurated in the 1830s by Irishman Ogle Gowan. Orange Orders were powerful organizations more akin to a Union or lobbying party than simply a social group. Prime Ministers John A. Macdonald and Wilfred Laurier were counted among their members and they were very influential in social and political realms and their Protestant identity granted their influence religious significance as well.

superior white race sat the Anglo-Saxon version. Lesser white races like Italians or Irish had the chance to rise through the social ranks depending on their ability to align themselves with dominant cultural norms. However, the other races deemed unsuitable for assimilation were actively campaigned against throughout the Dominion. Chief among the fears of the Anglo-Saxons was that of race-mixing because it was believed that so-called half breeds would weaken the hearty Anglo blood. Such beliefs would ultimately lead to the 1928 Alberta government's shameful use of Eugenics and forced sterilization. In the period covered in this chapter, such thinking also led to increasingly cruel and restrictive immigration policies.

Chinese immigrants were sought out for the construction of the railroad mostly because they were cheap labour and it was considered better to risk their lives than the lives of the white citizens of B.C. After its completion, Asians were no longer characterized as desirable immigrants and many were left to either starve in the wilderness of B.C. or join together in the Chinatowns of the urban centers. Their race, non-Christian religions, and different cultures made them, in the words of the day, a "yellow peril" against which white British Columbians needed to remain vigilant. The federal and provincial government of B.C. levelled a $50/head tax to any Chinese person wishing to enter the country. Finding that amount insufficient as a deterrent, the price was steadily raised so that by 1904, it was ten times the original amount.

In 1907, Vancouver made international headlines because of the anti-Oriental race riot that saw white British Columbians attacking both Chinatown and Japantown before Japanese immigrants were able to beat back their assailants. Future Prime Minister William Lyon MacKenzie King was dispatched to handle the embarrassing situation. His subsequent report inspired an amendment to the Immigration Act. In 1908, the Continuous Journey Regulation was enacted. It stated the Canadian government could "prohibit the landing in Canada of any specified class of immigrant who have come to Canada otherwise than by continuous journey from the country of which they are natives." In essence, this meant that anyone desiring to enter Canada had to do so on a ship that could make one continuous trip from the point of origin to the shores of Canada without stopping for any reason.

European ships could do this but ships from the Asian lands needed to find ports in order to re-fuel or re-supply. This not only restricted Chinese and Japanese immigrants but also excluded inhabitants of India. The Hindus were thus singled out as well, a particularly blatant attack because, as Smith noted, though "they are British subjects, they are not welcome into the Dominion of Canada."[9] I don't want to oversell this point and there would be few people who would be shocked to learn that 19th century popular ideologies were not exactly progressive when it came to race relations or gender equality. I do want to shed light on this because this time period gave birth to some myths that exist today.

THE MYTH OF THE COLD-LOVING CANADIAN

One of the most enduring myths that remains to this day is that Canadians thrive in the cold. No we do not. Canadian blood is no thicker than any other person's blood and I have spent enough time in this land to know that we lament the cold, and are just as prone to complain about it and avoid it, as any other nationality on earth. In the words of my son: "It's not that Canadians like the cold, it's just that we're used to it." However, we still cling to the notion of the hardy Canadian handling cold better than the inhabitants of other lands.

This myth has only been strengthened by a national obsession with hockey and the popularity of winter sports. On the surface, that may seem like a support of Canadian pro-winter toughness but then I simply offer to you the "snowbird" phenomenon as a rebuttal. A snowbird is a Canadian (usually of retirement age) who spends the duration of winter south of the

---

9   W.G. Smith, *Building the Nation: The Churches' Relation to the Immigrant*, (Toronto: Canadian Council of the Missionary Education Movement, 1922), 128.

border in warmer climates like Florida. Much like the Canada goose, such people are seen leaving this land in droves (usually in recreational vehicles) as the weather dips and the return of these people, much like the aforementioned bird, signals the return of spring.

Less anecdotal and more quantifiable, is any StatsCan map detailing where most Canadians live. From that alone, you can see just how much we detest the cold and just how false the winter-loving-Canadian trope really is.[10] An overwhelming amount of Canadians live as close to the southern border with America as humanly possible. Vast stretches of Canada have been declared uninhabitable by approximately 90% of Canadians and all of those regions are in the northern parts of this supposedly cold-loving land. This myth might seem innocuous or like just a bit of silly nationalist bragging that we can all enjoy. However, it becomes problematic when the belief that Canadians handle the cold better than other lands translates into an arrogance about immigrants from other lands. Handling the cold becomes a measure of "Canadianism" and, from that perspective, this myth has more potential for harm than we might care to believe.

Case in point, during the time of the postage stamp, cold weather was seen as one of Canada's assets. Those who were hard at work building the hearty Christian nation of Canada saw the snow and cold as forms of immigration policy given by God. The religious papers and writings of that time were filled with racial epithets denigrating undesirable immigrants and praising God for the sobering winters that would keep so-called weaker races from desiring to live here. It was taught that Anglo-Saxon blood held within it a toughness and durability that made all of that lineage much hardier in cold climates.

After all, England was peopled with Anglo-Saxons (another myth) and its global victories were thanks, in part, to its own

---

10   Canada FAQ reports that "the majority of Canadians live close to the border with the United States." http://www.canadafaq.ca/where+do+most+canadians+live/ Numerous other articles and sources show that anywhere from ¾ to 95% of Canadians live close to the border and the chief reason given is a more amenable climate.

cold and rainy climate. If you remember the last chapter you will recount that cold weather kept many desirable immigrants (British) from moving to Canada in favour of warmer American climates. Susanna Moodie and others published their hatred for the long cold winters. As the Dominion grew, some Protestants were able to spin Canada's winter into a sign of Providential blessing rather than a national weakness.

So, to recap, in just three chapters we have already seen several foundational theological reinterpretations of events designed as apologetics for Canada (I mean apologetics in the sense of a rational defense of an idea/view not the "I'm sorry" kind of way. Given Canadians' reputation for saying "Sorry" all the time, I do enjoy the humour in that). The Loss of the Revolutionary War was God cleansing the Empire of the insidious Republic; the power of French Catholics became contemporary versions of the biblical giants Joshua was called to fight (Protestant view); God spared the French Catholics from the American Revolution (Catholic view); now even the frigid and potentially fatal winter became further evidence of God's blessing. These weren't the only theological spins—and they won't be the last ones contained in this book—but I point it out because it reveals again Canadian Christians' inferiority complex. However, it also shows an aptitude for seeing God at work no matter the circumstance.

UNITING CHURCHES FOR CANADA

In conjunction with these ideas about Anglo superiority and celebration of the cold was a dominant national theology that viewed Canada as a centerpiece of the British Empire. A Dominion that needed to assert and promulgate God-honouring doctrine across its breadth. Thus the push for a United Church began. This enterprise would see increased revenue and influence offered to churches in much the same way capitalists and railway men sold Confederation to distant regions like British Columbia.

"If you join Confederation, we will bring the railway to

you and your local economy will burst with new import/ export opportunities and new merchandise as well."

"If you unite with our denomination, you will be granted access to the coffers that will allow for your church to pay a decent pastor's salary. You will have access to supplies, grow your congregation, and even free up money for missions."

Immigration and the railroad went hand in hand. The western world was being opened in order to compete with America's Manifest Destiny. Farmers began to head west in droves and by the 1880s initially smaller groups like the Mennonites almost rivaled Methodism's numbers in what is now Alberta and Saskatchewan. This was great for some but concerning for others.

Some asked what happened to the rugged Methodist pioneers of old? What happened to the ones who had traversed dangerous lands and won British North America for evangelicalism? Where were the Methodists? To answer that question, we welcome back our friend from the beginning of this chapter: Neville Trueman, the man who never died. This was overly dramatic because the reason he never died is because Neville Trueman never actually existed. He was a character in one of those pioneer books that became so popular during this time.

NEVILLE TRUEMAN

William Henry Withrow brought Trueman to life in his book *Neville Trueman: A Pioneer Preacher. A Tale of the War of 1812*. It is a hilariously scathing commentary on what Withrow saw as the weakening of Methodism. One of the reasons Mennonites and Methodists were growing closer to numerical equality in the west, it was argued, was Methodism's place in the higher levels of Ontario society. In short, Methodism had achieved the levels of influence men like Strachan had always tried to keep from them.

Withrow was clearly upset by such dalliances with influence and saw the Methodism of his day as a betrayal of its earlier, and better, character. He saw the church of his own time acting no differently than the fabled Anglican enemies of the past. The Methodist circuit riders had rightfully condemned such affluent Christians for their religiosity and fought them unceasingly for the souls of the colonists. The evangelicals had won, thanks be to God, but then became the very thing they had fought against. Withrow, in response, created a true man and his titular character was a true Methodist hero. A man of uncompromising values and rugged toughness from a time when Methodist men were real men. A time when the denomination wasn't caught up in the carnal and embarrassingly profane matters that were consuming the church of Withrow's day.

Like most myths, Withrow's book heralds the reader back to the good ol' days when Methodists were all about missionary zeal and conversion irrespective of natural or man-made obstacles. A time when Methodists were not warring with each other over unnecessary doctrines, or church buildings, or propriety. Like most nostalgic writings, it remembered a time that never really existed. Withrow's book does demonstrate that as the 19th century drew to a close, the growing wealth and stability of the land was causing some concerns about the spiritual health of Canadians. It was the 19th century version of more money, more problems.

While the west would always struggle with feelings of isolation and rail against Ontario's apparent lack of concern for them, the latter 19th century brought about a more unified Canadian church and a more unified Canadian nation with Christian values at its core. The Protestant, Anglo-Saxon, Masculine Christendom was well under way and structures were being established to see it last for generations. However, there was one notable, and frustrating, exception. Every time a Protestant missionary arrived in the west to build a new church and increase their national influence they kept discovering one very annoying and undermining fact.

The Catholics were already there.

CATHOLIC SUPERIORITY IN MISSIONS

Protestants weren't the only ones busy creating a Christian Canada in the wake of Confederation. While French and English were the official languages of Canada, many immigrants of German descent began to enter after 1867. So many, in fact, that German became the third language of the nation. This is not to say that Germans were new to Canada; they had been here since the 18th century and Halifax was largely built by German settlers in 1750. In fact, Lunenburg's population had grown to a whopping 10,000 within 10 years of the fort's completion. While many of these immigrants were Lutheran and Mennonite, the latter half of the 19th century saw many German Catholics leaving far-removed places like Odessa or closer locales like the United States and arriving in present-day Saskatchewan. Their industry and skills made them valuable members of society and their faith meant that priests were also needed.

In the west, places like Red River (Winnipeg) had enjoyed Catholic support for decades before either the railroad or Protestantism arrived. While Protestant pressures were making life rough on Catholics in Ontario (and to a lesser extent even Quebec), the west remained fairly untouched; most of the struggles there came as a result of internal Catholic tensions.

The dominant issue was language because many of the Catholics in places like Victoria were English-speaking, while the leadership was traditionally French. Ukrainians of the Eastern Rite (which had been joined with Rome since 1596) were offered precious few clergy because their ministers were married and were forbidden to emigrate to North America. Unfortunately, this 1894 anti-immigration decree coincided with one of the largest years of Ukrainian influx into Canada (not a coincidence). This increase in demand resulted in a similar problem for late 19th century Ukrainian Catholics as many early 19th century colonists faced: too many people, too few leaders.

Catholic dioceses had been opening since 1817, in spite

of the complaints of Anglican clergy, and by 1850 there were 983,680 Catholic Canadians. The nation had a total approximate population of 2.3 million by that time, making Catholics nearly one half. While there were technically more Protestants, don't forget the term included every denomination from Anglicans to Methodists, Mennonites to Moravians, Unitarians to Brethren in Christ; not one of which came anywhere numerically close to 900,000.

Thus were the Catholics better suited to national influence because they had the double blessing of being both ecclesiastically unified as well as sanctioned and supported by the British Government. As is the case with most successful church movements in history, those who are unified always accomplish more while those who are divided measure their influence in much smaller increments.

On the other side of the French Revolution, Catholic clergy in Canada were staunchly opposed to any idea of America taking over British land (hence the strange occurrence of French Catholic clergy actively telling people to fight for the British Protestant crown). In the wake of Napoleonic France, more Orders were created that increased Catholic missions around the globe. Republican France was hard on the church and that brought more Catholic Orders to Canadian shores. While Jesuits and The Brothers of Saint Vincent de Paul were numerous and influential, most western missions were the result of the Missionary Oblate of Mother Mary Immaculate, or Oblates for short.

While much of the early work of missions in the west was done by secular priests (priests who worked for a diocese but were not connected to a specific order) the Oblates were instrumental in bringing Catholicism to places as distant as James Bay, Red River, present-day Northern Saskatchewan, and British Columbia by the 1840s. Their vows of poverty and obedience made their influence even more palpable as the financial concerns Protestants faced were not as restrictive for Catholic missions. The Oblates often had little more than £10 on them as they arrived in whatever isolated location they had been called to serve.

Their vows, coupled with the fact that they didn't have families to support, meant that Catholic teaching came at a bargain basement price. These people became skilled trappers, builders, and hunters and similar to the Methodists of the early 19th century, were seen as one of the people they were serving rather than some distant reclusive spiritual academic. In fact, about the only scholarly work most of these men did was translate hymnals, Bibles, and prayer books into the various Indigenous languages closest to them. While they received no formal training in this area "all soon managed to [communicate] without interpreters...a condition essential to the success of the mission."[11]

The vow of obedience prepared these men for their work in ways that Protestants never could quite duplicate. While Baptists were arriving in Red River in the 1880s and finding the temperature and culture daunting, the Oblates had been there for decades and were well-established in those rugged and isolated locations. There are stories of Oblates and other priests literally saving the lives of Protestant missionaries who would become trapped in the cold. These men lived on next to nothing but were incredibly resourceful and their vow of obedience meant that people could be moved around quickly and with little fear of rebellion or resignation.

The Oblates found creative solutions to the problems of western missions that built on their existing Orders' rules but included a flexibility that made them pretty successful with both Settlers and First Nations. Like many of the early stories in Canadian religion, they served the people and simply lacked the resources or desire to force belief. Thus, as the institutions of power began to arrive in the early 1890s, coercive policies only gained a foothold after a season of substantial rebellion from the people. We will explore an example of this in a moment but first,

---

11 Robert Choquette, *The Oblate Assault on Canada's Northwest*, (Ottawa: University of Ottawa, 1995), 194.

let's talk about the Catholic women and all they accomplished.

I don't like to dedicate much space to numbers but there is one that is so staggering from this time period that I would feel remiss to not include it. In 1850, there were around 650 Sisters in all of Quebec. By 1900, that number had grown to over 6600. The Sisters of Charity, the preferred female coworkers of the Oblates, moved beyond their 19th century work in Montreal and established hospitals and schools in many of the same places as the Oblates during the later years of the century.

So too with The Sisters of Providence. However, the areas in which these women shone were in the realms of education and social services that complimented and surpassed that of their male counterparts. Social work will be an extensive part of our next chapter but as the needs of these rural communities grew, many of these sisters grew to meet the challenge in areas that were not necessarily their expertise. Education of the young, forming day schools, and boarding schools became one such area. From their arrival in Victoria in 1858, these sisters spread out through the burgeoning province and even into Alaska.

Therefore, as the railway connected the nation, more people began to go west into the vast prairie lands to build their futures. German, Hungarian, Polish, Ukrainian, Russian, Irish, Scottish, and English Catholics changed the demographic of Catholicism from the traditional French to a more multiethnic version of the faith. As the 19th century carried on, the Catholic leaders recognized the need for more English-speaking Bishops for this increasing collection of non-French Roman faithful in the west.

Missionary agencies had been instrumental to any church group desirous of western expansion which, as we have seen, meant smaller denominations were left out. Those that found their footing did so much later in the century after much of the religious landscape had been decided by the Anglicans, Presbyterians, Methodists, Mennonites, and Catholics. However, this attention to the west also meant that Atlantic Canada began to diminish on the national stage. A traditional stronghold of the

Baptists, Canada's oldest evangelical expression entered into a season of increased irrelevance.

Canada in the 19th century decided that it would be a westward facing nation and the transatlantic connections needed to wane. No longer was this a nation dependent on maritime connections, this nation's future was to be found in the fertile lands of the prairies and in the natural resources of British Columbia. Eventually the Baptists of the Atlantic would align with Baptists throughout the rest of Canada but the love affair with western expansion proved that the growth of one group frequently came at the expense of another group, even in as vast a land as Canada.

LOUIS RIEL: HERO AND CONTROVERSY

The Metis originated as children of French Voyageurs and First Nations that dated back to the first days of the fur trade. They blended both cultures but lived largely like their Indigenous ancestors even as they took some elements from their French lineage; like their language and religion. By the later part of the 19th century, the Metis were largely French speaking but, like most others in that region, were also fluent in English (a solid minority would consider English as their first language), and a multiplicity of Indigenous languages.

Louis Riel (1844-1885) was raised in Red River by a politically active father who was a leader in the Metis community—and who almost became an Oblate himself—and a mother who almost became a nun. Early on, the Catholic clergy of St. Boniface claimed Riel possessed a unique genius and was well-suited for the priesthood. Raised a devout Catholic, he left his home to be educated in Montreal, supported by none other than Bishop Alexandre Tache. He would do very well out east but eventually returned to Red River and began his life as a freedom fighter for the Metis.

In 1869, Canada began to move into the newly-purchased Rupert's Land. Unfortunately, surveyors and governor-elect McDougall jumped the gun and began surveying the land in order to break it into a more British style (the Metis lived around Hudson Bay Company outposts in allotments that took after a French style. There is a lot to explain about the differences but just know that the way the British and the French divide up land is different). They did this without taking existing borders into consideration. They also did this without taking into consideration the land was not actually the Hudson Bay Company's land to sell.

Desiring their concerns to be heard, the Metis National Committee appointed the Eastern-educated and skilled orator Riel as their president. The committee drafted the "Declaration of the People of Rupert's Land and the North-West," a document that rejected Canada's authority to govern their lands. They proposed to negotiate a settlement between Canada and this newly-formed provisional government. The Provisional Government of Assiniboia was included in the 1870 Manitoba Act that welcomed the province, including the respected lands of the Metis, into Confederation.

However, trouble was afoot that brought Riel into conflict with the Protestant leaders of Ontario. A Canadian military enterprise was underway during this time as well, hoping to convince Scottish Catholics from the Red River region to help destroy Riel's provisional government. This was discovered and the small collection of infiltrators was detained at Upper Fort Garry. Court martials were held and a young man by the name of Thomas Scott was ordered to die by firing squad. The killing of this member of an Ontario Orange Order on 4 March, 1870 made Riel a permanent target of the powerful Ontario Protestants. While celebrated in Catholic Quebec as a hero of Catholic concerns, Riel eventually fled to America to save his life.

During his time in America, Riel lived as a devout Catholic with a piety that would rival even the most ardent teetotaler of any age. However, Riel had a strangely evangelical experience in Washington D.C. on 8 December 1875.[12] In words that are

---

12   Robert Choquette notes what an important date 8 December is: "[I]t was on 8 December 1869 that the provisional government in Manitoba had been

shockingly close to that of Methodism's founder, John Wesley, Riel wrote: "I suddenly felt in my heart a joy which took... possession of me" and from that moment on, he saw his role as a prophet for his people.

Though he would return to Canada, his increasing insistence that he was tasked by God to usher in a new world led many friends to question his mental health. His life was very stressful and he was actually institutionalized twice against his will for erratic behaviour. During all this he began to distance himself intellectually from the Catholicism of his boyhood even as he kept up appearances as a devout Catholic by attending Mass regularly.

His admissions to receiving visions and revelations only increased and further deepened his belief that the Metis were to be emancipated from the oppression of the Canadian system. As we are going to see in the next chapter, Riel's belief that the Kingdom of God was soon to be established on earth was a concept growing in popularity at that time. Even his belief that the papacy would transfer from Rome to Montreal had basis in larger Ultramontane Catholicism that was very popular in Canada. I tell you the story of Louis Riel because it is unique as well as indicative.

His evangelical/mystical experience not only aligns him with more emotive faith but reminds us, once again, of America's importance on the Canadian scene. Despite receiving Catholic education in Red River and Montreal, Riel's prophetic call came in the capital of the United States and his life's theological passion was found south of the border. Riel's own journey away from Orthodox Catholicism also mirrors that of the prairies he called home. As we will see in subsequent chapters, these lands were destined to move from the rational Christianity of their founding missionaries to become the bedrock of conservative

---

proclaimed and that Pope Pius IX had opened the First Vatican Council... It was also on 8 December 1854 that the reigning pontiff Pius IX had proclaimed the dogma of the Immaculate Conception of Mary, and on 8 December 1864 that the same pope had issued his celebrated Syllabus of Errors, the foundational charter of ultramontane Catholicism." Choquette, *Religions*, 279.

evangelicalism in the following century; a theology built largely on prophetic beliefs of God's kingdom that closely resembled Riel's.

By 1884 Riel was attempting to do for the Metis in what is now southern Saskatchewan what he had earlier done for the Metis in present-day Manitoba. A provisional government had been set up to once again bargain with the Canadian government for the rights of the people. However, there was one powerful difference between the 1884 events and the 1870 successes in Manitoba: the railroad.

The violent disregard Canadians had for the Metis and other Indigenous people of the west was well-known during Riel's life. Despite popular sentiment of this age, many of the earlier missionaries and entrepreneurs had been more fraternal in their behaviour. The railway brought power and money that made peaceful interactions with the Metis a waste of time and resources, according to numerous leaders. Added to that was the hatred many Ontario Protestants had for Riel. This Metis leader was, even by the accounts of his critics and detractors, a faithful and good Catholic with morals and a clear intelligence. He taught school children and was well-educated and erudite. Yet he was unable to find an audience for his grievances within the growing power of Canadian Christendom.

His resistance against Canada came to a violent end as Riel surrendered to Canadian forces and was officially charged with treason. His lawyers attempted to plead insanity, a position Riel adamantly refused. He delivered a speech in court that not only displayed his rhetorical prowess but also proved his clarity of thought and ensured his sentence of death. Louis Riel was hanged in Regina on 16 November, 1885.

Finally, Riel's ability to combine faith with rebellion—while not anomalous in the Christian story—reminds us that beliefs are not formed in a vacuum. His theology, strange as many saw it to be, was based on a belief that God's justice would finally prevail against Canada if his followers were brave enough to follow him.

Louis Riel also wanted a Christian Kingdom, but the one he described looked much different than the ones Dominion churches were working to establish. Riel was a Christian but he didn't view mainstream Canadian Christianity—Catholic or Protestant—as an expression of faith, he saw it as oppressive to his people.

His life is proof that the lighter touch of a truly incarnational mission like the early Oblates or Sisters can yield generations of thoughtful and faithful followers from a variety of different backgrounds (though it must be noted the Oblates would abandon earlier models and also become agents of oppression as revealed by Indigenous children later in Canadian history—we will address this in the second last chapter). Riel's resistances in 1869 and 1884-5 remind us how quickly differing views of what the church is called to be can lead fellow followers of Christ into violent conflict with one another.

***

So, the stories of Bainton, Trueman, and Riel each show us elements of Canadian Christendom as well as the concerns Christendom created. Patriotism, political activism, and increased relationships with power brought cohesion for some and marginalization for others.

What was agreed upon by all was that the church had to help form and safeguard Canadian civilization. Christians of different denominations across the Dominion appeared willing to "accept a large measure of responsibility for the well-being of society."[13] The profound influence churches exerted over Canada during the years we have been looking at cannot be easily overstated.

Protestants built churches and support networks to compete with Catholics while Catholicism struggled to keep up with the demands from the non-French faithful. Despite all this change, most Canadians by the turn of the century were

---

13   John Webster Grant, *The Church in the Canadian Era*, (Vancouver: Regent, 1988), 212.

entrenched in the beliefs they already possessed.[14] Thus I make the argument that, while quiet in 1867, the following 100 years were a flurry of action and noise that took the ideas of the past and brought them to bear on the new reality of an industrialized Canada.

In order to understand what I'm talking about, we have to now explore the 20th century. If you remember the postage stamp from earlier in the chapter you know how important Canada was to the future of the world based on its connection to the Empire. However, those very connections to the ideas of Europe and England created some of the greatest challenges Canadian Christianity ever faced.

The 20th century would make and break decades-old alliances and create new denominations; it would witness Catholics aligning with Protestants against other Catholics; it would question all aspects of Christian thinking from creation to the nature of salvation. By 1967, an almost entirely new vocabulary was created as Canadian Christendom began to fall apart.

---

14   As John Webster Grant puts it, religious affiliations were "fixed, by and large, several decades before Confederation." Grant, *Canadian*, 223.

RESOURCES

Gordon L. Heath. *A War with a Silver Lining: Canadian Protestant Churches and the South African War*, 1899-1902. Montreal & Kingston: McGill-Queen's University, 2009.

- This academic work explores the ways in which the Boer War was interpreted for Canadians during its prosecution. Importantly, it shows how such attitudes influenced the way in which Canadians would interpret World War I.

Chester Brown. *Louis Riel: A Comic Strip Biography*. Toronto: Drawn and Quarterly, 2006.

- A beautifully drawn biography of Louis Riel. This graphic novel should be in every Canadians' library as it handles the story deftly and with great nuance that is visually stunning.

John Webster Grant. T*he Church in the Canadian Era*. Regent: Vancouver, 1988.

- Grant offers tremendous insight into many of the issues covered in this chapter. He explains how the churches of the later 19th century evolved from a British religion into a Canadian faith throughout the 20th century.

Alan Rayburn. *Naming Canada: Stories About Place Names from Canadian Geographic*. Toronto: University of Toronto, 1994.

- This is a very funny and insightful book that reads more like a popular level work than an academic work. Along with exploring the popularity of Moose within the Canadian lexicon, this book helps readers see and learn the stories behind some of the more popular and obscure place names throughout Canada. It is truly amazing to realize how many Canadian stories can be found simply paying attention to the names of various people. Rather than simply recount (boring) details about how places got their names, Rayburn takes the time to really show the heroes and scoundrels behind some of the most important locations in Canada. A fun way to understand Canadian history.

W. G. Smith. *Building the Nation: The Churches' Relation to the Immigrant.* Toronto: Canada Congregational Missionary Society, 1922.

- This first-hand account gives the reader insight into one Christian's research into the immigration issues of Dominion Canada. Smith's insights are compassionate and his research was helpful in this chapter's understanding of some of the immigration and racial attitudes present during this time. While a harder resource to find, it is well worth the exploration. For those interested in this topic, but unable to find this book, see Rich Janzen, Mark Chapman, and James Watson. "Integrating Immigrants into the Life of Canadian Urban Christian Congregations: Findings from a National Survey" (available online) for a more contemporary perspective by three sociologists of religion in Canada.

---

1 IDEA

Canadian Christendom (Dominion) granted the churches unprecedented influence superior even to American clergy. However, such influence was negatively viewed by the numerous groups that didn't benefit from this Protestant, Anglo-centric version of Canada. When we lament the passing of Christendom, we need a better understanding of the elements from that time that were abusive and problematic.

CHAPTER 4
LANGUAGE
1907 -

First thing we'd climb a tree
and maybe then we'd talk
or sit silently
and listen to our thoughts.
With illusions of someday
Cast in a golden light
No dress rehearsal
This is our life
— "Ahead by a Century"
The Tragically Hip

INTRODUCTION

When, in May of 1907, the Holy Spirit fell upon Ellen Hebden (1865-1923) she wrote:

> *My whole being seemed to be filled with praise and adoration such as I had never realized before... I said to the Lord "What does this mean?", and a very quiet, yet distinct, voice said "Tongues." I said "No Lord, not Tongues." Then followed a moment of deathlike stillness, when the voice again uttered the word "Tongues." This time I felt afraid of grieving the Lord and I said "Tongues, or anything that will please Thee and bring glory to Thy Name!"...Great peace filled my soul and I began to sing very quietly but to my amazement I was singing in another language.*[1]

From that moment, Mrs. Hebden's life began a trajectory of ministry, evangelization, and supernatural Christianity that anyone familiar with Pentecostalism will recognize. However, there are unique elements of this woman's story that deserve much deeper exploration; not the least of which was her disappointment in receiving the gift of tongues. Ellen Hebden's ministry in Toronto was dedicated to healing and she questioned the Lord's wisdom when Tongues, rather than healing, was the gift bestowed upon her. Strange or comical as that may seem, such a belief not only highlights the character of the woman, but also makes what followed a uniquely Canadian experience of Pentecostalism.

Mrs. Hebden's divine encounter occurred independently from Azusa Street and as far as we can tell, she had no idea similar events were transpiring in California at roughly the same time.[2] Another important element of this story for Canadian

---

1   Thomas William Miller, "The Canadian Jerusalem: The Story of James and Ellen Hebden and Their Toronto Mission Part 1," In *A/G Heritage*: 5-22 [Fall 1991], 6.

2   I desire this work to align with historians exploring the polygenetical theory of Pentecostal origins. Historians like Joe Creech, argue that the preponderance of the "Azusa paradigm" of Pentecostal origins is a result of the historical consciousness of the first generation of Pentecostal writers and eyewitnesses to the events of Azusa Street, which made it difficult for them to separate "historical events from their

Christianity is in the very un-Canadian trait that the Hebden Mission (where Ellen had her experience) became globally influential for a season. While this is the first time a Canadian Christian movement created such a global fervour, it would not be the last.

The Hebden Mission has been called at different times by different historians the "Canadian Azusa" or the "Canadian Jerusalem" and we can't understand the origins of Canadian Pentecostalism without taking the events of 651 Queen Street East, Toronto into account. As you are about to read, there was plenty that set The Mission apart but what made it a typical Canadian story was the ever-present tension of balancing European and American influences while creating something new.

The Mission began in the years following the 19th century program of building explained in John Webster Grant's *Profusion of Spires* and William Westfall's *Two Worlds*. These books are not simply tales of architecture but of architecture representing the worldviews, dreams, ambitions, goals, and ethos of the Ontario Protestantism discussed in the previous chapter.

Any traveler entering into Toronto in the early 1900s would be greeted by a horizon dotted with buildings and the aforementioned spires. Frequently, we see the religious landscape of Canada in much the same way. Our attention is drawn to those denominations who were, metaphorically speaking, large enough to be visible from a distance. However, the Hebden Mission offers us a reminder about the popular, literally ground-level expressions of the faith that were gaining influence and shaping Canadian Christianity.

Perhaps they were not as visible in this period of time but we overlook them to our own detriment; especially when one considers the longevity and growth of the PAOC (Pentecostal Assemblies of Canada). Some of these storefronts were designed

theological interpretations of them." Joe Creech, "Visions of Glory: The Place of the Azusa Street Revival in Pentecostal History," *Church History* 65, no. 3 (September, 1996), 407.

by, and for, smaller groups of immigrants but others, like the Mission, came out of beliefs that modernism was spreading through formerly great evangelical stalwarts like Methodism.

Ellen Hebden had been part of a similar house-based ministry in her native England called Bethshan, and it was during her time there that she had met her husband James. The two were inspired by the Keswick Movement: an annual, evangelical experience in the English town of Keswick that stressed personal conversion, biblical teaching, and holy living. The Hebdens believed they were called to live out their faith on the mission field and that brought them first to Jamaica and then on to Toronto. For a couple of years, the two set about establishing a home dedicated to contemplative life, prayer, and healing for all who believed. It was in this home that Canadian Pentecostalism was born.

Ellen would write that the day God spoke to her had begun with the final non-Mission tenants moving out. For her, that marked the moment the Queen Street space was properly sanctified to receive the Spirit of God. That evening at around 10pm, while a service was taking place on the main floor of the Mission, Ellen received the blessing that begun this chapter and changed this land.

Over the next few years, the Canadian Asuza's home became a gathering place for burgeoning Pentecostals from all around the world. The accounts of healings, utterances of prophecy, strange languages, and miracles brought skeptics and believers alike. One of those skeptics was George Chambers, a pastor who served a few blocks away. The early reports coming out of the Mission filled him with grave concern and he warned his congregants to fervently pray that such events would not invade their place of worship.

Their prayers, he would later note ruefully, were granted and the Hebden Mission remained the preeminent location for the Holy Spirit's presence in Toronto. Chambers would eventually leave his former church and become a staunch supporter of the Hebdens. This was the beginning of a new ministry for him that was cemented in 1919 when he became one of the founders of, and first superintendent over, the PAOC.

Before the PAOC's 1919 birth as a recognized Canadian denomination, the Hebdens spent years basking in God's seemingly unending blessing and building a respectable, if controversial, Canadian expression of the faith.

Newspaper articles explored the Mission and took some time to talk about the star of the show: Ellen Hebden. When questioned about the extremes this version of the faith caused and asked if this was some form of religious psychosis, Hebden simply replied: "Do I seem maniacal?"[3] To which the reporter had to respond that she did not. Through all the positive and negative attention, the Mission became globally significant due to its style of worship but also its abiding dedication to educate and send out missionaries.

Hebden-trained missionaries brought their Pentecostal teaching to locations as diverse as Ontario, Western Canada, Africa, Mongolia, China, America, and even Newfoundland (little joke there). Charles and Emma Chawner, Canada's first Pentecostal missionary family, were sent out from the Mission and China was the recipient of another Hebden alum: Robert Semple. However, it would be Semple's wife who was destined to profoundly shape Pentecostalism and who remains, in my humble opinion, one of the movement's most important theologians. I am speaking of Aimee Semple McPherson (1890-1944) or, as she is known in her Four-Square Gospel circles: Sister Aimee. Aimee always spoke about being a rural girl from Ontario who encountered God in humble circumstances and never dreamed of the kind of life she would end up leading. In a manner reminiscent of many stars of stage and screen, she moved past her humble roots and into the limelight of Los Angeles. While theatrical to say the least, Aimee's destiny was to become a world-famous preacher, not a star of the silver screen.

---

3 "Divines Indulge in Merry Moods," *The Toronto Star*, Monday, April 7, 1907, 1.

LANGUAGE

We will return to the Hebdens and Sister Aimee in a moment but this chapter is about language and so we begin with a brief Latin lesson. Ovid's Metamorphoses contains the following words: *et ignotas animum dimittit in artes* or, in the English, "and he turns his mind to unknown arts."[4] The challenges of the early 20th century created new words and understandings that the faithful had never encountered previously.

Christians had to contend with new ideas and, in so doing, turned their minds to unknown arts in order to explain and defend the faith in the face of such novel challenges. Twentieth-century Christianity was, in many respects, unchartered territory and terms like modernism, evolution, inerrancy, dispensational premillennialism, and Pentecostalism were created to explain the new world that was coming into being. This chapter explores not just the words, but the world that created those words.

Because Canada has always been a bilingual land, we will also take some time to address the changes that were taking place within Canadian Catholicism as well. In this chapter we are going to look at:

1. Aimee Semple-MacPherson and organizing the PAOC
2. Richard Bucke's cosmos and intellectual metaphysics
3. The growing respectability of English Catholicism and the tensions that created
4. Fundamentalist Christianity: a cartoon
5. Western Canadian Bible colleges
6. The United Church of Canada
7. Canadian social gospel movements

Somewhat ironically, it was Protestant and Catholic responses to the challenges of modernity that created the generations-long influence still dominant in today's Canadian Christianity.

---

4 Ovid, *Metamorphoses*, Book 8, Trans. By Brookes More (accessed 18/11/2021) http://www.theoi.com/Text/OvidMetamorphoses8.html *Metamorphoses*. Line 183.

AIMEE SEMPLE-MACPHERSON AND ORGANIZING THE PAOC

Sister Aimee, like Ellen Hebden, came to her Pentecostal faith independently of the famous Azusa Street revivals that took place in America in 1906. Her initial encounter with the Spirit took place at a revival close to her home, led by Irish preacher Robert Semple. After the two were married, she went with Semple to the Hebden Mission and received missionary training and validation for her impressive gifts from no less than Ellen herself. Aimee and Semple, inspired by the Mission's call to preach to the whole world, then moved to China as missionaries. Their time there was cut short when both became ill. Aimee survived the encounter, Semple's subsequent bout with dysentery proved fatal and the young mother of one returned to Canada. She would later marry an accountant by the name of McPherson and move to New York. However, motherhood was not her only call in life and she frequently thought of the passion she felt during her mission with Semple and the encouragement she had received from Hebden.

Although she and McPherson seemed to have had a good marriage, one that brought another child into her life, Sister Aimee packed up her kids and hit the road to preach from her car. Her husband soon joined but, after a year, found life on the road too unstable and returned to their New York home. He would file for divorce a year later. Aimee made her way to the city of Los Angeles and got down to the serious business of evangelization; she couldn't have picked a better town. The movie industry was making the city famous alongside many of its inhabitants, and a booming tourism industry made it a favourite vacation spot for thousands.

Thanks to those tourists, Aimee's message began to spread around the American nation. She was soon packing out places with her skilled, funny, theatrical, and poignant messages. The organization that grew up around her was able to purchase some space and soon the Angelus Temple was packing in upwards of 5000 on a regular basis. A Canadian Pentecostal superstar had arrived and set up shop not far from Pentecostalism's famous

Azusa Street.

While her ministry would make her a citizen of the world, Aimee returned to Canada as a powerful voice for change and spiritual renewal; a message that would impact her former home. After the healing of his wife's cancer in Ottawa, a gentleman by the name of Mr. Baker gave up his business and became a Pentecostal evangelist until his death in 1947. "Daddy" Baker—as he came to be known—directed an evangelistic thrust in Montreal and encouraged outreach to other parts of the province. He was the man responsible for inviting Aimee to the city in 1920 and her meetings that year were described by numerous attendees as the greatest revival in the history of predominantly Catholic Quebec.

Eugene Vaters (1898-1984), a disillusioned Methodist struggling with Modernism in his denomination (another topic we'll explore later in this chapter), investigated Baker's revival and four years later, after some time at the Moody Bible Institute, returned to Newfoundland as a reinvigorated Christian. Vaters and Pentecostal matriarch Alice Garigus (1858-1949) would join up and in 1925 the Bethesda Pentecostal Assemblies of Newfoundland was officially recognized as a denomination.

Two years later, Vaters would become the leader of the denomination, a position he held until the early 1960s. He would lean on Baker (including inviting Baker to preach at a revival) and that ensured the Montreal and Newfoundland connections would remain very strong. The strength of present-day Newfoundland Pentecostalism owes a debt to Garigus' vision, Vaters' theological concerns, Hebden's healing ministry, and Aimee's powerful Montreal revival.

Aimee held to a conservative theology but her presentation of the Gospel was anything but. She quickly adapted to the culture of her new home and brought props from local movie studios into her services. She once rode a motorcycle up on stage to illustrate a sermon about racing towards hell. She had elaborate costumes and sets and basically brought all the magic Hollywood could muster into her ministry.

Sometimes overshadowed by her theatrics was her theology. Her Foursquare church focused on what she believed to be the four elements that summarized the full Gospel: Jesus as Saviour, Jesus as healer, Jesus—along with the Holy Spirit—as baptizer, and Jesus as soon-coming King. Sister Aimee focused such teachings on personal salvation found only in Christ, the necessity of baptism, the reality of divine healing, and the defense of premillennial dispensationalism. Healing was a major part of the Hebden Mission and shows the ongoing influence that small Canadian mission held over the Pentecostal icon. But it is premillennial dispensationalism that will receive the lion's share of the attention in this chapter on the development of Christian language in the early 20th century.

I would like to return to Ellen for a moment because her belief that the Spirit should supersede organizational structure provides us with another insight into revivalism's nuanced history in Canada. Throughout 1910-11 Ellen's thinking became increasingly at odds with a growing segment of leaders within the movement. Likely due to her childhood religious experiences with her high church father, Ellen never took an official title and openly mocked designations like Reverend.

George Chambers and many others who had left denominations in which they held titles, possessed no such convictions. For Ellen, such organizations threatened proper ministry by usurping Jesus' leadership—most clearly seen in local churches—in favour of human organizations. Such structure, despite the rhetoric, reflected the motivations of this world, not God's kingdom. Ellen's staunch condemnations of such organizations alienated her from union talks and goes a long way to explain why the Hebdens were not part of the post WWI meetings that gave birth to the PAOC.

The Hebdens, like Alline in the 18th century, eschewed organization and the result was that both disappeared from the annals of the denominations they helped establish. In both cases, it would be historians of later generations who would rescue them from obscurity and grant them the influence they deserved. Like Alline, Ellen Hebden and her followers founded a vibrant Canadian faith that was exciting and unique to this land. She was influenced by her English home and the healing emphasis within the Keswick Movement. While her Latter Rain experience was separate from Azusa, she spent the remainder of her ministry interacting with, teaching, and learning from Pentecostals in the States. Both English and American influences can be seen in the Hebden Mission. Through missionary zeal and people like Sister Aimee, it also made a name globally and that made it unique among Canadian Christian experiences.

The Canadian Azusa really was ground zero for Canadian Pentecostalism and many PAOC churches across Canada can trace their origin to 651 Queen Street in Toronto. While this may seem to argue against my assertion that revival has little transformative value for Canada, the deeper point is that the revivals of the Hebden Mission and Henry Alline became influential because of institutional organization more than spiritual excitement. Like the Baptists of the Atlantic provinces, or the Methodists of Ontario, even a spiritually rambunctious denomination like the PAOC realized that organization—more than revivalism—was the key to success in Canada.

RICHARD BUCKE: A CASE STUDY OF INTELLECTUAL METAPHYSICS

Let's return to California and transport ourselves from sun-soaked Los Angeles to the snowy chill of the Rocky Mountains a few decades before Sister Aimee's arrival. We gaze in horror at a Canadian traveler about to freeze to death. Richard Bucke (1837-1902) had left Canada to pursue a life of adventure in the western frontier of America and found himself in a miner's cabin, recovering from near-fatal frostbite that would claim his feet but spare his life. That ordeal would prove religiously fruitful for the self-educated man and he would write later that while the experience cost him part of his feet, his new perspective was worth the price.

Returning to Canada once he was strong enough, Bucke

attended McGill and brought his new-found belief in the grandness of eternity to bear on his medical education. His California experience would never fully leave his mind and his near-death experience provided the motivation for his true spiritual quest.

Medicine offered him one avenue with which to explore his true passion for the life beyond. He read widely and deeply in the realms of poetry, literature, science, religion, French and German philosophy (two languages he taught himself), all the while maintaining grades sufficient to win a gold medal upon his 1867 graduation. He won awards and acclaim as a prolific writer who seemed to treat his rural Ontario medical practice as a means to support his academic pursuits.

A devotee of Walt Whitman, 1872 saw Bucke in England speaking at a conference about the influential American poet. After an evening of discussion, Bucke was returning to his lodgings when, in his words, he found himself "wrapped around as it were by a flame-coloured cloud." He originally took the dramatic appearance for an explosion in the city but came to realize that "the light was in himself."[5] Dr. Richard Bucke had just received a born-again experience.

Returning to Bucke's words, written in the third person, about that night: "[T]he Cosmos is not dead matter but a living Presence…the soul of man is immortal…all things work together for the good of each and all… the foundation principle of the world is what we call love and that the happiness of everyone is in the long run absolutely certain."[6] While scholars like Ramsay Cook argue this conversion was a later systematized reflection about pre-existing ideas, I hope you are able to hear in this episode echoes of other conversions like that of Henry Alline.

Unlike Alline, Bucke would not begin a new religious movement, per se, but would spend most of his career in London, Ontario as the Superintendent of the local Insane Asylum. In

---

5   Richard Maurice Bucke, *Cosmic Consciousness: A Study of the Evolution of the Human Mind*, (Philadelphia: Innes & Sons, 1905), 8.

6   Bucke, *Cosmic Consciousness*, 8.

this role he would again receive awards and acclaim for his humane and progressive treatments of the mentally ill. Similar to Alline, Bucke's experience with the light would inspire his writing and he would pen his most well-known work *The Cosmic Consciousness*.

Bucke's revival was religious in nature for sure, but it was not Christian. He would hold to a life-long belief that Jesus was a good man but not divine. He was a champion of evolution but not the Darwinian method as much as a cosmic advancement he believed to be at the heart of all life. Such beliefs would influence his treatment of the mentally ill because he began to believe that mental illness was not unnatural but was "closely linked to sanity through the evolutionary process."[7]

Sister Aimee and Dr. Bucke have many things in common. Both were rural-raised Canadians who underwent life-altering experiences that brought them into global prominence as pioneers in their respective fields. Both traveled to America and were inspired by the innovative nature of the Republican land. Both focused on the mystical elements of life and believed such intangible forces were the true powers of consciousness. But their religious differences provide a fitting picture of the spectrum that began to develop in the early years of 20th century Christianity. While controversial in her delivery, Sister Aimee reinforced conservative Christian views like inerrancy of Scripture, rejection of evolution, and a premillennial eschatology; worldviews that were increasingly under fire in the modern age. Bucke, in contrast, was clearly a genius who eschewed much church teaching as outdated, irrelevant, and just plain wrong. However, unlike many of his fellow academics, he believed in the afterlife and dedicated his superior intellect to explaining his illumination experience in England. Semple-McPherson illustrates the evangelical impulse while Dr. Bucke personifies the growing scientific and intellectual condemnations of classic Christianity.

---

7 Ramsay Cook, *The Regenerators: Social Criticism in Late Victorian English Canada*, (Toronto: University of Toronto, 1985), 94.

THE RESPECTABILITY OF ENGLISH CATHOLICISM AND THE TENSIONS THAT CREATED

We are going to return to such tensions that would dominate Canadian Christianity in the 20th century, but first we must take some time to explore a global event that had a profound impact on Canadian Catholics: World War I. The casualties this war created truly boggle the mind as death tolls rose to unprecedented numbers from the years 1914-1918. If you remember back to the previous chapter, Canada had first supplied soldiers for the British cause in South Africa at the turn of the century. You will remember the pride and nationalist language that came along with this as it was perceived to be a real step towards maturity and autonomy. That distant war did much to advance Canada's pride, sense of growth, and sense of global importance; ideas that were underpinning much of Canadian Christendom.

While such patriotism remained for the first world war, the catastrophic number of fatalities throughout the years did much to dampen earlier enthusiasm. Like most Christian rhetoric around war, Canadian churches raised the stakes of the conflict to cosmic levels in order to justify following the Prince of Peace while advocating for war. This was not simply nations of the earth battling for rival principles of government, this was a battle between good and evil and, as such, needed to be fought.

Increasing optimism of the early 20th century tended to condemn Christianity as a superstitious relic of an unscientific and unenlightened past, a belief most churches clearly did not enjoy. Christian teachings on human depravity were being overturned in light of the profound advances of the late 19th and early 20th centuries. With such optimism regarding the human species, religious rules and fears were losing their strength compared with the demonstrable evidence of human growth and development.

While the churches struggled with the theological and ecclesiastical consequences of this utopic optimism, they did seem to embrace certain facets as it pertained to war. The "war to end all wars" was dubbed such partly because it was believed that World War I was the last vestige of the ancient world's love of violence. It was the dramatic death of war and, at its conclusion, would usher in a new and peaceful world. With this interpretive paradigm in place, it only made sense that the last human war effort ever would be bigger than all previous incursions. Little did these people know, not only was WWI not going to be the last war, an even more destructive global war was only 20 short years away.

Before we get to that, an interesting development began to occur in Canada in the years following 1918. The willingness of Canadians, irrespective of faith or background, to engage in the costly conflict won Catholics respect in the national psyche. Actually, let me qualify that a bit better: their involvement in the war garnered *English-speaking* Catholics a new level of respect. While the French would remain a target of scorn and suspicion, their English co-religionists enjoyed new prestige and acceptance.

To be fair, Catholicism was crawling towards respectability due in large part to the prevalence of Catholic hospitals that both treated and employed people of other faiths. However, the influx of English-speaking Catholic immigrants threatened the French's hegemony over their church in Canada. The French Catholics had been the first to truly settle the west but their influence was being watered down by the aforementioned immigrants. English-speaking Catholics enjoyed their new prestige and, on a few occasions, even sided with Protestants against their French fellow Catholics. A notable story comes from Archbishop John J. Lynch of Toronto, who became so concerned about French Catholic influence that he demanded a halt to any French-speaking Catholics entering the province.

In essence, the times between both world wars saw an internal Catholic competition developing based on language more than theology and "seemed at times more interested in promoting...respective language rights than in sharing their common religion."[8] This is an important point to consider as we return to the language around modernism and fundamentalism because the underlying beliefs of both are much the same.

French-*Canadien* Catholics believed that their faith was superior to the Protestant version (nothing new there). Due to the marginalization they were experiencing in developing Christendom, they also became more vocal that the French language needed to be protected from English supremacy. For their part, English Canadian Catholics returned the favour and became more comfortable denigrating the French language and their French counterparts. The newer Catholic immigrants began to display a more Canadian nationalism that reflected Catholic convictions but, through the use of the English language, found greater sympathy in Protestant ears. This also shows the greatest rivalry in Canada is not, as some suspect, between Catholics and Protestants. The willingness of English-speaking Catholics to join forces with Protestants demonstrates that Canada's deepest internal divide remains between the French and the English.

The mantra of many Irish Catholics, for example, became fidelity to the Holy See, British Crown and, of course, an autonomous Canada. Autonomous is the important word there because these Catholics understood that independence was not something Canadian Christendom desired. These new Canadians were not only pro-Canadian but demonstrated their cultural savvy as well by becoming verbally anti-American. They learned quickly that a Canadian English Catholic was not only different from a French Canadian Catholic but was also different from an American English Catholic.

Thus was the monolith of Canadian Catholicism beginning to show cracks. Unlike the breaks being formed within Protestant circles around modernism (which we'll get to in a moment), Catholic cracks were due to actual linguistic differences, not theological ones. The two official tongues of this land created

---

8 Terrence J. Fay, *A History of Canadian Catholics*, (Montreal & Kingston: Mc-Gill-Queen's University Press, 2002), 158.

space for profound divisions to occur. The English wing of St. Peter's church in Canada found that condemning Francophone Catholics was the easiest way to gain ground in Christendom. This enmity had nothing to do with ecclesiology or theology but it would open the door for a cataclysmic reckoning within Canadian Catholicism only a few years later.

Linguistic enmity remained primarily between the French and English and, to be honest, has never been settled in any suitable fashion for the history of Canada. However, Christendom was also creating new vocabulary and the rivalries of the previous age were rearing their heads again, albeit in new forms. One element almost as divisive as the French/English tension was the new language surrounding biblical interpretation and authority. Although it would do little to unite various branches of the faith, all believers—Catholic and Protestant, French and English, American and Canadian—understood that traditional Christian teachings were under attack.

FUNDAMENTALISM: A CARTOON

To begin, let's look at the term Fundamentalist. This label was coined by Curtis Lee Laws, editor of the Baptist paper, "The Watchmen-Examiner," to describe Christians willing to "do battle royal for the fundamentals."[9] What were the Fundamentals? These were a series of 12 books written predominantly by American and British conservatives (with a few Canadians as well) between 1910-1915. They argued for the fundamental teachings of Christianity one must believe in order to call oneself a Christian. On the other side of this debate were the modernists/liberals who were willing to stress freedom from certain Christian doctrines and become more conversant with the modern trends of the age. With those two descriptions in mind, let's explore this cartoon from 1922:

I absolutely adore this comic. It says in one picture what many of us have attempted to do in entire books. If pictures are

9 George M. Marsden, *Understanding Fundamentalism and Evangelicalism*, (Grand Rapids: Eerdmans, 1991), 57.

worth 1000 words, then this picture is a library unto itself. So, I want to take a moment and dissect this cartoon because I think it has a lot to offer about the fundamentalists vs. modernist controversy and what it has to do with this chapter on language.

In the beginning we have a young man at the top of the stairs. He is youthful, handsome, and seems to be a model pastor as he is carrying a Bible (presumably) under his right arm. He has a full head of hair and, what is more important, he is not bespectacled. About the only negative thing we can say about him is that his back is turned to the light. Note the shadow which

The Descent of the Modernists. By E.J. Price, ca. 1922. This can found at wikimediacommons.com

indicates that even at this early point he is already on a dark and slippery slope down.

The name given to the first step is, quite simply, "Christianity." By that we can assume the artist means the more conservative version of the faith that held to traditional views, a faith that needed to be defended from modern assaults. "What kind of assaults?" you might ask and I am glad you did so because the rest of the comic will answer that exact question.

The next step is plainly titled, "Bible not infallible." In the early 20th century, when this strip was created, biblical higher criticism had made its way from Germany into Canada and was an established way of thinking. The University of Toronto, among other schools in larger metropolitan areas, contended with this issue and many careers were defined based on their viewpoints regarding the infallibility, or inerrancy, of Scripture. At stake was the authority of the Bible.

Although lacking nuance, essentially higher criticism looked at the Bible as it did other texts from the ancient world. Scholars discovered that even the Bible had been put together from multiple, and often anonymous, sources. Questions began to arise about, but not limited to, the first 11 chapters of Genesis. Was the Garden of Eden an actual place? Was there actually a global flood? If Adam and Eve only had two sons, where did the other people come from? If the first five books were written by Moses, how do we understand the passage that called him the humblest man on earth (which pretty much negates the statement)?[10] Is it possible some other anonymous author penned such a wonderful affirmation? Is it possible anonymous authors penned other sections as well?

While some pastors and scholars found such insights exciting, breathing new life into the Bible, others saw it as a challenge to divine inspiration. Many people in the pews at this time would not have wrestled with such questions and that is important to remember. Douglas Wilson makes the comment in his book *The Church Grows in Canada*, that "a lag between seminary and pew existed."[11] How much the trends of the academy pervaded the church is a matter of scholarly debate, but what is generally held is that increased attention to this matter caused concern among conservative ministers and leaders. The belief that the seminary shaped the pulpit and the pulpit shaped the nation meant that such teachings threatened, once again, the Christian character of Canada.

---

10 Numbers 12:3 - "Now Moses was a very humble man, more humble than anyone else on the face of the earth." (NIV)

11 Douglas Wilson, *The Church Grows in Canada*, (Toronto: Ryerson Press, 1966), 117.

While serious fights broke out in places like McMaster University, Hamilton, the greatest rebuttal to modernist teachings is seen in the proliferation of Confessional Bible colleges in the prairie provinces of Canada during the 1930s. These institutions of higher learning were dedicated to teaching the so-called faith of the fathers and offering theological foils to the more liberal institutions of the big cities.

There is very little time to cover the enormity of this topic in the space allotted so I will use the Presbyterians and Methodists as case studies. The Scottish tradition of possessing a broad and deep education helped the Presbyterian denomination during the period of intellectual struggle in Canada. George Monro Grant (1835-1902) was principal of Queen's University and held the Christian faith needed to be intellectually respectable if it hoped to retain relevance in Canada. He was instrumental in bringing philosopher John Watson to the school and promoting the newest streams in New Testament scholarship.

One of Watson's students, D.J. MacDonell was the minister of St. Andrew's in Toronto and was inspired by the social ramifications of the gospel; a characteristic of the so-called liberal faithful. His belief was that the Gospel called Christians to alleviate social ills and that Jesus' healing ministry and crucifixion showed that charity was superior to doctrine, action trumped rhetoric, and orthopraxy superseded orthodoxy.

To this end, the late 19th century saw MacDonell begin mission houses in the slums of his city and hold night classes for working girls. When talking to a reporter, he mentioned his belief that eternal punishment in hell was inconsistent with the biblical picture of a loving God. This caused some Presbyterians to wonder if he had departed from the Westminster Confession. He was called to account for such beliefs and 1876 began what has come to be known as the Last Heresy Trial in the Canadian Presbyterian Church. At the trial it was decided that no one can overthrow the tenets of the Westminster Confession but, as the title indicates, it was also the last heresy trial for the denomination. Officially MacDonell was chastised but, unofficially, the writing was on the wall and history shows us that the church was heading in a new direction.

In Methodism, the historical evangelical stronghold of Canada, Dr. George Jackson challenged the creation account in Genesis (1905) and was attacked repeatedly by Methodist Superintendent Dr. Albert Carman. Dr. George Workman of Victoria University refuted dictation theory—the notion that the Holy Spirit literally told the biblical writers what to write verbatim—and was forced to resign in 1899. He went to another college but was chased out by conservatives and forced to resign in 1907. However, Nathanael Burwash (Victoria College, Toronto) and laymen Chester Massey & Newton Rowell were vocal in their promotion of freedom within biblical interpretation. In the end, many preachers avoided the more controversial aspects of the debate and so we must acknowledge the earlier comment about the gap between the academy and the pew. That gap was not destined to last.

The Catholic Church also faced the pressures of modernism and to a large extent reacted in much the same way. The difference between Protestants and Catholic fundamentalists was that the latter had a strong, central governance upon which to lean for guidance and theological teachings. Catholic fundamentalists were known as Integrists because they supported the Catholic Church in its integrity. In 1878, under Pope Leo XIII, the Vatican instructed all of its seminaries, colleges and universities to teach only the philosophy and theology of Thomas Aquinas (Thomism). All other philosophies/theologies/new teachings if they were referenced at all were referenced in the footnotes or at the bottom of textbooks. The centrality and supremacy of Aquinas was extolled in order to combat such modern questions. Pius X also published the encyclicals *Lamentabili* in July 1907 and *Pascendi* in September. Pius argued that modernists supported agnosticism and seemed to claim that religious truth arose from man's need instead of God's special revelation. He argued modernism took the supernatural out of the study of history and weakened the faith as well as the sanctity of human life. It would not be until Vatican II in the 1960s that the Catholic Church examined the significance or challenges presented by higher criticism.

I hope you see why the artist chose biblical infallibility as the first step. The doctrine of inerrancy became important because the very core of the Protestant faith, the faith of *sola scriptura* was at stake. If the Bible was not handed down by God, then how can anyone know what is true about the faith? "This doctrine of 'inerrancy,' as it came to be known, was no invention of the late nineteenth century. Many Christians in the past had said or assumed much the same thing. But the fact that now some conservative Protestants were making biblical inerrancy a central doctrine, even sometimes virtually a test of faith, signaled the degree to which the new scientific and historical threats to the Bible were forcing everyone to shore up whatever he or she considered the most critical line of defense."[12] Like loyalty had been previously, inerrancy became one of the most important watch words of the day to determine the validity of one's Christianity.

The next, and increasingly darker, step reflects the belief that humanity no longer contained the *imago Dei*. Where did this idea come from? Well, in 1859 a gentleman by the name of Charles Darwin published a fairly influential book called *Origin of the Species*. This was followed in 1871 by his second work *The Descent of Man* which brought his theory of evolution to bear on the human species (the cartoon's title "The Descent of the Modernists" is likely a sarcastic nod to this second work of Darwin's). It is probably worth noting that when *Species* was first published many people in Christian circles welcomed it. On the other, more familiar, side scholars like Charles Hodge of Princeton also wrote against it. In his 1874 book *What is Darwinism?* Hodge answered his own question by stating that Darwinism is atheism.

However, response to Darwinism was varied within

---

12 Marsden, *Understanding Fundamentalism*, 37-8.

Protestant circles. Only in the southern United States was it consistently used as a barometer of orthodoxy. This is due, in large part, to the Civil War and the inherent suspicion the southern people had of anything that came from the north. In essence, Darwin's theory offered a counterpoint to the long established teaching of creation as explained in the Bible. Arguing that humans developed over generations removed the need for a creator God. In other words, we are no longer the pinnacle of creation but more the result of a random evolutionary accident. At least that's what the critics of evolution argued.

So, in the first two steps we see our handsome young pastor wrestling with the philosophical and scientific trends of his day. In order to contend with these challenges, our pastor was willing to concede to some of these theories. After all, where is the harm in recognizing the validity of scholarship and communicating a thoughtful and critical faith that can speak to these challenges? Well, the answer to that question is evident in the next steps.

The next step "No Miracles" just makes sense in the enlightened culture of the early 20th century. The idea that Jesus walked on water, or fed thousands of people with some little boy's lunch, or successfully battled demons sounds more like the fairy tales and myths of ignorant previous generations. However, modernists argued that these tales offered the reader important moral, ethical, and social lessons. Celestial events always heralded the birth of important people in the ancient world so we must not judge Matthew for adding the detail of the star to the nativity account.

Many of the truths of the Gospel, like the multiplying of food, were clearly exaggerations for literary effect and should be viewed as such. But the lesson the modern reader could take from such tales fit quite well into Canada's growing culture of social responsibility. If people pool their meager individual resources together, they multiply their symbolic loaves and fishes into a bounty substantial enough for everyone to enjoy. Thus the miracle can be revealed for what it was: a morality lesson about generosity and developing a social conscience that had ongoing relevance for Canadian Christians. The question was no longer "did this actually happen?" but shifted the gaze to present-day readers to ask them "will you help make it happen again?"

In such ways did certain Christians attempt to rescue the Bible from irrelevance by downplaying the mystical and miraculous for the ethical teachings contained therein. However, for other Christians, to do so was to strike at the very heart of the Gospel narratives. In effect, completely negating the power of Jesus over this world and the next. Arguably such concerns help explain the popularity of vibrant expressions like Pentecostalism or the variety of Holiness Movements that were born in the later 19th and early 20th centuries. They were seen to combat the spiritual dryness of established churches and the liberal stress on the ethical that challenged the power of the Gospels. These churches focused on dramatic conversions and powerful testimonies but also the second blessing or Latter Rain (as it was known in some circles) which set the person free, in the power of the Holy Spirit, to serve Christ in the world.

Biological evolution was not the only concern for the Fundamentalists; social evolution also presented a theological threat. It painted a very optimistic picture about the progress of humanity (remember the earlier beliefs about WWI being the "war to end all wars") that challenged the doctrine of depravity. Humans, it was argued, were capable of evolving to a moral and ethical level that made them more worthy to receive Christ at his second coming. Such beliefs spawned the conservative retaliation of premillennial dispensationalism made popular by conservatives like Aimee Semple-MacPherson.

Dispensationalism stated the role of the church was to win souls and await Christ's return to save the faithful from wretched and sinful wayward humanity. Proponents of this teaching divided history into ages and argued they lived in the sixth age: the age of the church. This age, like all those that had come before, was fated to end cataclysmically. Therefore, social evolution was just one more false ideology using science to entice the unsuspecting from their Christian beliefs in favour of earthly concerns.

The next step shows that clearly, in a world without miracles, the idea of the virgin birth is laughable. It makes sense, once again, from a literary point of view but not for anything connected to the real world. The idea of a virgin birth is not unique to the Christian story after all, unique births (even virgin births) were an ancient literary trope used to communicate the importance of a hero's life. The increased Greek scholasticism of the 20th century showed that the biblical word for virgin could also be translated as "young woman". Thus, Mary was a young woman who had given birth but later Christians changed "young woman" to "virgin" in order to give Jesus' birth a more messianic quality. In response, Marian centrality became a feature of Catholicism from the mid-19th to mid-20th century. Devotion to Mary was seen as a necessary corrective to this character assassination as well as foundational to support Catholic piety. This is evidenced in the numerous Catholic parishes named after her during this 100-year period.

Now that the miracle accounts of Jesus' life had been disproved and the virgin nature of Jesus' birth discounted, there was little point in defining him as divine. It is worth pausing in our description of the stairs to take a look at the character on the stairs. Note that our young pastor is not as young as he was when he first began. The Bible under his right arm is now a series of papers under his left; indicating that new and varied theories have replaced scripture as his dominant reading. His wardrobe has also changed and his eyes are now obscured by glasses, indicating his decreasing ability to see. This man, now more enveloped in darkness, has his foot on the step that challenges the atonement. Honestly, if Jesus is not miraculous nor divine, then there is little room left for this cornerstone theology. Jesus was fully human but not divine and his sacrifice was nothing more than another example of a good man being murdered by an oppressive regime. Tragic and poetic as that may be, it had no lasting salvific value.

With all these tenants of the Christian faith thus removed, no bodily resurrection was required. That would be the height of folly, even worse than a belief in the miracle accounts. And just like that, Jesus is relegated to the clubhouse with other great, though mythical, religious heroes. The final step, not surprisingly, is the embrace of agnosticism over Christianity. The camp of Dr. Bucke and his fellow spiritual academics; the camp of those scholars who, for all their intellectual acumen, had fallen prey to the deceptive spirit of the age. As we all know, agnosticism is just half a step up from full-blown atheism.

Atheism, for those who opposed the modernists, is the inevitable destination of the journey begun by our young pastor at the top of the stairs. To deny even one element of the traditional/ fundamental views of the faith is to descend into darkness and damnation. As evidence, our character is now completely ensconced in darkness, underneath his arm there no longer resides a Bible but a tome of academic literature, his respectable suit has been traded in for the robes of the academy, and his hair is completely gone.

Do you see what our young pastor has become? A German professor.

Seriously, how good is this comic strip? A blatant attack on the higher education that undermined the traditional teachings of the Bible in favour of the latest trend of the present age. However, conservatives were not the only ones who saw education as problematic for the future of Canadian faith. The more left-leaning Methodist Conference of 1892 met in Montreal and put forward the advice that a well-lived life was more important than one's adherence to a specific doctrine. Literally the exact opposite conclusion of the fundamentalists.

Although the two sides came at this point from diametrically opposed perspectives, both sides were attempting to achieve the same goal: fighting the perceived irrelevance of Christianity in Canada. However, the language they used to accomplish such ends made them anathema to each other. In the Anglo-Franco Catholic tensions and the conservative-liberal Protestant cases we have explored, language overshadowed shared faith and made enemies out of brothers. The great irony of these years is that both sides were incapable of seeing similarities and instead focused on their differences. For over 100 years now, Canadians have practiced their faith and their theology in the wake of that irony.

WESTERN CANADIAN BIBLE COLLEGES

As the novel ideas of the later 19th century became the curriculum of the early 20th, Canadian Christianity once again found itself in a crisis of faith. Some of this was brought on by the scientific and intellectual advances of the Victorian Age, but a large portion of this was brought on by the churches themselves.

New language, like premillennial dispensationalism, biblical inerrancy, evolution, dictation theory, six-day creation, and fundamentalism took over and formed the shibboleths of the new century. With educators being forced to contend with the issues of Darwinism and higher criticism and their ramifications for the church, many people began to question the validity of Christian higher education. Once again, I turn your attention to the explosion of Bible Colleges in the prairies of the west throughout the 1920s-1940s.

Not only did these schools act as a foil against the perceived liberal modernist tendencies of the big-city schools, they also ensured a more conservative climate for the west that exists to this day. More than 50% of Bible Schools in the west began in the 1930s. After 1952 many of these schools consolidated with others and began focusing on accreditation and academic respect but the numbers are impressive: Mennonites built 44% of the Bible schools, while Pentecostal/Apostolic made up 17% and the Baptists built 6% of these Bible Colleges.

Tommy Douglas is often—and correctly—seen as the quintessential Christian politician of this age. He is the architect of socialized medicine in Canada and made no secret that his policy was inspired by his Baptist beliefs. While Douglas' influence is beyond dispute, I want to introduce you to a lesser-known western Christian politician so that you can see a subtler, though pervasive, element of prairie faith.

William "Bible Bill" Aberhart founded the Social Credit Party and was the Premier of Alberta in the 1930s and 40s. He was largely responsible for bringing premillennial dispensationalism to Alberta (he became a believer after finding solace in the teachings of C.I. Scofield and soon adopted Scofield's teachings into his own theology). He taught that the church could never build a Christian society but must concentrate on conversion as the return of Christ was imminent. A theme made popular in various radio ministries like Scofield and Sister Aimee.

After being refused ordination, he became the unofficial pastor of Calgary's Westbourne Baptist and gave himself the designation "apostle," much to the annoyance of the actual pastor of the church. He began "The Prophetic Voice" newspaper and it became the vehicle for fundamentalism in Western Canada. The following quote is from there: "We believe that the final court of appeal is the infallible verbally inspired Word of God. We believe it all, and knowing that the original manuscripts have been lost long ago, we have no confidence in those individuals, here and there, who claim superior wisdom in the Greek and Hebrew that they attempt to correct what the Lord Jesus pronounced infallible and adamantine."[13] He held that the *Textus Receptus*, which is the main text for the KJV, was maintained by God in the Swiss Alps and was kept free from Catholic contamination. In 1927 he pulled Westbourne out of the Baptist Union of Western Canada because of a perceived modernist heresy at Brandon Bible College (which became secular in 1939). He then began the Calgary Prophetic Bible Institute Church in 1927 (W.B. Riley preached at the opening) but his personality drove many people back to Westbourne and his religious influence diminished as his political career grew.

His Social Credit idea deserves further exploration because it brought him into conflict with Prairie Bible Institute's

---

13   John G. Stackhouse, *Canadian Evangelicalism in the Twentieth Century: An Introduction to its Character*, (Toronto: University of Toronto, 1993), 38.

teachings that the drought of the 1930s was God's judgment on sinful Canada. They argued that Aberhart's solutions smacked of materialism and dismissed his socially-focused teaching as heretical. Aberhart was a rare breed of fundamentalist in that despite his belief that the church needed to focus on conversion over social issues, he, like Tommy, was a pioneer of the kind of socialized care that would become a trademark of Canadian politics.

THE BIRTH OF THE UNITED CHURCH OF CANADA (UCC)

In order to truly understand the impact of the fundamentalist vs. modernist debate we must also recall that much of this took place during the Great Depression. The 1930s in Canada saw the wages of the average worker fall by more than 40% and a quarter of Canadians became unemployed. The prairies' economy was absolutely devastated, and the young moved away in droves searching desperately for work.

However, another major development also took place in 1925 when the Methodists, Congregationalists, the majority of Presbyterians, and a smattering of small independent churches joined together to form the United Church of Canada.[14] Once again, the beginning of the 20th century created new terms as establishment returned to the Canadian scene but with all new emphases. Rather than propping up the Church of England, as the 19th century Establishment sought to do, this established church was a church of Canada and for Canada. It was a church with, in the words of Phyllis Airhart, the soul of a nation.[15] The United Church came to life at the height of the fundamentalist/modernist split and was only five years old when the Depression hit.[16] If its birth was during a tumultuous time, its childhood

---

14   This is also the year that Prime Minister William Lyon Mackenzie King first set up a government attempt to give Canada a new flag. It would take 40 years before the flag would be completed and officially endorsed. A large reason behind this delay was the power of Orange Orders who thought early plans to rid the nation of the Union Jack weakened Canada's Imperial and Christian connections.

15   Airhart, *Soul of a Nation*.

16   It also came into existence the very same year as the Newfoundland Pentecos-

during the largest economic crisis in Canadian history was no less dramatic. The question the UCC faced was how would it stand up to this challenge?

The UCC did quite well facing this first of its major crises. We have numerous records of pastors taking pay cuts and opening churches as food banks to protect the people of the prairies. As many as half of their churches were closed and most fell into disrepair as the UCC used their money to subsidize various prairie communities. The admirable actions of this new(ish) Canadian Church set it up to become the most dominant form of Protestantism in the post WWII period. However, the attention it paid to addressing both the material and spiritual needs of Canadians created some unintended consequences as well. Not only would the UCC become less conversant with conservative Protestants but, ultimately, its mission alienated it from many of its own constituency in subsequent decades. I will explain that more in a moment but, for now, I want to offer a quick survey of other Christian responses to the Depression.

The Presbyterians who had not joined with the UCC struggled as they were still reeling from the union. They were already tight on funds and resources and were incredibly limited in their ability to serve their people. The Anglicans, who had pulled out of Union talks in the later 19th century, suffered under reduced resources from England. The Catholic Church was, arguably, the strongest and most capable of shouldering the sufferings of its parishioners. Earlier tensions resurfaced as English Catholics, farther from the French strongholds, suffered more than their Francophone brothers and sisters.

All the churches cut their overseas missionary budgets drastically and this, maybe more than anything, contributed to the loss of Canadian Christianity on the global stage. One theme of this book is that Canada is an overlooked nation; the loss of missionary endeavours in the 1930s goes a long way to explain the diminishment of a global Canadian Christian presence.

---

tal Denomination we already discussed. An interesting juxtaposition of two different Canadian Christian expressions as we will see throughout the rest of this book.

While Baptists launched their "keeping the faith" campaign and Denton Massey's York Bible Class got so large that it needed to rent Maple Leaf Gardens, the overall character of the so-called dirty thirties was that stability and survival superseded innovation.

The 1930s, much like World War I, proved to be a powerful corrective to the ideas of social evolution. The economic devastations, theological controversies, and global conflict made holding such a position increasingly tenuous. The Fundamentalists had to do little more than point out their front windows in order to rebut their liberal rivals' belief in the goodness of people.

However, the 1930s also saw the birth of Canadian institutions like Air Canada and the CBC. Despite the challenges to social evolution that the world was providing, public events like the 1926 Scopes Monkey Trial in the United States had a devastating impact for the Fundamentalists. Due to this highly-publicized event, the media created the now-familiar tropes that painted Fundamentalists as unsophisticated and unlearned rubes. Liberals were equated with the intelligentsia of places like New York (or Toronto in Canada's case), places where higher criticism found more favourable audiences. Thus the die was cast and the Fundamentalists increasingly withdrew from the public sphere as they were viewed as anti-intellectual, anti-scientific, irrelevant, and destined to die off. But they did not die off, they went underground and prepared for a re-birth.

Between the growth of radios and the prairie Bible Colleges, conservative thinkers like Scofield found new and excited audiences and were able to reach numerous people across denominational boundaries. New Bible Colleges could hardly afford a wealth of books but they could tune in every day to hear American Fundamentalists, or Bible Bill, and their conservative teachings.

George Marsden comments that as the 1930's waned so did the influence of the Fundamentalist movement. However, he contends that the movement did not weaken but simply realigned as those closest to the movement went about doing what they did best: evangelizing and building local churches. One of the most fascinating aspects of these conservative groups is that while their thinking was considered regressive, their use of technology was very progressive. Radio was the great media outlet of those days and the Fundamentalists used it perfectly to garner more influence. Radio made it possible for them to make their triumphant return to the Canadian scene, seemingly from out of nowhere, only a few years later. They resurrected with such calm control and influence that you would be forgiven if you questioned whether they had ever diminished in the first place.

Splits within Protestantism helped these Fundamentalist and conservative Christians build small but increasingly loyal churches that were vehicles of their doctrines. Other institutional groups like InterVarsity and Campus Crusade can trace their roots back to Fundamentalist groups that desired to return universities to their Christian roots. Many evangelical movements (even the more moderate ones) are children of these earlier groups, and the more conservative tone of Western-Canadian Christianity attests to the strength these Bible colleges, Sunday School lessons, and radio ministries had over the Christian climate. It would not be until the neo-evangelical movement of the 1960s (most famously represented by Billy Graham) that some serious inroads could be made between Liberal and Conservative Protestants, as well as between Protestants and Catholics.

THE CANADIAN SOCIAL GOSPEL

Despite the troubles of the 1930s—or because of them?—many people returned to the faith of their fathers. Hard times brought neighbours together and the church had shown herself to be a good neighbour by offering material assistance as well as spiritual comfort. In the words of one witness of the time: "The bootleggers are gone, the movies have gone, credit is gone, social life is gone, but thank God the Church remains."[17]

The UCC proved its worth and cemented its place on the Canadian religious landscape. It would take a few more decades and one more World War, but the Canadian establishment experiment would soon make it the dominant form of Protestantism in Canada. Baptists and Presbyterians, two churches that were known for splits and internal fights in the early years of the 20th century, were humbled by the Depression and began to become more conciliatory. 1936 witnessed the recovery of fellowship between the Anglicans, Presbyterians & the UCC. That same year, the Baptists adopted the UCC Hymnody and two years later, the UCC and Presbyterians officially made up. The Anglicans developed a denominational pride in their ability to survive with less assistance from England but they had been scared enough to re-enter Union discussions with the UCC in 1943; ultimately to no avail.

Sadly, Catholic divisions along linguistic lines only deepened over the issue of separate school boards even though Georges-Henri Levesque opened Quebec cooperatives to non-Catholics in the 1940s; much to the chagrin of the Jesuit and Dominican orders. In all of this upheaval, both social and ecclesiastical, the modernist and fundamentalist continued to disagree and new rivalries became cemented. The Great Depression taught Canadians that when the chips were down, the church could be counted on to help and that brought people back into their former folds. Those with ears to hear, let them listen.

While the 1930s' social movements in the United States became increasingly removed from the church, the same was not the case in Canada. Society was still seen by notable academics as resting on the twin pillars of government and church.[18] Although this chapter has focused on the theological splits that occurred during this time, it needs to also communicate that

---

17   Eleanor J. Stebner. *"The 1930s" As Found in The United Church of Canada: A History*. Edited by Don Schweitzer, 39-56 (Waterloo: Wilfrid Laurier, 2012), 47.

18   Charlotte Whitton, Carl Dawson, E.J. Urwick, and sociologist Harry Cassidy are just some examples.

Protestantism was responsible for introducing and championing many modern institutions to Canadians.

I don't want to overstate the mainline churches' focus on social ills as being the central tenet of their gospel. Even during the Depression, progressive clergy of the 1930s argued that conversion, repentance, and worship needed to supersede social care within the church. While some scholars have argued that Protestants weakened their role in society by focusing more on social programs than evangelization, I disagree. I find the words of Nancy Christie and Michael Gauvreau to be a more accurate interpretation of this time. In their book *A Full-Orbed Christianity* they make the following argument:

> *While modern defenders of the secularization thesis have pointed to the declension of social evangelism as synonymous with the growth of a secular culture, early twentieth-century progressive clergymen did not view social evangelism as an eternally valid theology.*[19]

It is better to understand the actions of these clergy as a two-pronged approach. Rather than being unwitting actors in their own demise, the introduction of practical programs like social work, healthcare, and research councils into economic and social ills was seen as the visible outworking of the spirit of the Gospel. The influence of Protestantism over Christendom was closely linked to government-funded control over a variety of social programs.

These churches advocated scientific knowledge in social realms as an indispensable tool to help Canada navigate the catastrophic realities of the post-WWI world. Therefore, it is fair to state that many of the changes during this time were actually, and intentionally, created by Protestant Canadian Christianity. Despite the critiques of Fundamentalists, the vast majority of evangelical churches saw their role as "fed by two powerful streams, inner piety and social evangelism."[20]

---

19 Nancy Christie and Michael Gauvreau, *A Full-Orbed Christianity*, (Montreal and Kingston: McGill-Queen's Univeristy Press, 1996), 248.

20 Christie and Gauvreau, *Full-Orbed*, 249.

As the economic devastation of the 1930s turned into the more affluent 1940s, some churches grew concerned about the growing influence of American media. We have already examined the popularity of American Christian radio over Fundamentalism and the role of American marketing on Canada will be the focus of the next chapter. However, as it pertains to this topic, a new development—traditionally believed to be a more 1990s' than a 1940s' belief—was beginning to emerge.

Clergy became concerned that more affluent Canadians were attending church less and, much like today, placed the blame on the convenience and corruption of media. William Creighton Graham (1887-1955), the President of the United College Winnipeg, noted that a growing number of Canadians remained interested in faith but were growing less interested in church doctrine. In other words, these Canadians were spiritual but not religious. This formed another argument for the role of Christianity in the larger culture.

Graham argued that a church focused on its own internal workings failed to inculcate the people properly. Christendom was still strong within Canada at that time and many Protestants reiterated 19th century arguments that the best guide for public policy was Christian theology. It needed to be the skeletal system upon which the flesh and muscles of modern society would hang. Unfortunately for Protestants like Graham, their words were falling on increasingly deaf ears as the land was undergoing profound changes.

***

In conclusion, 20th century Canadian Christianity handled the new challenges thrown at it during this time well. Christendom was strong and many Canadians witnessed the benefit of church connection for both their spiritual and material needs. Once again, the churches willing to sacrifice and serve the needs of the people benefited, while those who focused on words alone tended to fade.

Canadian faith maintained a nuanced relationship to the scientific developments of the new century. They advocated for such advances to help aid in societal issues but also struggled with the challenges these advances brought to ancient interpretations of the faith. Christendom's influence over social programs differentiated Canada from America but such differences were beginning to pale in comparison to the advent and popularity of American media.

In the next chapter we will look at the ongoing development of liberal Christianity in the wake of the second world war, the end of Canadian Christendom, arguably the most important lesson all churches can learn from Quebec, and the celebration of freedom that can only happen when the time-honoured traditions of the past begin to crumble. In other words, it is time to see how Canadian Christianity would fare in the turbulent and transformative decade of the 1960s.

RESOURCES

Nancy Christie and Michael Gauvreau. *A Full-Orbed Christianity: The Protestant Churches and Social Welfare in Canada, 1900-1940*. Montreal & Kingston: McGill-Queen's University, 1996.

- This book looks at the social care that Protestants offered to Canadians in the first four decades of the 20th century. They contend that secularization is not something that the churches did to themselves. Instead, they use research to show that the churches consciously saw social activism as proof that the church helped usher in many modern Canadian institutions and ideas.

George M. Marsden. *Understanding Fundamentalism and Evangelicalism*. Grand Rapids: Eerdmans, 1991.

- One of the best historical works explaining the origins and developments of evangelical and fundamentalist thinking. Marsden traces the origins of the terms and explores the unique make-up of both groups as well as taking the time to explore the legacy of Christians that would fit into each of these categories.

Phyllis Airhart. *A Church with the Soul of a Nation: Making and Remaking the United Church of Canada.* Montreal & Kingston: McGill-Queen's University Press, 2013.

- This book is very important to understand just how related the UCC is to Canada and vice versa. It offers concise and accurate data to show the intertwining of our nation's official church with our nation's understanding of ourselves.

Michael Wilkinson and Linda M. Ambrose. *After the Revival: Pentecostalism and the Making of a Canadian Church*. McGill-Queen's University: Montreal & Kingston, 2020.

- A very important work tracking and explaining the

growth of Pentecostalism in Canada as a uniquely Canadian expression of a global faith. These two bring a staggering amount of depth, research, and understanding to what could be a very complicated set of stories. Easily one of the most readable and thorough accounts of Canadian Pentecostalism from two of the best scholars on this topic Canada has to offer.

Mark Noll. *A History of Christianity in the United States and Canada*. Grand Rapids: Eerdmans, 1992.

- Dr. Noll is a rare American historian of Christianity in that he is genuinely interested in Canadian religious history as well. This is a sweeping look at the developments of the faith in both lands. Like this book, it is wide in scope and misses some of the nuances within the Canadian story. However, it remains a valuable work especially for those who are interested in comparing and contrasting the American and Canadian experiences/developments of the faith.

---

1 IDEA

As Christianity came under increasing skepticism in the early 20th century, two camps within Protestantism began to form. There were those who stressed doctrinal purity and those who focused on the ethics of Jesus. Both groups sought to end Christianity's perceived irrelevance but both camps increasingly became at odds with each other.

CHAPTER 5
FREEDOM
1967 -

There's no simple explanation
for anything important, any of us do
and, yeah, the human tragedy
consists in the necessity
of living with the consequences
— "Courage,"
The Tragically Hip

INTRODUCTION

In St. Paul's second letter to the Corinthians he famously wrote: "Where the Spirit of the Lord is, there is freedom."[1] Popular ideas about the 1960s state that Canadians used the freedom they found in that turbulent and significant decade to, ironically, stop believing in God. This is the decade that is blamed for the end of traditional family values, decency, morality, and Canadian Christianity itself.[2] While that is not totally wrong, a better understanding of what happened during that time reveals that such beliefs are not totally correct either.

I hope you have seen throughout this book that perspective and context are everything. One person's freedom is another person's chaos. Methodist Reformers looked like Anarchists to 19th century Anglican Conservatives, suffragettes were seen as a threat to democracy, Pentecostalism was critiqued as unsophisticated make-believe, social evangelism was accused of undermining biblical authority, and vitriol aimed at feminists stated they wanted to destroy families.

People are rarely prepared to celebrate the fallout of moving from the old and familiar into the new and untested. Any church worker who has tried to do something new in his or her place of worship is probably familiar with the frustrating admonition: "Why are you trying to change this? We have always done it this way." Such sentiments invade every element of life and guarantee that cultural visionaries and societal guardians rarely see eye to eye.

Near the end of the very important year of 1967, the Canadian Minister of Justice made a comment that was destined to follow him all the days of his career. Not just because of its evocative pithiness, but also because it became a turning point in Canadian policy. Called to defend his overhauling of the

---

1 2 Corinthians 3:17

2 "Political changes in the early 1960s marked a beginning of the end for public Canadian life defined by traditional religion." Mark Noll. *What Happened to Christian Canada?*, (Vancouver: Regent, 2007), 27. "The 1960's marked the decade at which Christian Canada, long on life support, finally expired." D.B. Mack, "George Monro Grant and the Bow of Ulysses: An Ecumenical Vision in Victorian Canada."

Canadian Criminal Code, Pierre Elliott Trudeau stated: "The state has no business in the bedrooms of the nation."

What did he mean by that and what did such a statement mean for the Canadian churches? We'll return to the first part of that question in a moment but right now I want to address what this line meant for Canadian churches. The simple answer is: it meant plenty. It is not an overstatement to say that Trudeau's statement was a world-changer for traditional expressions of Canadian Christianity. But before we can dive into that, we need to travel back a few months to another paradigm-shifting event that occurred in the summer of 1967 (told you it was an important year).

You are currently looking at a dais in Ottawa, containing nine empty chairs. The majestic and austere Parliament buildings of Canada form the backdrop. The weather is beautiful, the date is July 1st and Canada is celebrating its 100th birthday. The stage was constructed so that throngs of eager Canadians could catch a glimpse of Prime Minister Lester B. Pearson, the Speakers of the Commons and Senate, or the Governor General. Although, if we're being honest, the largest draw of all was Queen Elizabeth II and her husband Prince Philip. Each one of these impressive guests was there to speak to the crowd about the nation of Canada. They were there to tell the Canadians gathered on those grassy hills and huddled around TVs and radios from coast to coast what they could expect from the next 100 years. 'Twas a time of real fervour and patriotism.

The tones struck on that July day were of hope, celebration, introspection, optimism, and excitement about what was to come. In order to set a proper tone, a worship service was scheduled before the speeches; and this is when things got interesting (a statement rarely uttered before a worship service). The empty chairs on the dais were beginning to fill and, if you were there, you might have noted that they were being filled by religious leaders and not the aforementioned famous speakers. If you were there and particularly attuned to Canadian religion, you might have been even more curious to note that, of the nine now full chairs, only three were occupied by a Protestant.

Given that I spent the last two chapters detailing the construction and success of the Protestant vision for Canada that straddled colonial dependence and autonomy without falling into American republicanism; and that I went into detail about the verbiage that came to define much of Protestant Christianity and Canadian nationalism even up to today; and that Protestantism exerted influence over arenas as diverse as commerce, immigration, social work, war efforts, literary criticism, and even international relations, I would not be surprised if you, gentle reader, are more than a little confused by this snubbing of Protestantism on, of all days, the nation's birthday.

The image of the chairs provides a very clear picture of the role Protestantism was called to play in Post-Centennial Canada. Like the Post-Confederation nation, the date marked a point of transition as Canada intentionally moved towards becoming something new. In the Dominion days of 1867 and beyond, Protestants had provided much of the language and cohesion that defined Canada; but this would not be the case after 1967. I don't want to overstate this because Protestantism would still loom large over the culture, but the dominance of Protestantism was going to change. These historically influential churches were still on the stage, but they had less seats to call their own and less authority from which to draw.

However, this diminishment of Protestant power did not equate to the diminishment of Christian influence. Though a frequent concern of those who discuss secularization, this is a sweeping generalization that doesn't take into account the numerous ways in which Canadian faith continued to speak into the larger culture. Rather, reducing the Protestant influence was seen as a desirable way to elevate the influence of other faiths. Officially, the time had come for Canadian Protestantism to quite literally sit alongside other religious groups.

The three Protestant chairs were occupied by The Right Reverend Wilfred C. Lockhart, Moderator of the UCC, the Right

Reverend John Logan-Vencta, Moderator of the Presbyterian Church of Canada, and the Most Reverend H.H. Clark, Anglican Bishop of Rupert's Land and Primate of All Canada. No surprises yet, the organizers of the Centennial picked their Protestants well, historically speaking.

The next chair held His Eminence Cardinal Maurice Roy, Archbishop of Quebec and Roman Catholic Primate of Canada. Given the Catholic nature of this nation, no one should be shocked by his inclusion either. However, the next three seats were occupied by a noveler collective: the Right Reverend Timotheos of the Ukrainian Orthodox Church, Rev. D.P. Neufeld of the Mennonite Central Committee (starting all those Bible schools had paid off well) and Rabbi S.M. Zambrowsky rounded out the diverse religious traditions on display in front of the nation.

For those of you who are paying attention, you might have noted that we have included only seven of the nine seats and that is because I want you to pay special attention to the last two. The next seated man was Prime Minister Lester B. Pearson and that, like Archbishop Roy, should not come as a surprise. While Canadian politics have always maintained a delicate touch when it comes to national religion, the absence of the PM during the Centennial's worship would have been negatively noted.

The last man, Lavy N. Becker, is the most interesting man on the stage that day. While ethnically Jewish, he was not there to represent the Jewish faithful in Canada, that job fell to Rabbi Zambrowsky. Mr. Becker was the chairman of the Canadian Interfaith Conference and he was there to represent the other religious groups who brought religion to bear on the Canadian milieu. His was the face of differing faiths, and he represented Canada's desire to include all, irrespective of creed or confession. And it was Mr. Becker who opened the service with a Call to Worship from the Psalms. The reading instructed the people of the religiously inclusive Canada to remember that the nation "whose God is the Lord" is blessed.[3]

I hope you see how important that moment was for Canada and for the churches of the Canadian Dominion. Divine blessing was no longer attached solely to the Protestant narrative that had shaped large sections of the culture. Instead it had shifted to define a blessed nation as one that safeguarded the beliefs of its multicultural inhabitants. While a Catholic, an Orthodox, a Mennonite, and two Jewish men (one of whom was not even representing Judaism) on a stage hardly fits the definition of diversity in our modern context, I hope you see what that worship service really meant.

Gary Miedema opens his work *For Canada's Sake* with this story and he makes a very important point. While Canada was predominantly Protestant, what can be seen on 1 July, 1967 is that "it was also making new room in national public life for other religious persuasions."[4] Lee Beach's *The Church in Exile* also begins with the Centennial story but his more theological treatise offers consolation and biblical guidance to those who feel the loss of Christendom in Canada.

The Centennial could be viewed as the undoing of Canadian Christendom, but not for the reasons many people believe. This was not a desire to remove God from public life but to recognize that God could be found in a multiplicity of expressions. The Canadian government had no stake in choosing which version of the faith was accurate and decided instead to grant them all space. While the policies and the issues were different, this was the secularization of the Clergy Reserves all over again.

And that is the importance of Trudeau's comments near the end of 1967. His campaign to overturn many outdated laws included legalizing abortion, homosexuality between consenting adults, providing family planning resources for Canadians and, in bill C-187, legalizing divorce. Churches across the land didn't

---

3 Psalm 33:12

4 Gary R. Miedema, *For Canada's Sake: Public Religion*, Centennial Celebrations, and the Re-Making of Canada in the 1960s, (Montreal & Kingston: McGill-Queen's University, 2005), xv.

take to this young man's new laws and many argued that his actions both doomed and damned Canadian society.

Trudeau doubled-down on his famous line by stating that decriminalizing an act was not a challenge to the moral teachings of any faith. As Andrew Thompson writes Trudeau "believed that private convictions should not be the basis for governance in the public realm."[5] If you take only one thing away from this chapter on freedom, let it be that Canadian faith became constitutionally privatized during this time.

Unlike the 19th century admonitions that the best government policies were inspired by Christianity (that we reviewed again in the previous chapter), the post 1960s' policies saw the wisdom in letting the government be the government and the church be the church. The Reformers' admonition to the King way back in 1828 had finally been realized: Canadians had guaranteed personal freedom to choose whatever faith they wanted, with no interference from their leaders and no cultural advantages to any one group.

FREEDOM

The stories of Becker and Trudeau teach us that 100 years after Christendom began in Canada, it began to end. Christendom had helped create the nation, but the next steps were to intentionally dismantle it in favour of a new picture of Canada. In 1965 the now famous red and white Canadian Maple Leaf flag was first unfurled as the official flag of Canada. A flag that was new and patriotic, not merely a handed down symbol from the colonial age. It was a flag that, despite numerous objections from various Orange Orders, no longer contained the Union Jack (a collection of three crosses). Although 22 of the early designs did contain crosses, no overt symbols of religion were ultimately included on Canada's flag.

The designer, George Stanley, argued that the single Maple

---

5   Andrew Thompson, "Slow to Leave the Bedrooms of the Nation," in *The Hidden Pierre Elliot Trudeau: The Faith Behind the Politics*, Edited by John English, Richard Gwyn and Whitney Lackenbauer, (Ottawa: Novalis, 2004), 25.

Leaf inspired unity between the three founding races of Canada (Indigenous, French, and English) and that the leaf itself was symbolic of the nation. The large white square upon which the Maple Leaf rested was also innovative as there existed no heraldic language at that time to define a background so large. A standard pale (the term for a vertical band on a flag) was supposed to be no larger than 1/3 of the total space, whereas the white on the Canadian flag takes up half. Conrad Swan, a Canadian officer in England, proposed the name "Canadian pale" for the larger white section and it became a part of subsequent heraldic vocabulary. While that might seem a little nerdy for most people, flags are incredibly important and to overlook the desire for unity, the lack of overt religion, and even the innovations on the flag is to miss a large clue about the nature of Canada at that time.[6]

Canada was a nation that was inclusive and modern, a nation that tipped its hat and owed a debt to the churches of the past but was now calling them into a new direction for the future. The churches willingly helped build the social programs that made such a thing possible, even though some later generations would argue these very actions dismantled Christendom.

Becker could easily read from the Psalms while still representing all faiths because Canada would always include the Bible as a foundational work. Trudeau could fight to legalize abortion even though, according to his wife, he staunchly opposed it personally. Both these men demonstrate how Canadian religion was shifting from public policy to the realm of private choice; Becker as the face of that change and Trudeau as the political force behind many of those changes. Canada began to intentionally build a society that created spaces for all people with as much fervour as the 19th century churches had fought for a Protestant Christendom. This was the Canada of 1967 and beyond and this is the Canada we will discuss in this chapter.

As we head into the next section take a moment to ponder

---

6   A brief video of this topic can be found on YouTube under the title "The Real Story Behind the Canadian Flag." Located at: https://youtu.be/qTMdH9-kmDk

just how successfully these plans were implemented. Trudeau was so committed to this conviction that many later Canadians believed he was actually a communist. Most would be shocked to learn that the former Prime Minister was a life-long, devoted Catholic. Protestants might be even more shocked to learn that this Catholic leader of our nation made some of these changes to public religion because of Jesus' Sermon on the Mount. Imagine that, Protestants enraged because they were living in a nation that literally tried to embody the Kingdom ethics of Jesus.

The 1960s are usually credited with birthing the radical changes of the 20th century but that is a simplistic reading that overlooks many cultural upheavals that lay just under the surface. Nancy Christie points out in her brilliant work on Protestant opinions regarding sex, that constructing the 60s as an era of revolt against earlier conservatism masks the "complex undercurrents of cultural change" that existed immediately after WWII.[7] While monumental shifts did occur in the 1960s, the seeds of such shifts were planted in the 1940s and 50s and only came to maturation later on. In this chapter we are going to look at the following as we examine the changes the 1960s brought to Canada:

1. The Baby Boom and importance of the suburbs on the faith

2. The Comfortable Pew

3. Expo '67 and more evangelical splits

4. The Quiet Revolution in Quebec

5. The Mad Men

6. The teenager: making rebellion sacred

7. An overlooked culprit for secularization

THE BABY BOOM & THE SUBURBS

The churches learned their lesson from WWI and were

---

7 Nancy Christie, "Sacred Sex: The United Church and the Privatization of the Family in Post-War Canada," In *Households of Faith: Family, Gender, and Community in Canada*, 1760-1969, Edited by Nancy Christie, (Montreal & Kingston: McGill-Queen's University, 2002), 348.

much less enthusiastic about the conflict with the Axis nations and Nazi Germany. The churches had had their wrists slapped in the 1920s in part because of their belief in the finality of that war, not to mention the Fundamentalist/Modernist controversies that took up so much press during that decade. They had bounced back during the Depression and showed their skills as agents for social advancement and a demonstrable love of their neighbour.

When war was declared in 1939, chaplains joined the military in droves to offer ongoing social assistance and comfort to the bereaved. Hitler was a tyrant, therefore Canada had to do its duty to keep him from gaining any more control. The churches reflected on the war with a more sober assessment and basically declared that fighting him was a dirty but necessary job. Churches included prayers for the Axis nations and the faithful that lived under Nazism. In 1942, the UCC became an important vocal and vehement resistor of conscription; a stance that aligned them with French Catholics.

Those who had a harder time during the war included the Jehovah's Witnesses, who were banned as a subversive organization. Germans everywhere likewise were suspect (nothing new there, in WWI Berlin, Ontario felt compelled to change its name to Kitchener) and the Hutterites were forced into alternative service during the war. While officially pacifist, Mennonites also felt the pressure to such an extent that some of their young enlisted—creating profound internal tensions within their respective communities. Despite later rhetoric about the reasons why we fought, Jewish Canadians didn't fare well during the war.[8] While some churches vocally and publicly opposed Japanese internment camps, they were impotent to prevent Canada from creating such atrocities.

However, Canadian churches did benefit from the post-war economic crash that accompanies any extended period

---

8   For a brutal examination of Canadian attitudes towards European Jews, see Irving Abella and Harold Troper, *None is too Many: Canada and the Jews of Europe*, 1933-1948, (Toronto: Lester & Orpen Dennys, 1983).

of conflict. The Canadian government needed to stimulate the economy and they did so by encouraging returning soldiers and other young people to get married and have babies. Basically, the government told young people to get together and have sex; Canadians enthusiastically embraced this—pun intended—call to action. Babies and families were a sure way to boost the economy and the baby boom of the 1940s and 50s was—pun intended again—born.

This pro-family stance was eagerly embraced by churches because each could marry and baptize their adherents and the Christian faith had much to say on this topic. Much like 100 years earlier, the 1950s' church growth was not due solely to successful evangelism, but more because the faith supported a popular cultural development. A development that had as much to do with the economy as it did with Christianity. In addition to this, the 1950s saw the boom of another interesting cultural development that was destined to change the face of Canadian Christianity: the suburbs.

Affordable houses also created a growing and stable economy and those that were able soon began to move from the cities into these smaller hamlets. Such new housing developments were not quite rural and not quite urban and they were quickly sought after by newly forming families. The churches followed these families to the suburbs and the remaining inner-city churches were left to deal with the social ills of poverty, crime, and overcrowding brought on by poorer immigrants.

For those of a middle-class socio-economic status, the suburbs were viewed as the safer destination to raise a family and climb various social ladders. Some churches abandoned their earlier commitment to social support and began serving people to whom such concerns were theoretical but not part of their lived experience. These churches offered financial support to the poor but the wealth of their congregants was creating homogenous churches filled with similar-looking people of nearly identical worldviews that lacked the variety of their urban counterparts.

A moralizing element also began to creep in as financial success was seen to be indicative of God's blessing (nothing new there); even if these churches saw saving the poor of the city as part of their Christian duty. In short, the suburban churches had the luxury of treating poverty at arms-length and began to focus more on the message, which was expected to be delivered by an erudite, educated, entertaining, and ordained minister. This was the respectable world of middle-class church and, as you will see through this chapter, class-based faith was destined to shape Canadian Christianity in surprising ways.

Evangelicals adjusted to the growth of the middle-class as they attempted to both honour their history as being the denomination of the everyman (which meant they could attract more people) while remaining intellectually viable and financially stable (which meant they could attract the right *kind* of people). Fundamentalist churches began to grow again during this time as their clear-cut delineations regarding Christian faith and salvation were seen as an antidote to the confusion of the post-war period.

Such tensions created numerous splits within the already varied forms of Protestantism. The Conservative/Evangelical/ Fundamentalist factions found their calling to clearly define the faith and enjoyed a resurrection of sorts, while the Liberal/ Mainline/Social Gospel churches continued their two-fold mission of social evangelism and personal piety. However, the inability of Mainline churches to speak into the changing landscape of modern Canada sparked the publication of one of the most seminal critiques of Canadian Christianity.

THE COMFORTABLE PEW

Concerns over church attendance inspired one of the most important works any Christian leader in Canada should read. In 1965, at the behest of the Anglican Church, Pierre Berton wrote *The Comfortable Pew*, a critical examination of the modern Canadian church.

To the Anglicans' credit, they commissioned the work in the hopes that their former son would offer them valid criticisms from his own journey out of Anglicanism, and the perspective of the growing demographic of un-churched Canadians. The book became a sensation but less because of the substance of the book and more, in the words of Berton himself, the event of the publication. In *Pew*, Berton made the argument that the church was to blame for Canadians' lack of religious interest.

Berton received a tremendous amount of criticism for his criticisms but the book did contain an element of the prophetic. *Pew* charged the clergy with using outdated language and "hackneyed phrases"[9] that most of their own people didn't understand. These preachers had betrayed their Founder's creative ability to draw on the lives of His audience to illustrate His points. Given the tumultuous times in which *Pew* was published, Berton questioned: "Where are the parables to fit the New Age?"[10] This was the age when the Cuban Missile Crisis, the Civil Rights movement in the States, Communism, homosexuality, and changing gender roles took up the front pages of every newspaper; yet the clergy were charged with rarely addressing any of these issues. To Berton, they preferred biblical stories and ethereal questions that did little to equip their people for life in the modern age.

Jesus' famous parable of the Good Samaritan contained no true power because Canadians didn't hate Samaritans. By the 1960s the word Samaritan was synonymous with a kind stranger rather than Israel's despised national rival. However, change the title to the Good Homosexual, or the Good Communist and now you have the kind of discomfort-inducing, paradigm-challenging message that would make Jesus proud. This was not to be, according to Berton, because the church of Canada put a premium on comfort over controversy. Their leaders said nothing new, rarely shared personal struggles, pulled punches

---

9 Pierre Berton, *The Comfortable Pew: A Critical Look at Christianity and the Religious Establishment in the New Age*, (Toronto: Hodder & Stoughton, 1965), 111.

10 Berton, *Comfortable Pew*, 113.

because of church pressure, and the average clergyman lost his dignity and conviction. In so doing, Canadian churches created a lukewarm pulpit; was it any wonder that Canadian Christians had become lukewarm as well?

In the age of communication, the inability of clergy to communicate was itself a sin. Berton argued that the church needed to reinvent old imagery and "breathe fresh vitality into a message that has lost much of its sting through familiarity."[11] Berton's argument wasn't that Canadians were biblically illiterate, it was that clergy were culturally illiterate. Canadians knew the stories—too well in fact—but the stories and messages they heard every Sunday were stale, outdated, and irrelevant. Through repetition and religiosity, they had done more to weaken Jesus than anything the early Roman Empire accomplished.

Were such accusations fair? Yes, and no.

Yes, because clearly there were numerous churches more invested in safe, repetitive messages that did little to challenge or inspire their adherents' beliefs. The notion that churches need to speak to issues with engaging and inspiring stories remains an important model today. I am not saying such beliefs are because of Berton's work, but he does provide a good example of a growing consensus within the educated middle-class of Canada around this time. Berton is important because he believed the church had an important role to play in society, but the way it was choosing to play that role left much to be desired. The Bible still had something to tell the Canadians of 1965 but, for Berton, a revolution needed to occur or else the church in Canada would be "abandoned."[12]

No, because Berton's solutions to the problems he raised about church relevance were even more problematic. Had the churches followed his suggestions, they could have become

---

11 Berton, *Comfortable Pew*, 116. He advocated replacing a sanctuary cross with a black man seated in an electric chair. The latter, while not technically biblical, did honour the spirit of the Gospel for the modern age.

12 Berton, *Comfortable Pew*, 129.

skilled in the art of communication, but they might have shared little in the way of biblical wisdom. The ancient language of the faith would be increasingly dismissed as "hackneyed" as Canadian Christianity simply editorialized on current events from a fairly liberal, left-leaning vantage point. Berton's churches would be very modern places where biblical stories would be read through a modern lens. Notions of scriptural authority like those defended by Conservative Evangelicals would have no place in Berton's churches. While some of the issues he raised were legitimate, his answers would have ignored much of Christianity's historic beliefs as outdated. In the words of Bruce Douville: "He didn't want the church to be church. He wanted it to be like his workplace."[13]

Another reason his critiques were unfair is that around the mid-1960s many churches already were more conversant with current trends. As we saw earlier in this chapter, numerous denominations had been outspoken on cultural and political issues since the Second World War. There is some debate as to whether *Pew* helped create this dynamic or that it simply requested something that was already happening. To my mind, the second explanation seems to make more sense and would explain why Berton's work—for all its claims to be critical—was such a commercial success.

What should be noted is that Berton's call for a modern expression of the faith was answered on a national scale just two short years after *Pew*'s publication. The sweet irony is that one of the most effective responses came from the kind of Christians Berton seemed to respect the least.

EXPO '67

In the same year as the Centennial, Expo '67 was taking place in Montreal. That was the year that Canada presented itself to the world and one of the few times the world appears to have shown up. Running from April to October of that year, Expo

---

13   This is from a conversation I had with Dr. Douville.

housed pavilions that explained and entertained visitors with numerous creative displays of traditional "Canadiana" as well as clever innovations to showcase the nation as a progressive force on the globe.[14] For our purposes, I want to focus on two pavilions: The Christian Pavilion and the Sermons from Science Pavilion. Both of these pavilions make sense in light of our discussions around scripture and modernism in the preceding chapter as well as the politics and cultural developments we have begun to explore in this chapter. Expo truly reinforces these earlier points and shows how the teachings of these two camps have echoed loudly for generations.

The Christian Pavilion was created by the more Liberal/ Mainline Christian denominations with a more visionary design. Sometimes aligning with the nationalistic goals of the fair and at other times contradicting and challenging it, the Christian Pavilion desired religion to remain a vital and challenging force on the Canadian landscape. The building itself was simple with the exception of the roof, which was in the shape of a giant checkmark that dipped dramatically, and then jutted into the sky with equal flair. Outside the building was a simple Tau cross (the one that looks like a capital letter "T") and the words "Christian Pavilion." But it is the interior I want to focus on.

The Pavilion was divided into three sections—or Zones— and each section was filled with photographs that occasionally featured excerpts from the Bible. The pictures themselves were hung in creative fashion and drew the attendees' eyes towards different themes displayed stylistically (the Christian Pavilion was doing in 1967 what many churches think is edgy and *avant garde* even by today's standards). By the time people reached the third and final section, they were given space and time to contemplate what they had just experienced. The Christian Pavilion embodied the new mentality of Canadian Christianity and they found a very artistic way to accomplish this task. In fact,

---

14 "The general theme of the fair was 'Man and his World,' a tribute to human achievement that reflected the secular spirit of Canada and especially that of French Canada one hundred years after Confederation." Grant, *Canadian*, 225.

the artistic nature of the pavilion *was* the way they accomplished this task. The pictures invited people to interpret the faith in ways that made sense to them and purposefully eschewed doctrinal or dogmatic statements in favour of personal interpretation.

In contrast, the Sermons from Science Pavilion was more about proselytization.[15] They held lectures and talks to validate the traditional teachings of Christianity from, in their opinion, a defensible scientific angle. Created as a lecture theatre, topics were introduced that focused on the previous century's challenges to the traditional interpretations of the faith. State of the art technology like listening devices and films were employed to show just how modern their views were, even if they reiterated older beliefs.

Topics like evolution, dinosaurs, and the age of the earth were discussed and debunked as the Sermons from Science Pavilion invited their attendees to see God at work in the physical realm around them. If the Christian Pavilion opened the floor up for discussion, introspection, and interpretation, the Sermons from Science Pavilion provided clear cut answers and evidence that left little room for personal opinion. They challenged people to choose following Christ, an idea the Christian Pavilion rejected. Sermons from Science was as declarative as the Christian Pavilion was ambiguous, as literal as the other was allegorical.

These two groups displayed their respective origin stories even if they had evolved to incorporate new information, technology, argumentation, and interpretations. It must also be noted that the two pavilions originated as one but split when disagreements over style and mission became insurmountable. The more evangelical collective found the open-ended nature of the plans problematic due to a lack of evangelization. The idea of leaving people to arrive at their own conclusions felt like spiritual neglect. It was incumbent, they would argue, to place before rational and intelligent people arguments in favour of a

---

15 Defined by Merriam-Webster as 1: to induce someone to convert to one's faith.
2: to recruit someone to join one's party, institution, or cause.

Creator God and demand, on that day, the people choose whom they were going to serve.

For the mainline group, such arguments were relics of a former age that only drove people further from the faith. It was better, they would argue, to show the compelling and creative nature of the faith reflected in the world all around. The fact that several pictures featured Canadians living in poverty also served to remind people that social responsibility was a key element of the Christian faith.

The Canadian culture increasingly desired religion, in the words of Gary Miedema, to "celebrate what all Canadians held in common and to avoid what divided them. As a result, particular religious beliefs and doctrines were to be de-emphasized in public life, while such things as the cultivation of love, self-sacrifice, and loyalty for the sake of the common good were put to the fore. Difference was to be downplayed. Commonality was to be celebrated."[16] For the Sermons from Science organizers, that mentality was a death knell for faithful Christianity.

Whatever your thoughts are, the point I am trying to make is that these two Pavilions continue to demonstrate the ways in which Protestants were struggling to bring their faith to the masses. One side retained their historic stance that Jesus offered the truth above which all other truths must be measured. The other side offered a faith that challenged the power dynamics and evangelization tactics of old by honouring the importance of individual conviction over dogmatic teaching.

What both sides took for granted was that their audience would be educated and intelligent and capable of making rational decisions on matters of faith. Sermons from Science literally debated scientific ideas, assuming their attendees would have enough education to make sense of such arguments. The Christian Pavilion believed education equipped people to draw their own conclusions without religious leaders walking them

16 Gary R. Miedema, *For Canada's Sake: Public Religion, Centennial Celebrations, and the Re-Making of Canada in the 1960s*, (Montreal & Kingston: McGill-Queen's University, 2005), 204.

down the primrose path of faith. The important element to note is that both groups assumed a level of academic sophistication from their audience and tailored their respective messages accordingly.

It took years of planning to make both these pavilions and that fact should also not be lost on you; these were not thrown up overnight. I want you to note this because it shows that the ecumenical and inclusive nature of Canada presented at the Centenary celebrations in Ottawa did not signal the end of Christendom. Rather, it should be viewed as a response to a cultural trend that was already well underway. It should also be noted that the Christian Pavilion's artistic representations attempted to live out what Berton believed to be the only way forward for Canadian Christianity. This, again, argues that Berton's book was less trail-blazing than first thought as numerous churches were already engaging the culture innovatively.

But there is a fun irony in this as well as it pertains to Berton. The Sermons from Science Pavilion was an unequivocal rejection of *Pew*'s ideas as heretical and blasphemous. However, Berton did call churches to make better use of modern communication technology—to adapt to life in the media age. The more evangelical group—Christians that Berton clearly disdained—did this much better than their mainline church competitors (a theme we'll see again in the next chapter on televangelism).

The Sermons from Science Pavilion developed media savvy modes to communicate the Christian faith as *the* truth, not just *a* truth. They embodied the technological innovations of the day and then used them to advance their historic interpretations of the faith—the very interpretations Berton dismissed as outdated. The Christian Pavilion, in contrast, used stagnant (though creative) images to advance their more modern understandings. Therein lies the irony: historically, conservative evangelicals tend to be more modern in style while more traditional in content, while the mainline Protestants are the exact opposite.

Again, both sides were responding to the climate of the time but, again, both sides approached it from antithetical perspectives. For the Christian Pavilion, the inclusive and innovative nature of Canada blended quite well with their artistic representation of Christian truths. For the Sermons Pavilion, the faith needed to be defended from the dangerously inclusive voices that sought to undermine it. While the words and technology and culture was different in the 1960s, both camps remained entrenched in the positions established 50 years earlier.

THE QUIET REVOLUTION IN QUEBEC

As scary as these new cultural trends were for the divided camps of Protestantism, Catholicism also retained its title as an enemy of true faith. Catholicism was large, well-funded, unified, and commanded the loyalty of the French as well as large sections of English, Ukrainian, German, Polish, and Irish immigrants across the land. Even though English-speaking Catholics had won some favour in post WWI Canada, the Church of St. Peter's seeming impenetrability to the devastating effects of modernism only added to Protestant concerns. It was the great and perpetual threat to Canadian Christendom because it was an ancient and consistently stable version of Canadian Christianity. To Canadian Protestants, Catholicism had always appeared as a monolithic structure of fear and dread—a religious Death Star, if you will.

That was a Protestant opinion, but the Quebec of the 1960s had a much different view. In the words of Canadian Catholic historian, Terrence Fay the "external image of a stable church in a secure province did not correspond to reality."[17]

Such changes didn't happen overnight and while the 1960s are credited with the Quiet Revolution, the impact is really only seen when we take the rest of the 20th century into account.

---

17 Fay, *Canadian Catholics*, 279.

There is a ton of debate about what the Quiet Revolution was, what a better name for it should be, and what caused it. For the sake of this book, I am going to focus on the clerical choices that I think helped it along. However, such internal decisions must be read against the one backdrop all sociologists and historians of this period can agree on: when the province took social services away from the church, the nation effectively replaced the church as "the locus of francophone identity."[18]

To begin, the church in Quebec enjoyed an 87% attendance rate in the late 1950s (when someone attends Mass at least once a week) with only a 4% decrease by the end of the 1960s. Concerning, sure, but not overly dramatic yet. In 1959, the first major change occurred when priest and professor Angelo Roncalli was elected Pope John XXIII. In a symbolic act in which he literally opened up windows, the new Pope allowed a gust of fresh air into the stale Catholic Church. The Church Council known as Vatican II ran from 1962-64 and is, in my opinion, the most important act of Western Christianity in the 20th century. The impact of this pope's council was felt all around the world and Quebec was no different.[19] Chief amongst such changes was the increased role of the laity in decision-making processes and influence in their local parishes.

1960s Catholics were beginning to see a church increasingly out of touch with the reality of the modern age and nowhere was this clearer than in Quebec's response to the 1968 papal teaching forbidding contraception. If the church was supposed to take the opinions of the laity into consideration, this approach was seen as an unwelcome invasion into the bedrooms of the faithful. Where did such an idea come from? Well, from the beginning of this chapter (not literally) and Trudeau's comments about the nation having no business in the bedrooms of the people.

18   Brian P. Clark and Stuart Macdonald, *Leaving Christianity: Changing Allegiances in Canada Since 1945*, (Montreal and Kingston: McGill-Queen's University Press, 2017), 159.

19   "Canadians were sometimes more open to the influence of such international events as the Vatican Council…than were the more self-sufficient Americans." Grant, *Canadian*, 219.

Quebec Catholics believed that such an admonition included the church as well.

Women were increasing in the workplace, had education, and were living their lives well beyond the former confines of the home. They were fully capable of making such decisions for themselves and didn't need the church to make it for them. The freedom we are talking about in this chapter gave rise to an increased sense of personal autonomy and autonomy in sexual matters was arguably one of the most important (especially in the 1960s). The church handled this situation poorly and, rather than wasting time fighting against such irrelevant beliefs, Catholics did what Canadians have done since the 1800s: they walked away. From the 1970s and on, Baby Boomers began to disappear from a church that was seen as entirely too authoritative and outdated to speak with any meaning into their daily lives.

After the changes implemented by Vatican II, Catholicism was not so different from other versions of the faith. Positively, this meant that Protestants and Catholics could enjoy more cordial dialogue as their religious cultures and rules were less alien to each other. Another interesting result was that this is also when modernism began to invade the Canadian branch of St. Peter's ancient church.

Not surprisingly, the youth were the most conversant with, and vocal about, such issues. While seminary enrollment declined by over 16% in the 60s, those who were becoming priests began experimenting with new forms of worship (including more evangelistic/revivalist styles) to align their new, post-Vatican II beliefs with the spirit of the times. While such innovations did nothing to reverse the moderate decline in numbers, it did show that young Catholics were becoming more involved in social reforms that included a desire to reform their church.

The groups of young reformers broke into two camps that largely looked like the ones we have already seen in Protestantism: traditionalists and modernists. The traditionalists, like the conservative Protestants, focused on personal piety and faith but remained vested in social concerns like the alleviation of poverty. However, they were unwilling to challenge their church and believed the answers lay in greater attention to the Mass and the servant nature of Christianity.

The modernists, like their Protestant counterparts, believed the views of the church needed to be challenged and held up to intellectual and philosophical scrutiny. They believed the traditionalists' faith to be blind adherence to outdated structures and they had the teaching of Vatican II to support them. These modernists read political literature like Trudeau's *Cite Libre*, and they believed authentic faith would create a better human being and strengthen society. These two groups approached the secularization of their age in two distinct ways: the former saw it as a threat and the latter saw it as an opportunity for positive change.

Whenever I talk about this topic I stress how absolutely vital this one story is for Canadian Christianity. This is the secularization story of Canada because in a shockingly short period of time, French-Catholic *Canadiens* removed one of the two pillars upon which their entire culture had been sustained up until that decade.

In the Quebec Act of the 18th century, all the way back to the Plains of Abraham, Britain had promised to constitutionally protect the French language and the Catholic religion. Then, in 1960, the Liberal government of Jean Lesage basically said: "You know what? We don't actually need the church anymore." They began programs to remove education, healthcare, social services, and even trade unions from the clerical sphere (to be fair, Catholic leaders had been very supportive of these unions, believing them to be a way to strengthen the influence of the common working person).

So, picture yourself as a thoughtful Quebec Catholic during this time. You have issues with church teachings, you find the church to be hypocritical, out of touch, and in true Canadian fashion, too powerful to be trusted. But what are you really going to do? If you want to be educated you need the church. If you need to go to the hospital, you need the church. If you want to educate your kids, you need the church. If you want to get married or buried or access to better jobs, or even some assistance while you look for work, you need the church. And, in less than a year, your government removes all those institutions from the church's control.

"So," you ask, "I don't need to go to Mass in order to go to school or get health care or social aid?" And your provincial government responds, "Not if you don't want to. You don't need the church for any of those services anymore." What are you going to do? Well, if you are like almost half of the population of Quebec after the 1960s, I am going to tell you exactly what you are going to do: you are going to enjoy sleeping in next Sunday morning, indulging in fun activities without the ensuing guilt, and spending your growing collection of disposable income on vacations and stuff for your family, rather than giving it to the church.

Just that simply and quickly, the Catholic Church lost control over the most Catholic place in the nation. The numbers put together by Reginald Bibby's Project Canada are truly staggering as it pertains to church attendance. When asked if they attended mass at least once a week, 87% of the Quebec Catholics in the late 1950s said they did. In 1975 only 42% fit into this category; by 2000 that number was 20%; a decline of 67%.[20] If we use the biblical definition of a generation as 40 years, then in one generation modern Quebec literally experienced a religious apocalypse of biblical proportions.

As John Webster Grant stated succinctly, "when French Canadians realized that their survival as a people no longer depended on the support of the church the old bonds snapped with a suddenness that startled the entire nation."[21] Revolution had come to Canadian Catholicism and humorously, this Canadian Revolution proved to be just as polite and quiet as the

20 Taken from Clarke and Macdonald, *Leaving*, 140.

21 Grant, *Church in the Canadian Era*, 218.

stereotypical view of this land would dictate.

However, in 2003 Donald Cuccioletta and Martin Lubin cleverly re-defined the Quiet Revolution as a noisy evolution.[22] Their point was that Canadian religious history has given this event a mythological character that tends towards simplistic interpretations. Seeing only the dramatic fall out can make us blind to the building social outcries that are more to blame. I think that title change, and the ways it helps us see the subtle evolution of the revolution, can help Canadian Christians beyond Quebec's borders learn some important lessons.

The first lesson reiterates my point from the first chapter that Canadians vote with their feet. This has always meant that Canadians will simply walk away from any institution, religious or otherwise, that doesn't hold to the values of minimal interference in daily life and maximum willingness to offer assistance when called upon. If the church becomes too focused on teachings and lessons but neglects social obligations, Canadians will manifest their disapproval through their departure.

The other lesson we can learn from the Quiet Revolution is that we can thank Catholic leadership for the quietness of the whole event. Bishop Roy (one of the seat occupants on the dais at the beginning of this chapter) saw the wisdom in letting go of the financial burden these institutions placed on the church. Like the Protestant social reformers on the prairies, these leaders opted to return to a more community-based pastoral role and let the government run the programs and the Universities train the professionals.

All of this was tied up in Quebec politics as well but it was an "amicable secularization" as Fay puts it that "allowed Catholics to retain a pastoral presence in those institutions. A humbler, more modest and receptive church continued to support the people's right to determine their own political future."[23] The church actually began to listen to the needs and complaints of

---

22 Donald Cuccioletta and Martin Lubin, "The Quebec Quiet Revolution: A Noisy Evolution," *Quebec Studies* (Vol. 36): Fall-Winter 2003.

23 Fay, *Catholics*, 282.

the people and even started to embrace a multiethnic society and one that championed democratic rights.[24]

This was of extreme importance throughout and beyond the 1960s as Quebec was on a nationalistic journey as well. Desiring to rid the land of Anglo-centric business interests, the weakening of Catholicism had the potential to weaken this new autonomous, pro-French stance as well. However, Trudeau argued convincingly that the church wasn't needed for French autonomy. For example, he cited the Labour Unions in Quebec, arguing they needed to be brought out from the sphere of Roman Catholicism. He believed the church restrained practical pro-French solutions because of "unrealistic corporatist ideology... influenced by a reactionary and anti-modern clergy."[25]

The familiar lament that a weakened church meant a weakened moral fabric of society also circulated throughout the province. Such concerns proved to little avail, the people embraced the Revolution thanks, in some part, to thinkers like Trudeau and even Archbishop Roy. The decline of Quebec Catholicism's influence in the later 20th century was more dramatic, but similar in motivations and outcomes to the Canadian Protestant experience. Granted, Quebec's Quiet Revolution (or noisy evolution) must be treated as unique based on some Quebec-centric reasons, but most denominations' experience of that time was noticeably similar.

I want to be very clear about the message this evolution/revolution teaches us: if Quebec society can effectively oust the church and continue on, then so can *anyone* in Canada. There is no region, culture, or section of Canada that needs the church and this is an idea we'll see developing even more in the next chapter.

These changes were slower moving than popular opinion might dictate; but they have also proven to be deep and abiding

24 "The Roman Catholic Church became one social institution among many, just as the French Canadians became one ethnic community among a multitude." John English et al (eds.), *The Hidden Pierre Elliot Trudeau: The Faith Behind the Politics*, (Ottawa: Novalis, 2004), 54.

25 English et al (eds), *Trudeau*, 52.

changes. The Catholics were proving resilient as they adjusted to their new role as cultural partner rather than cultural guardian. In that decade they began leaving the rooms of power and control but also set the church up to be a sought-after critic on a variety of social issues from prison reform to Aboriginal rights, from unemployment to immigration.

Catholicism had a lot to atone for and the more authoritarian its behaviour, the quicker it lost adherents. If interest in the faith is to return, it will largely be due to curiosity of the young, generations removed from the still skeptical Baby-Boomer Catholics. Those skeptics are now the grandparents of the youth of today and, naturally, their issues with the church are not likely to have the same emotive impact on the present generation. Like the other seasons of church growth in this land, any future growth for Quebec Catholicism will come from a perceived cultural desire, not necessarily a church movement. While there is some interesting re-branding of old cathedrals taking place in Montreal to make them centers of cultural and social influence once again, immigration seems the most likely hope for any Canadian Catholic resurgence.[26]

MAD MEN

As this chapter begins to wind down, how do we define the freedom these stories are illustrating? We can define it in one word: autonomy. The elevation of the self, and self-interest, as the chief motivator for life decisions. Quebec Catholicism is just one of the examples of the ways in which Canadians were increasingly ignoring the church as the gatekeepers of meaning. But we must look at two other factors before concluding this chapter—because both of these contributors to 20th century secularization tend to be overlooked.

---

26   To this end, and to somewhat support this statement for the potential of a Quebec revival, Sam Reimer notes that the PAOC (another denomination with strong growth due to immigration) has more congregations and attendees than any of the other Protestant denomination in Quebec combined. See Reimer, Sam, "Pentecostal Assemblies of Canada's Congregations", *Canadian Journal of Pentecostal-Charismatic Christianity* 3, no. 1 (2012): 41-69.

The first factor has to do with Canadian wallets.

Not their actual wallets (although that could be interesting for certain aficionados of the wallet/purse industry), but the fact that many Canadians enjoyed fuller wallets in the 1960s. The increase of disposable incomes introduced Canadians to the greatest cultural influence of the modern western world. Institutions that dwarfed the influence of the church over culture. Institutions many churches themselves gladly and eagerly gave themselves over to as well (even if they said the exact opposite). Institutions that convinced us all that desirable terms like "freedom" and "independence" were available to purchase. I am speaking, of course, of marketing agencies.

Specifically, the advertisers known to history as the Mad Men; so named because the heart of their industry was located on Madison Avenue in New York. The advertisement agencies and creative thinkers in this zip code forever changed the world— both the spiritual and secular worlds. The Mad Men created worlds that the average American (and Canadian) wanted to live in. Worlds of success and joy and fun and adventure that, if you purchased the right product, were waiting for you.

Think about the simple impact of this philosophy: it doesn't matter if you're selling cars, coffee, kitty litter, or pants; the most efficient way to inform the public about your product is to have a person stand in front of a camera and simply show the product, briefly explain what the product does, and then state the price. But that is not how advertising works. Advertising creates a desirable world, or a desirable state of being, and then attaches a product to the attainment of that world or state. The only time cost is even mentioned in ads is to highlight how little the attainment of said desires actually costs. What the Mad Men figured out was much more comprehensive than simply increasing public awareness of a product. A truly great marketing campaign also helps create brand recognition and customer loyalty. That has done more to shape the later 20th century church than most realize.

In order to demonstrate how such thinking shaped

Canadian church ministries I am going to split my argument into two parts: the first will happen right now, and then we will return to the second part in the next chapter. My argument explores marketers' targeting of a specific demographic: the teenager.

THE TEENAGER: MAKING REBELLION SACRED

The teenager is a strange creature indeed. Not only physically with all the hormones, voice-cracking and awkwardness, but as a cultural development as well. The idea of this in-between time of human development had been around for a while by the 1960s. A phase when young people needed to discover their own identity in order to become independent and autonomous adult members of society. A time to build friend groups and begin establishing distance between themselves and their parents. A time of exploration, a time society recognized as not quite adult, but also not quite childhood. An in-between time with all sorts of developmental milestones. A time many Christians believed needed its own brand of Christianity. Ladies and gentlemen, I present to you: youth ministry.

Para-church youth organizations like CGIT, Youth for Christ, Inter-Varsity Christian Fellowship, and TUXIS had been successfully operating for decades. The YMCA and YWCA had been giving young men and women activities and Christian teaching for a century by the 1960s. Denominations like the UCC had their Youth Wing, Pentecostals had Ambassadors for Christ, and the Anglicans had the Anglican Young People's Association bringing the faith to their younger adherents. As established as these programs were, they really hit their strides in the 1950s and 60s and a lot of that had to do with marketing.

The youth culture of the 1960s made marketing to the young make sense. While a bit of a "chicken or the egg" conundrum, the question is whether the marketing created the culture, or the culture created the demand. While not the only answer, one of the most important elements to keep in mind is that the general financial prosperity of the post-war period helped both along. Simply put, parents could afford to buy their kids more youth-focused products like music and clothes that were deemed essential for their self-expression and autonomy.

And churches bought in too. The role of youth pastor is not a biblical—nor even a historical—Christian calling; it came in large part as a result of this marketing push (and I say that as a former youth pastor). The church hired fun, usually younger people for the job of relating Jesus in ways their parents' preachers never could. Take a second to think about this: Sunday Schools for children were nothing new but now there was a growing desire for a separate stage of Christian education within the church. The generation who made famous the phrase: "Never trust anyone over 30" required a leader who was, at the very least, under 30.

The Christian youth counter-culture of the 1960s and beyond attempted to repackage their version of godliness as a form of rebellion. But not rebellion against the church, rebellion against their fellow youth. Church youth groups sanctified the teen culture's desire for rebellion by teaching their youth to rebel against the godlessness of their peers.

Some of the leaders in the more Left-leaning Mainline churches seemed to understand that a youth pastor should be an insightful person more akin to a spiritual director. A person who could lead young people into the exploration of their faith and invigorate their curiosity. A person who understood that the church youth room should be the most dangerous room in the church. Teenage Christians should exist to challenge the beliefs and forms of their elders. Youth services should be problematic and confrontational and uncomfortable to those who spent their Sundays in the sanctuary. These leaders saw the youth group as somewhat of a microcosm of the larger cultural wars that were happening at that time. They re-examined their teachings to show Jesus as a social and political radical that had plenty to say to the activist youth of the late 1960s.

But there were plenty of churches that wanted politics out of their young people's heads. Given the tumultuous times, who can blame them? These churches hired youth ministers to teach young people the faith and to keep them in the church. I hope you can see how difficult that mission was, given the pervasive role of marketing and the motif of rebellion that undergirded all elements of teenage culture (it is just as difficult today for the same reasons). Teens in the 1960s and 70s were on a journey of self-exploration and self-gratification and the churches' taboos around sex especially became increasingly seen as oppressive and contrary to true spirituality. As we will see in the next chapter, Protestant teachings on chastity—especially focusing on women's sexuality—and their condemnations of drug culture alienated their young in much the same way the Catholic Church of Quebec had. Even a cursory view of statistics shows a noticeable pattern of steady decline from the late 1970s to the early 21st century.

To blame the young for such rejection misses the point. Church leaders failed to take into account that Canadian youths' autonomy was increasing along with their parents. While anti-drug sermons and stances that only supported sex after marriage worked for the older members, the Boomers had, frankly, a more vested interest in a pro-drug, pro-sex worldview. At the risk of sounding like a broken record (not that it is possible to *sound* like anything at all in a book) Canadian youth did what all Canadians do when faced with a religious power system deemed over-bearing and non-pragmatic: they voted with their feet and simply left.

But why was this generation's departure so dramatic?

For starters, the Boomer generation is the largest in human history and so their departure left a vacuum never seen before. Such safety in numbers made it possible for these youth to impact formidable cultural institutions like the church and government. The sheer amount of young Boomers also made them a desirable demographic for the Mad Men. Their youth culture was economically formidable and at the heart of that culture was a celebration of teenage autonomy.

For example, Elvis Presley's vulgar, sexual, hip-shaking

gyrations on the Ed Sullivan show in 1956 was condemned by cultural guardians, but it was also the most watched television episode of the entire decade.[27] By the late 1960s, Presley's crooning was increasingly passé and was replaced by the even more radical message of groups like The Beatles. This band's song "Revolution" told those invested in the institution to "free your mind instead" and their legions of fans eagerly sang along. It wasn't just music but also fashion, literature, art, films, and, in the relative youth of men like Kennedy and Trudeau, even politics itself began to skew younger. Such was the power of this young and numerically massive generation.

The growing collection of youth-specific merchandise increased the influence of the young over the larger culture. The decline in church attendance proved that the majority of church messages had fallen behind the times. Arguably for the first time, the young had the language, influence, and—thanks to a growing economy—even the money to move themselves from the youth room to the sanctuary with or without their parents' permission. What the decades that followed demonstrate was that even the sanctuary no longer held much appeal. Thus, a large portion of the largest generation in human history simply walked out the front door. To the Beatles' rhetorical question "You say you want a revolution?" These young Canadian Christians answered, "yes."

What is often overlooked in discussions around the secularization of the 1960s and beyond is what it did to those youths who remained in the church. Those who took to heart the message of sacred teenage rebellion against the evils of their day became leaders in the church by the 1980s. Their survival of the mass Canadian exodus shaped their ministry and took on similar characteristics to the UEL sermons almost 200 years earlier. Canadian Christianity was still declining but these new

---

27   With 60 million viewers—or 82.6 percent of TV viewers at the time—tuning in, the appearance garnered the show's best ratings in two years and became the most-watched TV broadcast of the 1950s. Accessed at https://www.history.com/this-day-in-history/elvis-presley-first-appearance-the-ed-sullivan-show

leaders had an appreciation for cultural relevance and their role within it. They saw an opportunity to revision church and began to cast themselves in the role of the faithful remnant. Similar to the Loyalists, they framed their losses in spiritual terms to give hope, meaning, and mission to their churches going forward.

Did such beliefs take a lighter stance on the moral/spiritual issues that had alienated their peers? Absolutely not, many actually doubled down on such stances. These were the people who had faithfully rebelled against the experimentations of their day and were hardly going to abandon such beliefs when they were in charge. Instead, they took the styles and formats of the services they had enjoyed when they were younger and made them mainstream.

Services designed like the youth models of old brought teachings of the church into popular culture. These so-called "Attractional Models" of church featured modern music, superior technology, and relevant messaging in language anyone inside or out of the church could understand. These models assumed a level of biblical illiteracy and set about re-educating the predominantly middle-class Canadians who had left church in their youth about the faith in easy-to-understand ways.

They focused a lot of resources on family-based programming that covered every developmental stage from infancy up to college with unique curriculum for each. Many of these leaders had been the recipient of such targeted teaching and believed the future of the church lay in such innovations. They recognized that many of those who had left were now parents themselves and would appreciate a church that was family-friendly. They weren't wrong. Such churches became incredibly popular and the statistics of the 1980s and onward show a noticeable trend upward in attendance, baptisms, and activity throughout the decade.[28] These churches tended to be more evangelical and conservative in tone and while some Mainline and Catholic churches attempted similar models, they

---

28   See Clarke and Macdonald, *Leaving*, 102-21.

did so to much less avail.

We will examine such models in greater detail in the next chapter because I don't want us to move past the importance of 1960s teen culture just yet. For all my focus on the young in this section, the greatest legacy of the Mad Men was not their hand in helping to form modern teenage culture. Their greatest legacy over Canadian churches was the ability to change the definition of evangelism from a life-long journey of personal conversion and religious development to a focus on numbers as the barometer for success.

A STRANGE CULPRIT OF SECULARIZATION

We are told that Canada is in the midst of a spiritual crisis. That is a loaded term that, I argue, is influenced as much by marketing as it is by theology. All we really know is that less Canadians are going to church. From a market-share perspective, that is a crisis; but is it really a spiritual one?

Sam Reimer's *Evangelicals and the Continental Divide* and Clarke and Macdonald's *Leaving Christianity* both focus on the loss of belief during this time; and that is not something that should be overlooked. Pierre Berton's concern that Canadians knew the biblical stories too well was not a 1970s problem at all. But I would like to close this chapter focusing on a second overlooked element.

Secularization discussions today have largely been reduced to conversations around loss of numbers in church attendance and membership. I hope you have seen that every generation has dealt with some kind of secularization and that every generation has dealt with perceived loss of influence. Whether we're talking about American Methodist influence, Clergy Reserves, pro-immigration laws, or multiculturalism, each generation's secularization teaches us about the culture and norms of that time. And that gives us insight into the culture and norms of our own time.

As Nancy Christie and Michael Gauvreau argue, the secularization of this age is not to be found only in Canadians' lack of faith brought on by the encroachment of modern ideas. Rather, they remind us the "increasing diversity of spiritual choice"[29] is also a culprit. The myriad ways in which the churches responded to the post-war period, the Fundamentalist/ Modernist divisions (which we saw in the last chapter) and the advent of TV and newer styles of church (which we'll see in the next chapter) was not something that happened to the churches but something the churches orchestrated.

Thus, when we talk of secularization in Canada we should consider the post-WWII era and the "fragmentation of the evangelical experience" as one of the reasons behind secularization.[30] Mainline churches like the UCC lost adherents while more populist evangelical churches gained them. These conservative churches were accused of going to war with modern ideas, something that should've precluded them from the larger Canadian culture. However, they did so through progressive use of technology and a greater attention to cultural tones that made their potentially problematic messages palatable. These evangelical groups, on first look, brought new life into Canadian Protestantism but they were also viewed by many middle-class Canadians outside the church as anti-intellectual and bigoted.

As the Canadian economy strengthened in the 1960s, such rifts only deepened. While consumerism did impact the church, it did so in ways that many of us have overlooked or misunderstood. Middle-class Canadians demanded their brand of faith be geared toward the respectable and intellectually defensible. However, these people were also busier, had more money, and tended to view church as a viable Sunday plan when other plans fell through. Regular attendance in such groups tended to become less about going to church every week and more about going once or twice a month. While Methodism had been the evangelical church of the common person in the 19th century, the UCC (which Methodism had opted into) was the more respectable middle-class church of the later 20th century.

29 Christie and Gauvreau, *Fully Orbed*, 250.

30 Christie and Gauvreau, *Fully Orbed*, 250.

They were being replaced as the "everyman" church by groups like the PAOC, The Christian and Missionary Alliance (CMA), or one of the growing collections of non-denominational churches. The PAOC, as one example, had grown from their humble origins in the early 20th century to gain a staggering amount of adherents. Pentecostals had grown from 26,000 members in 1931 to a whopping 220,390 by 1971. They had grown over 300% from 1961 to 1971 and that meteoric rise has been explained a few different ways. Some have argued that Mainline churches' switch to more liberal ideologies caused an exodus into conservative evangelicalism. While that does make sense, there is little statistical data to support that claim. Increased immigration combined with the global nature of evangelical groups like the Pentecostals provide some answers for such surprising statistics.

Also, the rebellion against the godlessness of the "world" raised the stakes for these evangelical adherents and made church attendance a matter of spiritual survival. Simply put, their salvation depended more on church attendance than their Mainstream counterparts, to whom church was more a valuable social institution among many. We'll look into this more in the next chapter because the only point I am making now is that Canadian churches' offering of multiple, and often competing, versions of the faith weakened the Canadian Christian voice across the land. This is nothing new as the familiar dynamic of respectability versus popularity from chapter two reared its head once more (See? I told you reading those early chapters would come in handy).

And here we have a better way to understand the trend that has dominated in Canada for the latter half of the 20th century in regards to attendance and decline. The lament of many respectable churches (those who engage with popular philosophy or scientific arguments and don't view them as enemies of the faith) is that their numbers stagnate or decline despite their best efforts to show the relevance of intelligent Christianity. On the other side, popular Protestant evangelical churches with teachings seemingly at odds with Canadian norms seem to consistently attract more members.

Evangelical churches believe their numerical increases indicate their fidelity to God, an idea that the Mainline churches obviously can't stomach. Whatever your thoughts on this are, an important element we are going to look at in the next chapter is that the growth of the CMA or PAOC did nothing to raise the national attendance average. The doctrines of these churches tend to resonate with other self-professed evangelical Protestants and there is little statistical evidence to show these churches grew due to evangelization (just like in other seasons of Canadian church growth). In fact, some of the teachings of these churches provide barriers to those outside their walls because they are perceived as outdated, judgmental, or anti-intellectual. Thus, while the individual churches do well numerically, they can also contribute to the overall societal trend towards decreased institutional religion that has come to define the latter half of the century.

And this is an important irony with which Canadian Christians must wrestle. Secularization, despite its name, is not just the successful creation of the secular world but can also be understood as the unintended offspring of the fragmented Christian one.

RESOURCES

Pierre Berton. *The Comfortable Pew: A Critical Look at Christianity and the Religious Establishment in the New Age.* Toronto: Hodder & Stoughton, 1965.

- One of the most important books any Canadian Christian leader can read. While some of the issues dealt within it are outdated, it provides fantastic insight into the struggles of the churches during the 1960s.

Gary R. Miedema. *Canada's Sake: Public Religion, Centennial Celebrations, and the Re-Making of Canada in the 1960s.* Montreal & Kingston: McGill-Queen's University, 2005.

- This book provides a sweeping historical look into the ways public Christiantiy was defined and created in the 1960s.

Terrence Fay. *A History of Canadian Catholics.* Montreal and Kingston: McGill-Queen's, 2002

- A thorough examination of the complex developments of Canadian Catholicism that shows it as unique among the world's Catholics and uniquely Canadian.

English, John, Gwyn, Richard and Lackenbauer, P. Whitney (eds). *The Hidden Pierre Elliott Trudeau: The Faith Behind the Politics.* Novalis: Ottawa, 2004.

- This book is a true find for anyone interested in religion and politics in Canada. This is a series of essays from a variety of scholars that focus on former Prime Minister Trudeau's religious motivations and writings. This book is very accessible and the chapters are instructive as well as engaging as they explore this often overlooked element of the man's life.

Mad Men the Series. Presented by the AMC Network from 2007-2015.

- While it seems strange to endorse a TV show in an historical work I think this show is incredibly valuable for modern audiences. The show will give hours of insight in the materialist culture that existed behind the scenes in one of the most formative decades in recent memory.

---

1 IDEA

Secularism can be seen as a result of competing Protestant opinions, and Catholic abuses of power. Canadians don't need any one version of the faith in order to live spiritually-full lives.

CHAPTER 6
REALITY
1980 -

Come on in, sit right down
No, you're not the first to show
We've all been here since, God, who knows?
— "Looking for A Place to Happen,"
The Tragically Hip

INTRODUCTION

Jesus stood in the city of Jerusalem and declared "I am the light of the world." He was attending the Festival of Booths, or Sukkot, a celebration that includes the lighting of torches and candles in the evening. As Israel's holiest city became awash in the warm glow of the flames, Jesus made his famous "I am" declaration—one of seven recorded in the Gospel of John.

With the darkness of the desert as his backdrop, Jesus compared himself to the light embracing the people at that moment. In typical fashion, the Nazarene carpenter then extended the circumference of the illuminated circle of safety. He instructed the attendees that he was not simply their Messiah but the Saviour of all those in the realm of darkness. Jesus used the community created by the light to teach that the Messiah's mission was universal, not regional.[1]

Two thousand years later, a Victoria-based follower of the Light of the world also found himself awash in lights. While Jesus' use of lights was designed to teach on the expansive inclusiveness of God's salvation, the electronic lights of the late 20th century British Columbian church became a tool of isolating exclusion. Those lights are symbolic of the changes taking place in Canadian Christianity of the 1980s and 90s.

Randy Hein grew up in an Evangelical, Baptist, Mennonite Christian subculture during the 1970s and 1980s. He was raised on notions of Jesus' imminent return and Christian films like *Thief in the Night* kept him, and scores of other evangelical youth, on guard against the impending apocalypse. They remained vigilant against the temptations of the world because one day soon the faithful would be carried into heaven while the heathen world was left to wallow in seven years of misery. Once completed, the final and awesome Day of the Lord would end it all: classic premillennial dispensationalism as taught by Sister Aimee or C.I. Scofield.

As we discussed in the last chapter, one of the dominant

1   This is taken from Kevin Quast's *Reading the Gospel of John*. (New Jersey: Paulist Press, 1991). Quast was a well-known Canadian Johannine Scholar.

narratives of those days was to transform the growing irrelevancy of the church into the tale of a faithful remnant in a world literally going to hell. Although his post-secondary education took him to the (gasp) secular world of Simon Fraser University, Randy never stopped thinking about the church. Despite being "left leaning" he took up the mantle of youth group leadership in a large evangelical church.[2]

This was also the grunge era and the khakis and polo shirts of the 1980s' Christian culture was being replaced by flannel shirts, combat boots, baggy pants, goatees, and shaved heads. Canadian-based theologian Stanley Grenz was one of the first people Randy encountered who was talking about doing church differently. While exciting, most took up Grenz's challenge in more cosmetic, rather than substantive, ways. In his own words, and in keeping with the middle class suburban white kids of that decade, Randy's evolving ecclesiology was "pretending to be dangerous" while doing nothing new or revolutionary.

Throughout the 90s, Bill Hybels' Willow Creek Church was increasingly the Mecca (pun intended) of attractional ministry with growing scores of books, music, studies, conferences, and a multi-million-dollar cultural influence that hit a zenith in 2000. Randy's church, like other churches in Canada's suburbs, borrowed heavily from Hybels' model and others like it because they seemed to work. Further reflection would have shown these leaders that their reach to the unchurched was still almost non-existent. Some churches during this time experienced substantial growth but the Canadian nation saw steadily declining numbers in attendance (as discussed in the previous chapter).[3]

Randy's youth group promoted morals and created a space that appealed to many parents in the area. They were happy to send their teens somewhere that taught against profanity and

---

2 This quote, and all subsequent quotes, are from Randy in an interview I had with him.

3 One example shows that, in 1981, slightly over 600,000 Canadians from ages 25-44 identified as having "No Religion." By 2001, that number had more than doubled to north of 1,600,000. See Clarke and Macdonald, *Leaving*, 166-73 for more.

drug use, even if the parents remained uninterested in the Light of the world themselves.

This was Randy's world as he stepped on to the stage of his church to speak to 500 young people about Jesus. As the final notes of the worship music faded and the buzz of the teens' voices diminished, Randy was alone on stage. Whereas Jesus' lights brought him into community with those around him, Randy became aware he couldn't see a single face. Though in the light and in a room full of people, he felt totally alone. "At that moment," Randy would later recall, "I lost confidence in that church model."

The personal crisis this seemingly innocuous moment created began Randy on a journey from a flannel-based fashion change into a fundamental one. The plasticity of Christianity could not be remedied by cooler clothes but had to be stripped down to the studs and rebuilt. The next three years Randy focused on theology and ecclesiology. He began to challenge the church on gender issues, homosexuality, women's rights, the environment, First Nations, corruption, commercialism and the myriad of other church teachings that were crumbling in the first years of what many refer to as the post-modern period.

In 1990, a lot of people were on the same page but, by the end of that transformative decade, many churches ignored the call to reimagine church. They maintained the corporate model and avoided the concerns emerging Christians like Randy were raising. These churches possessed a successful model that attracted many people. Like most of us, such churches asked the rhetorical question: "If it isn't broken, why fix it?" The 1990s began creating vocabulary that called out overly-stylized faith and cautioned against chasing numerical growth as a false god of consumerism. Such desires, it was argued, were echoes of past materialism, not signs for the church of the future.

Replacing the former vocabulary of conversion with a new vocabulary of conversation or focusing on social justice over morality seemed to be the old heresies of the early 20th century returning. The Christian youth of the 1960s and 70s were leaders by the 1980s and their beliefs were changing the face of Canadian Christianity. Despite such revolutionary beginnings, the process of institutionalizing their earlier radicalism made them somewhat deaf to the concerns of Generation X. The generation that "never trusted anyone over 30" were over 30 themselves and had begun to embody—in spirit at least—the very structures they had earlier rebelled against.

Unfortunately for Generation X Christians, the old guard were young and numerically larger and were going to remain in power for many more years. The emerging faiths of some younger Canadian Christians went underground, but many simply stopped attending church. Randy sums this up perfectly when he states that "by the early 2000s" due to struggles with leadership, and his need for change "my season of influence was over."

REALITY

The experience of Randy and others like him were the natural outworking of events begun in the 1960s. The more liberal Christians believed that faith had ramifications for this world and taught about the obligation Christians had towards society. The youth from this realm would be inspired to create a series of activist groups on campuses around the nation that would come to be known as the New Left. Other groups in places like Toronto, Banff, and Vancouver embraced the hippie ideals of that time but applied them to their Christian faith. Jesus' long hair, sandal-clad feet, and teachings on peace and love fit beautifully within this narrative. For the so-called Jesus People, the Nazarene Messiah was the poster boy for the pro-love, pacifist, and anti-institutionalism they preached.

The premillennial dispensationalism of some conservative churches rejected such socially-focused theology, stating it was as useless as polishing the brass on the Titanic.[4] University

---

4 I remember a t-shirt one of my friends wore to church in the late 1980s that stated "forget the whales, save the humans" and that is a good summary of where such

groups like InterVarsity and Campus Crusade for Christ also addressed the tensions of the day but approached them from a more doctrinal angle focused on Christian living, accountability, and logical defenses of the faith. One group focused on the intellectual assent to fundamental Christian truths while awaiting the end of days, and the other was criticized for having "become a civics lesson."[5] What concerned both sides, and what continues to dominate much of the conversation today, is the perceived lack of Christian influence over society in either civics or theology.

Later 20th century churches began a period "on the periphery of power" that was lamented by some but, in the words of John Webster Grant, released "Christian energies that have been smothered for centuries."[6] Economic growth brought new professions onto the Canadian scene, more programs of education, more government help to alleviate the church of its responsibility, and social care was increasingly in the hands of trained professionals. Secularization, from this vantage point, was a gift that freed churches to embrace their vocation within Canada.

This chapter will examine the final decades of the 20th century as the most secular time Canadians have ever seen. The 1990s was the decade in which the church quietly but noticeably diminished from the larger cultural conversation to such an extent that it even became less of a target for criticism. Despite the proliferation of televangelism and the growth of evangelical denominations, the larger picture of Canadian society was largely irreligious as the other-worldliness of the church was usurped by the satisfactory answers the material world had to offer.

Sure, there was a sense of a spiritual malaise but few people saw the church as able to offer any relief. This was the

---

theology tended to lead its followers.

5 Ramsay Cook. *The Regenerators: Social Criticism in Late Victorian English Canada*, (Toronto: University of Toronto, 1985), 230.

6 Grant, *Canadian*, 217.

decade that brought the maxim "I am spiritual not religious" to the forefront. While not the first generation to utter such beliefs, this pro-metaphysical and anti-institutional worldview became so ubiquitous in the 90s it became passé. However, that idea was destined to die spectacularly and horrifically and would shake the western world with such an impact that none of us have stopped talking about religion since. The last day the western world ignored religion as a dominant cultural influence was September 10, 2001.

This chapter will explore the following:

1. The leftward slide of the UCC
2. The Jesus People
3. The ordination of women
4. Gay Rights
5. Televangelism
6. The Toronto Blessing (because it's time to challenge my own assertions about revivalism in Canada)
7. The 1990s
8. Actual Canadian beliefs

THE UCC MOVES LEFT

Bruce Douville's perfectly titled *The Uncomfortable Pew* tracks the emergence and relevance of young radical and countercultural Christians in the 1960s and early 1970s (thanks to the previous chapter, you understand why his title is fitting and funny...see? You're becoming a history nerd). His doctoral dissertation about the revolutionary, hip culture not only plays off Pierre Berton's book, it also communicates the discomfort many of these movements brought to older, established Canadian Christians.[7] The kind of discomfort Berton deemed necessary for the Canadian church to grow once again. Similar to Randy's conclusions about 1990s suburban Christian counter-culture,

---

7 Douville has also published a book by the same name. His book, like most books written from a dissertation, has a tighter focus. In it, Douville focuses on the interactions between Christianity and radical student left in Toronto, from the 1960s to the early 1970s. His dissertation can be downloaded for free in PDF form.

Douville contends the "dissemination of hip culture was evident in the late sixties, but it was the early seventies when it became the dominant culture of white North American youth."[8]

While this section will track the growth of these young white Christians' social conscience, there are two major takeaways from the late 70s culture that we need to observe. The first is that thanks to interest in Eastern religions, transcendental meditation, and the growth of marijuana use, the "spiritual smorgasbord had gone mainstream."[9] The inability of mainline churches to create relevant biblical teachings opened the door for other traditions. The freedom of the 1960s created a new reality in the 1970s that offered plenty of appealing spiritual alternatives to the Christian narrative. Although these teachings and spiritual practices were well beyond the Protestant world, they came largely as a result of the fragmented Canadian Christian ethos and the lack of a universal Christian response to a myriad of issues.

The second take away is a resurgence in anti-Americanism that would have made John Strachan proud (you likely get that reference as well...see how much you're learning?). An increasing number of Canadian youths desired to rid themselves of American corporate greed and its impact on the Canadian economy. While I posited the lack of missionary endeavours after the 1920s as one of the reasons for the loss of a global Canadian presence, the Christian activists of the 1970s blamed an external cause. Building on the popularity of South American Liberation Theology, many of these Christians saw their *raison d'etre* as championing the impoverished and marginalized within Canada. Such people groups included First Nations, the Metis, Inuit, French Canadians, and vast collections of immigrants. Each of these people groups were seen as systematically disenfranchised by an economy too tied to the imperialism and

---

8 Bruce Michael Douville. "The Uncomfortable Pew: Christianity, the New Left and HIp Counterculture in Toronto, 1965-1975." (Ph.D. Dissertation: York University, 2011), 369.

9 Douville, "Uncomfortable," 372.

greed of American corporations.

Student groups began to insist on more Canadian faculty for Canadian universities and increasing attention paid to the Canadian context as different from, and in many ways superior to, America. I want you to hear the echoes of earlier chapters regarding education and anti-Americanism. A patriotism was growing that believed Canada's lack of global significance was a secret strength. Groups like the SCM (Student Christian Movement) shared similar concerns with 19th century ministers like Robert Easton. Remember, he warned of the impact American greed could have over the more socially-minded environment of Canada. Liberation Theology's argument that God holds a special place for the poor only strengthened this group's resolve to create a socialist and anti-capitalist Canadian culture. A culture that stood as a condemnation of the same American manners Easton had condemned all the way back in 1815.

During the Vietnam War, Canada also received a substantial collection of draft-dodgers from the States. Given the age of these refugees, it is no surprise that Canadian youth saw this as an important issue. Some scholars argue this was one of the moments when the UCC began a leftward slide. Others see the condemnations of the Vietnam War as further evidence of a Canadian desire to separate from America, but that opinion is not supported by church sources from the time. What can be seen is churches responding to the needs of these young Americans for humanitarian, rather than political, motivations.

Anti-American rhetoric was substantial and while draft-dodging was a perpetual topic of controversy, some clerics vocally supported American youth who chose to flee rather than fight. These discussions walked a fine line stating the church needed to help anyone who looked to Canada as a haven, whether or not the churches supported their reasons for doing so. This is how churches like the UCC were able to address the concerns of Christian young people without necessarily endorsing their more progressive stances on issues like American imperialism or third world solidarity.

These youth movements lost influence as the young aged and entered the work force. The optimism, communalism, and spirituality of the 1960s movements morphed into the more individualistic self-improvement fads of the 1970s and 1980s. However, in one arena did these youth movements command a generational legacy that needs to be noted for Canadian Christians.

Whether it was dealing with Vietnam, women's issues, gay rights (more on both of these in a moment), or the role of the church in political activism, it is fair to say that the 1970s is when the UCC embraced more progressive Leftist leanings. Many of the clergy and leaders during that time had been inspired by the struggles of the 1960s and early 70s and created a church that could house both Christianity and progressive politics. A small number of these activists found employment within churches and believed they had the manifesto for Canadian Christianity moving forward.

Canadian Catholics also embraced more progressive attitudes in the wake of Vatican II but their ecclesiology made institutional restructuring more difficult. While there existed progressive writings from influential laity and substantial support for draft-dodgers, the only real changes of that time was the inclusion of folk music and guitars in the Mass. The messages from the Vatican in the 1970s and 1980s boomeranged back towards conservatism and the changes that took place in Quebec Christianity had more to do with rejecting the Church rather than finding new ways to exist within it.

Motivations are tricky to discern or understand, and few of us do anything in our lives for just one reason; our motivations tend to be a mosaic. I don't want to come off sounding like all the churches cared about was numbers, that is unfair and lacks nuance. There was concern over the theology of the time and church leaders across the board spoke about the theological imperative to remain relevant and conversant. Genuine theological concern for the faith of the young—similar to the concerns Anglicans displayed about American Methodism—went hand in hand with desires to engage youth and grow churches.

What can be said is that other mainstream/liberal Protestant denominations had limited success interacting with the attitudes of that day. In order to retain their own youth it was argued that denominations needed to be conversant with social issues. It was hoped that intelligent Christian responses to these concerns would ensure that the young who self-identified as Christians would remain. Even a cursory examination of numbers from the later 1970s and 1980s prove just how incorrect such beliefs were. The 1980s saw steady declines in numbers for the liberal Canadian churches and the only rise in Catholicism was thanks, once again, to immigration.

Ironically, conservative evangelical churches saw a definite upswing in attendance during the same time. I say ironic because these churches were antithetical to popular Canadian sensibilities of the time and yet their oppositional stance resulted in greater numerical success. Why? The answers are multifaceted, but one has to do with Pierre Berton's hypothesis. He argued that churches needed to be more interactive with the issues of the day if the church hoped to remain. The UCC and other mainstream groups did that by genuinely engaging with complex social issues.

However, what Berton didn't predict was that interest in religion could be reignited through simple cosmetic changes as well. As we began to cover in the last chapter, conservative churches changed little about their theology but they gave their style a much-needed face lift. That sounds dismissive but, historically speaking, that cosmetic change proved much more effective in garnering numbers than the UCC's engagement. While some churches struggled to create Christian social progressivism, others created Christian pop culture.

THE JESUS PEOPLE

In short, the Jesus people beautifully wed the style of 1970s counterculture with the message of evangelicalism. These people could have the long hair and radical clothes of their non-Christian friends while maintaining their Christian identity. Because evangelicalism stresses the importance of conversion and separation from the world, there is a sense of specialness its members share that the young of the liberal churches don't. Evangelical youth are the recipients of more attention because their theology is all about being saved from a doomed world. There are plenty of social and cultural pressures from a very early age to keep evangelical youth on board the proverbial ark of the church, and to prevent them from jumping into the destructive floodwaters of the world.

As important as such theology was (and is), music was the key to these churches' success. Jesus Rock incorporated the cultural sound and created an entire Christian music industry that looked and sounded like all the popular songs/artists on the radio. The key difference was that these artists sang Christian lyrics. From that came the fashion, movies, books, comics, conferences, and a very successful *counter*-counter culture that gave these churches niche relevance.

Many older Christians within these groups were able to embrace such youthful changes jubilantly because the message was still very conservative. I don't want to oversell their acceptance because many remained disdainful toward long hair and believed rock n' roll was the devil's music. However, the point I'm making is the re-imaginings in the UCC were even more challenging to time-tested beliefs (as we'll see a little later in this chapter). Older evangelicals looked much hipper than their liberal counterparts because they accepted new forms with greater speed. In many ways it was easier for them because, in essence, they were simply altering the appearance of the church with precious few changes to the actual theology. Once again, innovation is more palatable when connected to stabilizing and familiar elements from the past.

The Jesus People's origins were in California (a fact that should surprise absolutely no one) and by the early 1980s many had begun to form into increasingly organized collectives. One of these groups began to emphasize the creative role of the Holy Spirit and embraced a Christian perspective on freedom. They stressed relaxed attitudes towards clothes but a more stringent dependence on the Bible. In 1982, one of these collectives formed the Vineyard Denomination; a direct child of the 1970s Jesus People. Praise bands and stylish clothes went from counter-culture to mainstream culture. Books were being written—and sold—that celebrated such stylistic changes as the new and improved ecclesiology. Some of the Jesus People had also been draft dodgers, so there existed a significant collection of American ex-patriots in places like the Okanagan Valley, B.C., to bring such changes to the Canadian scene.[10]

Pipe (and even electronic) organs increasingly changed from a traditional instrument associated with grandeur to symbolic of the old and irrelevant way of doing church. By the 1990s the so-called "worship wars" began in earnest that pitted praise bands and choirs against each other for the role of preferred Sunday musical style. For some, the problem was solved by introducing two Sunday morning services: one billed as Traditional and the other as Contemporary. The sermon and prayers could be the exact same in both but the music was expected to be different. You could ascertain the ecclesiology of a church you were attending based solely on which of the two formats was later. If the contemporary service was first, chances are it was run by the youth group and was a consolation service. Whichever service held the later time slot was still the main event.

Canadian Evangelicalism has always embraced an outsider

---

10   I don't want to give the impression that this was a unified stream of church thinking. These were more independent collections that shared common themes and beliefs. Included in such groups were Jesus people known as the Yorkville hippie scene, the Jesus Forever Family at Rochdale College, and Saint Margaret's Reformed Episcopal in East Vancouver. For more on the Vineyard Denomination in Canada, see vineyard.ca and check out their history section.

role opposed to the religious establishment of the day. The Jesus people were the 1970s iteration of that impulse. Their emphasis on the Holy Spirit, so-called authentic faith, and even their belief that Christianity is a relationship, not a religion, gave them cultural influence not enjoyed by their more liberal co-religionists. While the Jesus People truly embodied an attempt to radically live out their faith, the ways in which their 1980s and 90s evangelical children did so left much to be desired. Despite the growth of denominations like the Vineyard and PAOC during the 1980s, their "in the world not of the world" ecclesiology became increasingly at odds with accepted Canadian attitudes towards the role of religion.

For all their stylistic innovation, their stance on numerous key issues only further entrenched nominal Canadian Christians in their belief that church should play a diminished role in the modern age. To build on the concluding point from the previous chapter: the numerical growth of conservative evangelical Protestants also contributed to the increased numerical growth of secularized Canadians.

This is not to place blame on conservative evangelicals, but to reiterate that the variety of Christian voices is more the culprit. In the Leftism of the UCC or the innovative conservatism of the Jesus People, I hope you can see just further developments of the Anglican/Methodist rivalries of the 19th century, or the Modernist/Fundamentalist debates of the early 20th century, or the Sermons from Science/Christian Pavilions of 1967. Although the UCC brought Canadian social concerns into a Christian framework, their efforts were not rewarded with increased adherents. And despite their anti-institutional, casual, seeker-friendly approach, conservative evangelicals were unable to meet the challenge posed by 1990s Gen-X skepticism.

However, these churches did have one thing in common: all of them were struggling when it came to the topic of gender and sexual identity in their new reality.

THE ORDINATION OF WOMEN

Arguably the most important new reality of Canadian religion in the 1980s was the presence of women in all facets of church leadership. By the 1970s Presbyterians, Anglicans, Lutherans, Convention Baptists, Mennonites, and the UCC had ordained women for ministry—the UCC leading the pack with over 400. Obviously, the Catholic Church didn't change its teachings regarding female priests, bishops, or cardinals, and other higher levels of control remained the exclusive vocation of men alone. However, that is more indicative of Rome because, as Grant puts it: "[T]he situation might be different if the decisions were made in Canada."[11] Several prominent conservative evangelical Protestant groups also held to an ecclesiology that precluded women from leadership. Such a stance, as in the case of the Fellowship and Convention Baptists, irreparably divided two branches connected to the same denominational tree.

Education returned to the forefront and this was largely thanks to the enrollment of women in theological schooling around the nation. From 1975 to 1981, the amount of students rose by a whopping 50% and in the 1980s some theological student bodies were more than half female.

This is important to note because gender roles went through a lot of changes in Canada during the later 20th century. Some denominations, likewise, became intentional in their scrutiny of religious language. In the UCC, Chairman became Chairperson, the denominational hymnal Voices United greatly decreased the number of times God was referred to as Father, and gender inclusive language was desired for all biblical readings.

Rev. Bob Mutlow of Woodcliff United Church in Calgary explained such teachings to me in the following way: when a female minister read the advent text: "Glory to God in the highest, and on earth peace, goodwill toward men!" she had to do one more mental step to recognize that the word "men" was not specifically for males but was indicative of all humanity.

---

11 Grant, *Canadian*, 234.

However, that extra mental step reinforced earlier subjugated roles for women and, it was argued, replacing "men" with "people" was a legitimate translation of the Greek.[12] Such changes within the church reflected the larger Canadian climate as it pertained to women in the workplace.

The journey to acceptance for working women was fraught with many perils and the church weighed in on such potentially problematic matters. The increase of ordained women was partly the result of the feminist movement—which reached its zenith in the 1970s. This was also a time some historians refer to as the Age of Evangelical Moral Panic. For some churches, the rise of female clergy was just one more example of secularization and they held grave concerns what such developments meant for the nation.

Following WWII, the family sphere was considered an almost sacred environment and, as such, needed to be protected. Christianity's ongoing shift from the centre of power meant the home was increasingly seen as the primary space for the cultivation of faith. Several denominations began to look into the role of marriage and began to form new arguments about the importance of the nuclear family as a building block for society.

In the UCC, it was the United Church Commission on Marriage and Divorce, begun in 1957. They argued that the family unit was the building block of the nation and marital structures needed to be maintained for the sake of society. Nothing new so far as many Christians make similar arguments today to oppose same-sex unions. What was novel was that many clergy (mostly male) began stating that a good marriage took the wife's desires into account. Whatever could have spawned such a revolutionary idea as this? Clearly, this was an awakening to the historic marginalization of women. Perhaps it was a cry to correct the imbalances in domestic life? No, it was none of those, it came out of concern that more women entering the workplace would undermine men's traditional role as the

---

12 He taught me this in a meeting in his office in early 1998 when I was hired to be a youth minister at the church.

family breadwinner.

In addition to the increased earning power of women, the decriminalization of birth control in 1969 also offered another tool for women to determine their own life beyond the traditional private sphere of the home. The ethics of the baby boom were being reinterpreted both legally and, with an increasing number of female clergy, from the pulpits as well. For some Protestant groups such cultural shifts only strengthened their end-times theology and created a new focus on the so-called traditional family. Their teachings around roles in the traditional family are just as fascinating to explore.

One of the new focuses on the family unit was around romantic love between a man and a woman. The ways in which such romantic attraction could, in a Christian union, be symbolic of "Creative love itself."[13] Marriage was no longer about procreation or social order (as it had been since the dawn of the institution) but gave new impetus to romance as a tool for female empowerment and equality. In a twisting of the 1960s' sexual liberation movement, sexual equality within a marriage was seen as a path to purer faith and much less dangerous to social order than economic equality.

As Nancy Christie writes: "Sex...would lead the modern woman back to the welcoming family circle."[14] In order to combat women's materialistic desire to join the workforce, men were encouraged to satisfy their women in the bedroom in order to keep them home. As the former gender roles of moral mother and provider father blurred in this new reality, some church leaders hoped to reinforce them in the realm of marital sex.

Propping up the myth that men are more interested in sex than women, some churches argued that sex was the key to true female empowerment. While similar arguments were made in some feminist literature of the time, these churches were not embracing such writings. Rather, they placed women in the role of gatekeeper, because she decided when, and how often,

---

13 Christie, "Sacred Sex," 359.

14 Christie, "Sacred Sex," 363.

sex would happen within the confines of the marriage. Such a role, it was argued, gave women their power in the home. This kind of domestic influence was seen as a far superior recourse to women having multiple sexual partners or entering the work force. This is just one example of some of the issues women faced as they entered into higher education for the sake of ordination.

The UCC eventually embraced many of the tenets of the new morality in the late 1960s and released marriage to the realm of the secular state. It was argued that a marriage was between two adults and could be dissolved through mutual consent, with no church interference. By the 1970s it was no longer seen as a social disease but as a consequence of the modern age. At its heart, most of the issues around women in ministry have to do with the ongoing fear of women's sexuality and that is why the next round of trouble came specifically due to women's reproductive rights.

Feminism remains a divisive term even today and so no one should be surprised to see the legalization of birth control and abortion quickly used to point out the moral failings of the cause.[15] Rarely was it seen to be combating the countless ways in which women's autonomy had been marginalized throughout Canada's history including, but not limited to, forced sterilizations and innumerable cases of domestic violence. Even equating feminism with abortion or birth control reveals the belief that a woman's chief role is as wife and mother. To offer alternatives to either of those roles is a moral failure on the part of the so-called, "weaker sex."

As Robert Choquette writes the "restricted and second-class place of women in society had been reinforced and rationalized by value-judgments and stereotypes to the effect that women were physically, emotionally, and intellectually weaker than men" and when such beliefs were proven to be "patently false and unfounded" some churches were less than thrilled to welcome women into an equal place in church or

---

15 To be fair, many Feminists also saw abortion as a central issue to their cause.

society.[16] While many in the PAOC argued the decriminalization of abortion was proof the end of times was upon them, it should be noted that the 1971 official stance of the denomination stated abortion was "justifiable, both theologically and medically, under specific circumstances."[17]

Let's stay with the PAOC for a moment because they offer an interesting perspective for a few reasons: 1) their origin in the 20th century made them one of the more recent Christian movements, potentially more sympathetic to modern sensibilities; 2) they were a revival-based expression of the faith that historically empowered pious women to lead and preach and; 3) they were one of the Christian groups actually experiencing growth in the late 20th century.

While the modern character of, and Pentecostalism's track record for, empowering the traditionally disenfranchised had the potential to make it a champion of women's equality, that turned out to be untrue. Well into the 1980s, the PAOC consistently taught a complementarian message to its women.[18] While there were large collections of active women's groups, females were encouraged to facilitate change as helpmates to male leaders and through personal prayer. Michael Wilkinson and Linda Ambrose write that the PAOC repeatedly emphasized three characteristics for women throughout the later part of the 20th century:

> 1. Women should embrace their roles as ancillary support workers...2. Women should do their unpaid work in the home and the church motivated by love, not money. 3. Women should expect to participate in the organization covertly from their private prayer closets, not directly as strategists who challenge, counsel, or give advice to

16 Choquette, *Religions*, 298.

17 Wilkinson and Ambrose, *Revival*, 112.

18 A theological perspective that argues men and women have different, but complementary, roles in marriage, family, life, and roles in the church. For a longer definition from a pro-complementarian female Canadian author see: Mary Kassian, "Complementarianism for Dummies." Downloaded at https://www.thegospelcoalition.org/article/complementarianism-for-dummies/

men.[19]

By the 1980s, while mainline denominational schools were filling with future female leaders, the PAOC finally began to ordain women. However, this growing Protestant collective struggled to find women preachers, evangelists, and church planters. Given the nature of their teaching, that fact is not surprising.

PAOC attitudes toward abortion saw them aligning more with the Moral Majority in the States. Numerous documents reflected more American-style political activism than their own Canadian denomination's earlier arguments. They also echoed some of the mainline Protestant churches' earlier recognition that they needed to focus energies more on theological matters and less on changing the morals of an increasingly secular world. Despite the tardiness of several church groups like the PAOC, the outright hostility of some para-church organizations, and the ongoing complementarian teaching of several prominent evangelical churches, the reality of 20th century Canada was that women had several paths to church leadership. Concerns about sexual identity and ethics remained, and many of these issues have continued to hound women up to this present day. Equality between the sexes as mandated by law meant that female voices would be heard in the halls of power as well as from the pulpit.

GAY RIGHTS

In 1988 the UCC made a landmark decision that same-sex attraction should not be an obstacle to ordination. Many people saw this as the natural next step in the increasing acceptance of new sexual identities of the 20th century. Many Canadian Christians also believed such a step was beyond the pale and the UCC splintered after 1988.

Scientific research weighed in on the matter, arguing that sexual preference was a biological predetermination not a

19 Wilkinson and Ambrose, *Revival*, 93-4.

personal choice. If sexuality was like eye colour, then the moral arguments against it had no merit. This was one of the main arguments for those who stood in favour of allowing same-sex attracted ministers into leadership.

In Toronto, Metropolitan Community Church brought together faithful followers who desired to worship God in a space that affirmed their sexuality.[20] While the UCC decision was greeted with respect in many circles, the dominant story for most gay men and women in Christian Canada was one of exclusion. The vast majority of Christian voices either ignored gay rights or condemned it. Even those who were speaking more positively tended to frame the debate over the immorality of the homosexual act versus the homosexual person. This "hate the sin, love the sinner" argument sought to include people without condoning their actions. Throughout the 1980s churches like the UCC began to amend such opinions in a fairly rapid, though controversial, turn of events. While it would prove damaging to the numerical base, the UCC was able to declare support for same-sex attraction and create a space for those in active same-sex relationships to fully belong to the church.

While same-sex marriages would not be officially sanctioned in Canada until the 21st century (therefore beyond the scope of this book) it is worth noting that evangelicals opposed to this were simply unable to mount any kind of sustainable action. This is not to say that church groups sat idly by. The Evangelical Fellowship, Roman Catholics, PAOC, Evangelical Baptist, CBOQ, and Free Methodists teamed up with the Canadian Organization of Small Businesses to defend what they called traditional family values. Throughout the 1980s such groups vocally challenged what they believed was the undermining of Canada's Christian character. Such threats included homosexuality, but also

---

20 "Since 1973, MCC Toronto has been helping shape Canadian values of inclusion, diversity, and equality. A place of worship and a place of action, MCC Toronto is a vibrant and progressive church rooted in the Christian tradition and the LGBTQ2+ community that is open and welcoming to everyone, and a Human Rights Centre that is fiercely committed to social justice." Taken from the MCC homepage. https://www.mcctoronto.com/about-us/

included drunk driving, sexual promiscuity, increased divorce rates, women in the workplace, Dungeons & Dragons, rampant Satanism, and pornography. The solutions were revival, prayer, fasting, prophetic preaching, and a return of Christianity to the public market place of influential ideas.

This topic also introduces another tension worthy of reflection: which of these responses was actually more "Canadian"? While the UCC suffered as a result of their decision, that decision also better reflected the changing norms of many Canadians. Conservative evangelicals were adamant in their opposition—a stance that should have alienated and weakened them—yet they benefitted numerically. However, their growth largely came from immigration, and some former UCCers jumping ship for churches that better reflected their theological beliefs. Once again, Canadian Christian culture was revealed to be a vast and expansive domain with room enough for competing ideologies to claim space. Such diversity within Christian teaching is not unique to Canada, but this story offers a uniquely Canadian example.

Despite being more in touch with the norms of the day, the UCC was unable to parlay such alignment into actual attendance. This landmark decision from the ecclesiastical perspective barely registered on the larger Canadian scene. Support of inclusion was not rewarded in Canada; perhaps it was merely expected. Those who decided to take a stand against gay rights were shamed by unchurched Canadians as bigots and homophobes. These churches provided another valid reason for Canadians to avoid church and also gave the unchurched a moral reason for doing so. Yet conservative numbers grew and such growth strengthened their theology of a faithful remnant in an unfaithful world. Thanks to the 1988 ruling, these churches could also point to the UCC as included among the unfaithful.

This also strengthened an ecumenical push between evangelicals and Catholics that had been growing modestly since the end of WWII. The Catholic rejection of same-sex unions made them surprising allies with conservative

Protestants (as well as with some conservative Jewish groups). While conservative evangelicals had often been champions of anti-Catholicism—arguing frequently it was a diabolical and idolatrous superstition—they became more conversant thanks to their shared concerns over Canadian sexual morality. The size and influence of Canadian Catholicism, the increasing influence of conservative evangelicals, and the declining numbers of liberal Protestants made the anti-same-sex camp a formidable Canadian Christian perspective.

Thus the tension of which side better represents the "Canadian" response. The UCC provided a Christian response that aligned with shifting Canadian norms, while the conservatives and Catholics presented a Christian response that challenged and rejected them. More importantly, the tension highlighted for the churches of the 1980s that Canadians easily ignored their teachings, even the most sexually progressive ones. In other words, the churches were damned if they did and damned if they didn't.

TELEVANGELISM

However, what did gain media attention were the outlandish actions of televangelists from the States like Jim and Tammy Faye Bakker. The land that had always bred Messiahs now had the advent of television to bring their messages of prosperity and flash into Canadian homes. The average Canadian had access to fun churches with polished routines and charismatic characters offering exciting and salacious church from the comfort of their own living rooms. All you needed was a good TV—an item most Canadians possessed by that time—and this well-marketed version of the faith further reduced the significance of Canadian Christianity.[21]

100 Huntley Street brought a Canadian version of American Christian television, but millions continued to flow from Canada

---

21 "[I]ndustrialization and the provision of urban amenities were producing a new breed of Canadian whose outlook owed more to salesmanship and the mass media than to Bible-reading and the mass." Grant, *Canadian*, 216.

to support various American-based television ministries.[22] David Mainse's creation began in 1977 and has enjoyed success across the nation ever since. While Huntley would never garner the attention of its American counterparts, neither did it succumb to the greed and hypocrisy that defined televangelism in the minds of many. Mainse must be credited for an authenticity and integrity that kept him above all the scandals that, for the most part, went hand in hand with TV church. Ironically, his ability to host with integrity is also likely one of the reasons why his show never really hit big numbers. Success stories like that of the American televangelists had as much to do with their scandals and lavish lifestyles as their views on God. Whether it was Tammy's trademark eye shadow, or Swaggart's sweeping hair, these people were marketing masters and put their mastery to good use.

Those outside the church mocked these preachers ceaselessly and pitied anyone who donated to their causes. What such critics failed to realize was the genius that made televangelism so powerful. While accused of being the modern incarnation of the Depression-era snake-oil salesman, they were actually something else entirely. Televangelists built a brand of the faith that people recognized and trusted. They used the TV to display their lives in order to breed the kind of familiarity and transparency preachers are supposed to have. The cadence of their speech (preacher voice) was used to communicate sound bites possessing an air of deep truth that elicited emotive responses from their audience. Their shows created pandenominational communities—previous evangelicals had done the same with radio—giving people a sense of belonging.

They looked directly into the camera (breaking the fourth wall), talked directly to their TV audience, and often prayed for people by name. They used their celebrity as a spiritual tool. They literally embodied a distant spiritual entity but TV granted them an illusory intimacy because people worshipped with them

22 1984 saw as much as $19 million donated to America.

in their living rooms. Fame is a powerful concept and has very god-esque qualities, and Jim and Tammy Faye were celebrities that felt like friends. Their personas were built on the familial nature of church, boosted by the power of television.

Giving to such a church was no different from tithing, and the elaborate promises of what such financial fidelity would bring to the audience made perfect sense. The material success of the 1980s was given spiritual significance and the promises of God's blessings switched from the ethereal to the material, from the hereafter to the here and now. While there is plenty of evidence that donations largely came from those of a lower socio-economic bracket, that also makes sense given how desirable this prosperity gospel looked to those struggling to make ends meet. Televangelists weren't snake oil salesmen; they were Mad Men. They used the Bible, TV, and marketing tools to literally monetize faith.

While topical and desirous of engaging with political and cultural issues from a Christian perspective, David Mainse never turned into a brand. He should be applauded because he quietly and consistently produced Christian content for Canadians while never chasing the lavishness of the Americans. While *100 Huntley Street* provides a clear contrast between American and Canadian versions of televangelism, it should be noted that many of Mainse's guests were well-known American evangelists and celebrities. While both had the same access to technology and both were attempting to engage the faith in creative new ways, the American version would always be bigger, shinier, flashier, and more successful than the Canadian. But it would also be more visibly problematic and damaging to the faith.

Perhaps the main legacy of televangelism is how it influenced non-televised worship. Televangelism's success proved there was a market for church. Resources in larger evangelical churches increasingly went into audio/visual equipment to duplicate televangelism's style in their sanctuaries. Church leaders combined 1970s youthful church style with televangelism to remedy their concern about Christian irrelevance in Canada. In the blazingly neon decade of the 1980s they created a new brand of church especially tuned to modern tastes: Seeker Sensitive.

SEEKER SENSITIVE CHURCH

Evangelization always remained a central element of churches and the seeker sensitive model was born out of a desire to show the growing pack of exodus-inclined Canadians that Christianity could, with its guitars, relaxed attitudes towards clothing, and high production values, be cool. The church of the 1980s desired greater relevancy and showed people that the ancient teachings of Jesus were as relevant in that materially rich decade as they had been to the rebels of the 1960s (many of whom were now rich themselves).

While the 21st century would usher in the astonishing success of Willow Creek or Rick Warren's Saddleback models, the 1980s and 90s witnessed substantial growth in Christian materialism that would lay the groundwork for these later models. Clothing, music, and films all communicated cultural connection as well as Christian distinctness. The clothes and music mimicked (and mocked) popular "secular" phrases, trends, and tropes but gave them Christian meaning. They literally provided a way to purchase and then display the theology of being *in* but not *of* the world.

All of it designed to intrigue the unchurched and possibly make them curious about church as well. And the churches they were calling Canadians to attend would be likewise hip, relevant, entertaining, and engaging. For a while, it seemed to work and somewhat stem the tide of departure. Weekly Protestant attendance grew 2% in the 1980s from 28% of Canadians attending at least one service a week to a hopeful total of 30%.[23] Conservative groups grew faster than their liberal counterparts as usual but many of their moral teachings kept them increasingly out of touch with shifting Canadian values.

---

23 Clarke and Macdonald, *Leaving*, 112.

An unintended consequence of this desire to relate the faith to the culture was that it empowered Canadian Christians to reject any practice or teaching that didn't fit into their individual worldview. Evangelicalism has always focused on the individual's role in his or her salvation and that emphasis combined with marketing, increased education, a multiplicity of faith expressions, and a booming economy made church shopping an acceptable spiritual enterprise. Canadian Reginald Bibby described this time in his famous book *Fragmented Gods*.[24] While people still attended church, most didn't pray or tithe regularly and were prone to blend their faith with other pseudo-spiritual elements in the culture. Reginald Bibby summed such thinking up when he quipped that more Canadians read their horoscope than their Bible.[25]

Canadians sought out churches that satisfied their perceived needs and the balance shifted in Protestant churches around the land. Laity approached their faith in the same way they approached buying shoes and the churches scrambled to hold on to their spiritual customers. Televangelism and Seeker churches helped people draw these conclusions with their focus on divine material blessings and terminology that aped the psychological language of the age. Educated and literate masses demanded creative and engaging material with demonstrable benefits, so many preachers hopped on the self-help bandwagon. They began to show how Jesus could help a person find true inner peace but that inner peace was interpreted less through the Bible and more through the lens of psychology or the influential positive thinking movement pioneered by Norman

---

24   Reginald Bibby. *Fragmented Gods: The Poverty and Potential of Religion in Canada*. Toronto: Stoddart, 1990. As did Wade Clark Roof from an American perspective in *Spiritual Marketplace: Baby Boomers and the Remaking of American Religion*. New Jersey: Princeton, 2001.

25   Bibby, *Fragmented*, 74. The numbers he cited were 75% of Canadians read their horoscope on occasion whereas 45% read their Bible. To demonstrate the growth of the spiritual smorgasbord referenced in the previous chapter, Bibby also found 35% of Canadians believed in Astrology, 61% in Extra-Sensory perception, 22% believed in communicating with the dead, and 63% of Canadians believed psychic powers were real and could be used to predict the future.

Vincent Peale.

Canadians were less willing to entertain Christian teachings around sacred suffering—ditto for Americans. In an attempt to maintain relevance, many preachers began to sound like self-help gurus, or popular televangelists as they offered their parishioners multiple-step programs for personal fulfillment. This was the decade in which children and youth ministries exploded as various denominations appealed to the Boomers' family values by offering Christianity for kids. Dozens of VBS programs, Teen Bibles, Christian rock music, and stylish clothing began to fill sections of Christian bookstores (another Mad Men innovation). Christian pop culture proved financially successful, but tangentially relating modern values to the ancient faith weakened the uniqueness of the church. Many of these ideas eventually fell flat and to those outside the church such measures were, in the words of one Canadian band: "Close but kind of meatless / like actors who play Jesus."[26]

THE TORONTO BLESSING

Now it is time to address the elephant in this book. I have written numerous sentences challenging the belief in the transformative nature of revivalism in Canada. Anyone who rejects this stance needs look no further than the mid-1990s and the Toronto Blessing. You are right to do so, gentle reader, I mean, what *was* that?

It began humbly enough, in a building near a runway at the Pearson Airport in Toronto. Pastors John and Carol Arnott invited Missourian Randy Brown to speak to their congregation in January of 1994. At the time, the church was known as the Toronto Airport Vineyard Church but was destined to move well past their denomination of origin and become The Toronto Blessing. Brown recalled the first meeting had an attendance just north of 100 and as he spoke, people began to succumb to laughter, falling down, and increasingly bizarre behaviour. Thus

---

26   The Odds. "Someone Who's Cool," released in 1996.

began the most influential revival in the history of Canada. For the next 12 years, six nights a week the Toronto Blessing held services that literally impacted the lives of millions of people around the world. The Blessing inspired Canadian expressions from Kelowna, B.C. to St. John's, Newfoundland and for the first time since the Hebden Mission, Canada was a leader in a global Christian movement.

In a true inversion of historical precedent, the Blessing is also responsible for inspiring the largest revival in American history. I need to write that again just to make sure it sinks in: a Canadian church is credited with beginning the largest revival in the very pro-revival land of America. It is one thing to be big in Canada, but to be responsible for the biggest revival in the States is truly a feat. The Brownsville Assembly of God revival began in June of 1995 and lasted for just over six years, about half the time as the Toronto experience. The Toronto Blessing also reversed the historic flow of Transatlantic faith by commanding the attention of the U.K. for over a decade. The last time a North American movement was that popular across the pond, Jonathan Edwards was the key leader. It is fair to say that the Toronto Blessing was as big as it gets in 20th century western Christian history, and definitely as it pertains to Canada.

However, even the massive and hitherto unseen level of success the Toronto movement achieved in every conceivable category, was unable to effect lasting change. As big as it was internally to Canada and internationally to the world, stats from the 90s show that the impact remained largely unfelt. The Toronto Blessing made waves mostly in previously Christian markets and most notably in pre-existing evangelical and charismatic churches. It drew impressive media attention but the oddity of the worship and strange miracle claims—like people receiving golden teeth in their mouths—also garnered negative press. Unfortunately, such reports mirrored the skepticism televangelism inspired and unfairly caricatured Charismatic Christianity. These people were unfairly mocked as a ridiculous, anti-intellectual, and suffering from a hysteria or mass mental illness; but not genuine faith. This did nothing to enamour the Blessing to unchurched Canadians.

There is a lesson to be learned here as it pertains to the Canadian religious landscape. I will always remain sympathetic to those Christians who believe Canada needs revival, but I continue to offer cautions as well. Canadians couldn't ask for a more grandiose event than the Toronto Blessing and yet it, like all revival movements, eventually came to a close. Today the Blessing is Catch the Fire church and I am genuinely curious to see how the church will handle its revivalist legacy. The numbers for the Blessing were off the charts, manifestations of it went from coast to coast, it changed the religious landscape of America, and the duration was truly impressive. The impact it had over global faith is easily the most any Canadian church has ever enjoyed in the history of this land.

In the interest of transparency, I should state that I periodically attended a similar service in Calgary known as Tehillah Monday. It was there that I converted to Christianity so, for all my skepticism, I must admit that my own life has been impacted by Canadian revivalism. If it wasn't for the Toronto Blessing, you wouldn't be reading this book right now. Radio personality Tara Jean Stevens was likewise impacted. In season 1 of her podcast, *Heaven Bent*, she explores the phenomena and notes that her Northern B.C. church was inspired deeply by the Blessing in Toronto. This five-episode season is a fair, funny, sympathetic, and insightful chronicle of the Blessing's history. Peppered throughout her study are personal recollections of growing up in Charismatic Christianity; but she notes from the beginning that she no longer self-identifies as Christian.

She is a perfect example of a Canadian Done (the name for someone who was raised in the church but made a decision to leave) because she is not angry, bitter, or dismissive but is actually quite appreciative of her church upbringing. Stevens is at peace with her decision to leave not only the church, but the faith as well. The disconnect between the church's teaching and her life experiences proved too substantial to overlook.

For those who see revivalism as an antidote to spiritual illness, I caution that other cultural factors must be considered as well. Stevens embodies the first of those factors because the church's teachings—like many other popular evangelical churches' teachings—became increasingly at odds with Canadian norms. As much as we may think the faith should transcend such norms, historically this is not the case. The churches that advance conservative taboos around sex, drugs, movies, and morality eventually force their young to choose which ethic speaks to them. Given the multi-faceted nature of Canadian Protestantism, even revivalist culture isn't as strong as some think. When push comes to shove, an inclusive and humble national culture like the one Canada promotes can prove much more appealing than a restrictive and judgmental Christian culture.

Therefore, my earlier assertion about the importance of organization remains as true in this case as in any other. The Vineyard's rejection of the Blessing experience was problematic in the mid-90s but did little to minimize the denomination's impact over Canada in subsequent years. The Vineyard remains a vital expression of the faith and its adherents are active Canadian Christians, especially in the province of Alberta. While lacking the explosiveness of the Blessing, the Vineyard impacted numerous people over a longer span of time and I can't help wondering which version has proven more formative. I don't want to minimize the Toronto Blessing's accomplishments, but the attentive reader must also pay attention to the limits of its impact. Even this success story did little in the way of evangelizing unchurched Canadians or returning Canadian Christianity to pre-1960s significance. Revival is exciting and provides new energy around matters of faith. While less dramatic, the legacy of Canadian Christianity belongs more to the quieter, daily witness of small churches operating well removed from the spotlight.

The Toronto Blessing was successful by every conceivable measure. Was it numerically huge? Yes, it was massive. Did it bring international attention to Canadian religion? Yes. Was it long lasting? Yes, 12 years (a good biblical number). Did it excite people about Christianity? Yes, even the skeptical were intrigued and some of them even converted. Did it create disciples? Yes, absolutely. The Blessing created people who were very excited about their faith. Did it change the tide of secularization as we talk about it? No.

I thought I might argue that the Blessing is the exception that proves the rule about Canadian revivalism. But that's not quite accurate. In many ways, the uniqueness of the Toronto Blessing makes it the case study that, as it pertains to secularization and our focus on numbers, proves the rule.

THE 1990s

Despite the startling success of the Toronto-based movement, skepticism remained one of the chief descriptions of the 1990s. In 1996, UK writer Dave Tomlinson released *The Post Evangelical* and this work somewhat captured the growing feeling that change was in the wind. The church had become too predictable and no longer spoke into the lived experiences of most people, even those it claimed to represent (echoes of Berton). Tomlinson argued that the ongoing binary nature of evangelical theology (conservative/liberal, good/bad, heaven/hell) needed to be discarded to remain in conversation with the larger culture. Early 20th century language around denominationalism, ecclesiology, theological convictions, and views on scripture was increasingly viewed as irrelevant and problematic. It was the language of a bygone age that few could relate to and even fewer had any desire to see again.

By the 1980s a problematic new generation was maturing as the children of the Boomers (labelled Generation X by Canadian author Douglas Coupland) challenged the notion that truth was a commodity. Gen X was immediately suspicious of any one person or institution arguing that their way was *the* way. These were the children raised on the idea that Christianity's exclusivist teachings were not welcome in the inclusivity of modern Canada. Apparently, that message had been faithfully taught because Gen X rejected exclusive truth claims almost across the board.

It is hard to pinpoint the moment things changed in that decade but there was an anger in the films, music, fashion, books, and culture about the hypocrisy and corrupt corporate nature of those who had come before. It is no coincidence that the 90s saw another Woodstock and that the quasi-hippie fashion of grunge became all the rage (pun intended). Suddenly, thrift stores were cool as the young rebelled against materialism and followed the trend of buying ill-fitting, second-hand, lumber-jack clothes to symbolize their rejection of Mad Men materialism. Anything too polished, too plastic, too manufactured, too new, or too neat was suspect of mainstream corruption. If there was a moment that such feelings coalesced I would argue that the moment Nirvana's "Smells Like Teen Spirit" exploded onto the airwaves is that moment.

Teen Spirit was the name of a deodorant of the time, aimed at capturing the quintessential and desired teenage smell. Truly marketing at its most ridiculous and an idea that anti-rock star Kurt Cobain lambasted in his band's monstrous 1991 hit. Cobain was notoriously anti-establishment (a word I hope has new meaning for you) and he pretty much personified the rejection of all things corporate. Famously, he wore a self-made shirt on the cover of a 1992 Rolling Stone issue that stated: "Corporate magazines still suck." This nose-thumbing on the cover of the very magazine celebrating his music made him a hero to Gen Xers like myself. He gave words to all who felt that the morals of their predecessors were nothing but hypocritical rhetoric designed to sell stuff and make money.

Cobain's "Grunge Rock" sounded rough and organic and was a direct challenge to over-produced 1980s Glam Rock that had monetized and commercialized the spirit of rebellion— similar to the ways certain evangelical teachings spiritualized rebellion as well. It was not long until this mentality grabbed the hearts of young Canadian Christians across the land. A desire for authenticity began to question the production of slick services that were accused of being closer to Madison Avenue than Golgotha. I like to refer to this developing ecclesiology as "Cobain Christianity" that stated, in many more words, that corporate Christianity sucked. The rebellious nature of the 1960s' New Left and Jesus People had effected some change, but the more pleasant and popular seeker-sensitive movements of the 1980s and 1990s smacked of selling out.

If you remember one thing about the 1990s, remember that Gen-X skepticism was powerful enough to kill Superman (co-created by Canadian Joe Shuster in the 1930s). While the comic character Doomsday is credited with the actual deed, the deeper truth is that my generation had no use for the indestructible Kryptonian. He was too powerful to relate to our weakness; he was too good to offer advice about our increasingly grey ethical world; he drew power from the sun so he couldn't speak to our darker Nietzsche-esque worldview.[27] Superman was the cheesy, literally unstoppable perfect hero of previous ages that held no value for Gen X. The only thing left to do was to kill him. That is how my generation's skepticism became personified in the character of Doomsday—a name with resonance in both the secular and sacred realms if ever there was one.

Room had to be made for a superhero with more 1990s' values and it is no coincidence that Superman died while Batman (aka the Dark Knight) enjoyed a renaissance. Christian leaders of that time largely failed to wrestle with the ramifications killing Superman had for the church. If Superman was determined to be fatally irrelevant, how long would it be until the perfect-man Jesus succumbed to the same fate?

This was also the time when churches like the Crystal Cathedral, Saddleback, and Willow Creek were creating their international influence and Canadian Christians began

---

27 Nietzsche's creation of the superman and the comic *Superman* offer very strange parallels and contradictions that almost summarize the differences between Gen-X and their parents' generation all on their own; but there is not the space in this book to dig into that.

borrowing heavily from these successful American models. Despite earlier concerns about American influence over Canadian culture, Christian Evangelical culture believed much of what took place in America could be duplicated in Canada as well. Sam Reimer's *Evangelicals and the Continental Divide* did exceptional research showing Canadian Evangelicals had more in common with American Evangelicals than they did with fellow Canadian non-Evangelicals. While the Canadian/ U.S. border has always been porous, Reimer's work shows that 20th century technology united Christians through shared theological beliefs even more than the dominant nationalism of preceding generations. The point I want to make is that Gen-X disillusionment infected Canadian and American youth alike in both the secular and sacred realms.

However, Canada's march towards inclusivity in religion, immigration, and a variety of previously taboo social constructs like sexuality meant that more conservative views of the faith invited ridicule and rejection from unchurched Canadians. Michael Adams' Fire & Ice offers a foil to Reimer by tracking the growing disparity between Canadian and American values that began in the 1990s.[28] Adams' research argued that conservative 1990s Canadians still landed to the left of even the most progressive Americans.[29]

Such leanings inspired a conservative pushback in some areas. Social conservatives, political conservatives, and religious conservatives grew stronger in the 1990s, especially in the west. Conservative ideologies tend to be appealing in times of perceived instability and the proliferation of denominations like the PAOC, CMA, Alliance, and Vineyard in the west—as well as

---

28   Adams argues that such similarities are a one-way street that only Canadians focus on. He quips: "although it may sometimes seem that Canada and the U.S. are 'on the same page,' that's usually because we're reading over their shoulder." Michael Adams. *Fire & Ice: The United States, Canada and the Myth of Converging Values*, (Toronto: Penguin, 2009), 49.

29   As it pertains to patriarchy, Adams writes: "*all* American regions agree more strongly than *any* Canadian region that Father knows best." Adams, *Fire & Ice*, 87. Italics part of the original quote.

the Toronto Blessing's influence over Canada from the mid-90s and on—bolstered Christian conservatism. This is when Sam Reimer's Continental Divide captured the influence American evangelicalism had over numerous Canadian churches. While baptisms in the PAOC, for example, continued to drop in the 1990s, that decade also displayed the highest rates of attendance and activity in the denomination's Canadian history.

Many of these denominations failed to take seriously the post-1960s push towards a public faith that focused on commonalities. Such a culture had precious little room for the exclusiveness of evangelical claims. Those who took stands against moral issues found much smaller audiences than their American counterparts and claims that Jesus was the only way to heaven smacked of arrogance. In response to such trends, and a lack of known Canadian voices on this issue, conservative denominations continued to borrow from American evangelical resources. This made sense in light of the shared beliefs and ongoing Christian consumer culture of both America and Canada. However, it did overlook a key difference between Canada and the United States that somewhat lessened these products' impact north of the border.

Throughout the late 1980s and 90s statistical evidence shows the regionalism we have spent so much time exploring in this book was beginning to lessen. There were fewer differences than ever before between Atlantic Canada, historically possessing the strongest national attendance rates, and the much more prone-to-skip-church Victoria-based Christians. More importantly, despite some strong Christian centers like the Fraser Valley in B.C., or Three Hills Alta., or Carleton County N.B., the 1990s proved Canada doesn't actually have a Bible belt. There is literally no region in Canada churches can count on for adherents. Put another way: "In all regions, a major section of the population never attends a religious service."[30]

Again we return to the loser theology from chapter one

---

30 Clarke and Macdonald, *Leaving*, 117.

because American evangelicalism is powerful in ways the Canadian version never has been. While the Bible Belt gives American evangelicalism an established and stable power base from which to draw, Canada has no such entity. As the advent of television and telecommunications was unifying Canadians— and minimizing regionalisms—the culture of a polite public faith focused on bringing people together and overlooking theological differences was making inroads into even the most active evangelical sections of this nation.

For all their anger, young Cobain Christians saw ecumenism as a virtue; they embraced a more theologically generous and open spirit on issues like salvation. They dismissed theological differences as unnecessary and sought more mystical teachings promising unity where once there was only division. Even evangelical Cobains were showing sympathy for, if not complete solidarity with, the "spiritual not religious" refrain of their non-churched friends. While such a cooperative spirit had some real potential, and while some individual denominations were growing, the story of 1990s' Canadian Christianity is that churches weren't growing enough to offset the number of Canadians leaving.

The malaise that shaped the 1990s came from a desire for true connection in all experiences of life, including religious ones. In the words of David Fincher's classic 90s film *Fight Club*, "We're the middle children of history, man. No purpose or place. We have no Great War. No Great Depression. Our Great War's a spiritual war... our Great Depression is our lives." (Sadly, the 21st century has provided more than enough actual wars and financial depressions to make any person long for the complaints of the 90s). Christianity was only one of the casualties of the 1990s. Many of the institutions that helped form Canadian culture were viewed with suspicion. This was a generation that celebrated questions and trusted few of the answers. How could the Gospel of Jesus—a gospel increasingly preached as providing answers to life's toughest questions—speak to such people? The leaders didn't take the challenges seriously and instead demonized the spirit of the age.

Frustration at the previous decade's religion was moralized and dismissed and forced many Christians (like Randy) to create alternative Christian narratives and alternative Christian communities. These places didn't register in census materials and there was a pride in being off the religious radar.

Young Gen Xers spent times in coffee shops and art houses and trendy, largely urban, locations discussing Kerouac, Nietzsche, Cohen, and Chomsky. Many Gen-Xers strove to be philosophers and poets, artists and thinkers. We were accused of lacking, and actually eschewing, the work ethic of our parents. A closer examination from the Boomers would have revealed an important development they were overlooking.

There are many factors to consider but I want to return to an idea we have already explored. If I can offer you one simplistic, though accurate, image about the shifts within Canadian Christianity in the 90s it is this: Boomers found their ecclesiology in the suburbs, Gen X found theirs by returning to the cities. The urban renewal of the 1990s impacted where Gen X worked and played and built their communities—both religious and non. While we were accused of being too philosophically-minded to be any practical good, the slacker generation (what my generation was called until Coupland's moniker Generation X caught on) turned out to be truly revolutionary. Unlike the Boomers, our revolution wasn't commercial or even social necessarily, it was technological. From the perspective of leaders in the church, it looked like Gen X would never commit to, or amount to, anything. How could such people impact the world? I'll tell you how: the slackers of the 1990s created the internet (insert sarcastic bow here); you're welcome.

So, if the suburbs shaped Boomer ecclesiology, and Gen X faith was inspired by cities, thanks to the web, the next generations will shape their views on Christ in a virtual world connected to, and distinct from, the material world. A dichotomous world that needs to blend together seemingly contrary experiences into something that is a little of both and something that is neither. Where have we read that before?

WHAT CANADIANS ACTUALLY BELIEVE

Despite some growing paranoia in certain sections of the population, there is still not a large collection of Muslims, Hindus, Sikhs, or other religions in Canada. The most dramatic and sustainable growth is in those Canadians who ascribe to No Religion. Despite this, most people in this land, when asked about a deity, will describe God using a somewhat stereotypical Christian(ish) picture. Most Canadians know about Jesus, even if they have no idea how Jesus is both God's son and God at the same time. Granted they will be theologically and biblically illiterate, but in the 1990s there was still some connection to Christian teaching. It is impossible to get away from the Christian God in this part of the world even today. For this reason, I don't think secularism is the issue many Christians think it is.

God is all over 21st century Canadian holidays, ethics, schools, hospitals, and our national anthem. A few years ago controversy erupted over changing some of the lyrics in the national anthem. Many Canadians were incensed and cried foul against those who deemed the language to be exclusionary or outdated. What struck me most was the outdated term in question wasn't the use of God in our anthem—no one said a word about that. It was out of concern that the lyric "True patriot love in all our sons command" excluded women. Whatever your thoughts are on that, don't miss the bigger point: when our so-called secular land engaged in a debate about changing our national anthem it had to do with gender; no one cared about the religious element.

Time is also still measured in largely Christian terms from Christmas to Easter, to the popular Saints days (Valentine's and Patrick's) so that even the true god of this age, consumerism, must bow a knee and confess that the Christian calendar is still lord. For the time being anyway.

From the vantage point of Canadians of other religions, it is debatable to say that Canada is a post-Christian land. This is not to say that things didn't change in the 1970s, far from it. What most Canadian churches fail to understand about our own land is that Canadians did not really stop believing in God, they stopped trusting the church. All our conversations and resources and attempts to reframe church seem to be addressing the wrong questions. Our attempts to fix this issue fail to address the most important reality of the contemporary religious landscape.

In Michael Adams' other famous book, *Sex in the Snow*, he brilliantly diagnosed the heart of post-Christendom Canada in a couple of sentences, and then moved on. For me, I read and re-read that sentence dozens of times because it remains the most important fact largely overlooked and misunderstood even today.

Adams argues that the challenge against religious authority can be seen as a rejection of the church's monopoly over eternal destiny. As the parents in Randy's neighbourhood can attest, there remains an appeal to the morality and ethics of the church, when they are taught with a light hand and stay out of the bedroom. They liked Randy's church because it promoted good values without being overly preachy. These parents placed almost no value on the Christian idea of salvation because his church was providing a service for this world, not the next one.

For Adams, Canadian secularization is a rejection of the shame and guilt-based threat of hell as an interpretive and manipulative tool. Without hell, people become free to explore their faith and their life without the specter of eternal torment keeping them in line (the exact opposite of Henry Alline's early faith journey). Church morality thus becomes important only for people who go to church, it is easily ignored by those who don't. This stands up historically as well when we think of Quebec Catholics rejecting the 1968 encyclical opposing contraception or the inability of Protestants to mount any kind of national opposition to same-sex marriage. That is an important distinction to remember. Canadians seem to have a fairly high view of most other Canadians. Few of us seem willing to get up early on a Sunday morning to hear that our non-church neighbours, people we genuinely like, are damned.

For any Christian who wants to serve this so-called secular, post-Christian Canada, there is one reality you must contend with and one thing you must know. The reality of contemporary Canadian spirituality originates from one point that many people have overlooked or misunderstood: from the 1970s to the 1990s Canadians did not stop believing in God, they stopped believing in the devil.[31]

31   "[P]erhaps it is the Devil who is dead…Fear and guilt were often the greatest factors sustaining church-attendance numbers, and motivating Canadians to behave according to the dictates of religious structures… the slaying of lesser gods—including any once-unquestioned authorities—became much less intimidating, if not inevitable." Michael Adams. *Sex in the Snow: The Surprising Revolution in Canadian Social Values*. Tenth Anniversary Edition, (Toronto: Penguin, 2006), 25.

RESOURCES

Bruce Douville. *The Uncomfortable Pew: Christianity and the New Left in Toronto*. Montreal & Kingston: McGill-Queen's University, 2020.

- This book treats the youth movements of the 1960s and 1970s and shows through solid research how they impacted subsequent generations of Christian leaders and how they changed the face of Canadian Christianity.

Heaven Bent Podcast: Season 1.
Found at https://frequencypodcastnetwork.com/shows/heaven-bent

- A wonderful and powerful exploration of the Toronto Blessing from a balanced, though respectful, journalist with a personal connection to the phenomenon. This series provides commentary as well as solid historiography of the movement and its impact.

Lee Beach and Gordon L. Heath. *Centre for Post-Christendom Studies*. Available at the following website: pcs.mcmasterdivinity.ca

- This think-tank out of McMaster Divinity College in Hamilton, Ontario addresses the shift of culture as it has moved away from the influence of the church. This site has numerous videos, academic articles, interviews, and resources for church leaders and thinkers who want to wrestle with this reality. Several of their videos can be found on YouTube and it provides a multiplicity of perspectives in an engaging fashion.

Michael Adams. *Fire & Ice: The United States, Canada and the Myth of Converging Values*. Toronto: Penguin Books, 2009.

- This book corrects the notion that Canada and America have similar social values. This chapter has dealt with the influence of American thinking over Canadian Christianity without taking into consideration the differences between the two nations. This book offers a detailed and statistical analysis of the nuances in such beliefs.

Brian Clarke and Stuart Macdonald. *Leaving Christianity: Changing Allegiances in Canada Since 1945.* Montreal and Kingston: McGill-Queen's University Press, 2017.

- Easily one of the most important books any Christian interested in the story of secularization since the end of WWII should read. They offer concise statistical information and well-reasoned explanations from a very academic, and sympathetic, perspective. I have used this book frequently to help understand the shifting Canadian landscape.

---

1 IDEA

Canada's views on female ordination, among many other social issues, kept it left of American social issues. While this worked numerically for numerous smaller evangelical churches, the more socialist impulse in Canada meant that such churches had little impact on the nation overall.

CHAPTER 7
RECONCILIATION

I am the stranger
Do you know what I mean?
That is not my dad
My dad is not a wild man
Doesn't even drink
My daddy's not a wild man
On a secret path
— "The Stranger,"
(Gord Downie's Secret Path)

"I probably sound testy, and I suppose part of me is.
But I shouldn't be. After all, Dead Indians
are the only antiquity that North America has."
— Thomas King
The Inconvenient Indian

"Societies are known by their victims."
— Richard Drinnon

In the beginning there was a great void. Gitchie Manito (the Creator) spoke and sent His thoughts out to travel through the void. They found nothing so He called his thoughts back. The return of those thoughts to the Creator made the stars in the sky.

Next, Gitchie Manito created Geesis (the sun) and placed Mother Earth close enough so that Geesis and Neebageesis (the moon) could take turns walking around and watching over Earth.

When Ah-ki (the earth) was young she was filled with beauty. Gitchie Manito filled her with singing birds that spread seeds of her trees in all four directions. Gitchie Manito gave life to all creatures on the land and in the sea and placed the four-legged creatures upon Mother Earth. Each lived in harmony with the others.

From each of the four directions, Gitchie Manito gathered an element and breathed over it. From the combination of these four elements and the breath of the Creator, man came to be. The original man was called Aninishinaabe

Ani-"from whence"

Nishina-"lowered"

Abe-"the male of the species."

All tribes come from this original man and it was this man's job to walk the earth and name the owayseug (animals), the nibi (water), and the valleys in the Creator's gitigan (garden). Original man came to learn that Mother Earth had four seasons and each one brought new revelations about the rhythm of the world. Some plants were good to eat and others were good for mushkeeki (medicine). Original man became lonely; he noticed that all the animals were in pairs while he alone.

He asked Gitchie Manito for a partner and was given Maengun (the wolf) in response. The two explored the earth and became friends. When they were done, Gitchie Manito told them to go their separate ways and warned them "each of you will be feared, respected and misunderstood by the people that will later join you in this Earth."

This turned out to be true as both the Aninishinaabe and the wolf would be hunted for their weenessisee (hair), and both would have to flee from their lands. The descendants of Aninishinaabe looked to the wolf because the destinies of the two were linked. From the wolf came humanity's greatest companion: ahnimooshug (the dog). It was dogs who first taught humans that tying six dogs together at the front of a sled would help the humans go farther and faster. The combination of six dogs and one human meant that the number seven would have deep spiritual meaning for the people.

Aninishinaabe journeyed more and met more celestial guides before meeting up with the Firekeeper's daughter. Her beauty was like that of the setting sun and Aninishinaabe fell deeply in love. From their union came four sons, each of whom likewise journeyed throughout the world. Each one found his own partner and fathered children; these brought the tribes of the world into being. Each of the sons traveled to a different realm of the four directions and found that each part had its own unique qualities. The tribes they created were separated by language and culture but each was called to remember that, despite their differences, they were all family.

Sadly, this union and harmony was not to last. Men and women no longer accepted the marital unions, families began to fight each other, villages began to fight each other, and brother began to kill brother. Gitchie Manito was greatly saddened by this but kept waiting "hoping that the evil ways would cease and that brotherhood, sisterhood, and respect for all things would again come to rule over the people." As people grew even worse, Gitchie Manito decided to purify the earth with a mushkobewun (flood) of water.

Soon the world was clean but how was it to begin again? One man, Waynaboozhoo, had managed to stay alive by resting on a giant piece of wood. Onto that wood, the animals gathered and the birds would rest. Once the animals gathered their strength they would hop back into the water and let another animal rest for a while. After many days, Waynaboozhoo told the animals that he would swim to the bottom of the great waters and grab some earth from which they could rebuild.

He dove down and was gone for so long that many animals believed he had drowned. Finally, he emerged and told them he was unable to reach the bottom. Other animals like the Loon, the otter, the mink, and even the turtle all took their turns but to no avail. Then the tiny Wazhushk (muskrat) offered to go. Because he was so small the other animals laughed at his offer. Waynaboozhoo chastised the animals saying, "It is not our place to judge, only the Creator can do that! If our friend wants to try, we must let him."

Again, much time passed and everyone was convinced that muskrat had drowned. What they didn't know is that muskrat had made it to the bottom. He used his last bit of strength to grab some earth and then push off towards the surface. On his way back to the surface, he died. His lifeless body floated up near Waynaboozhoo and the other animals. Great songs of lament were sung for the bravery of the small creature and it was then that they noticed his hand. Within that tiny paw lay a small clump of Mother Earth. Waynaboozhoo exclaimed that Earth could now be rebuilt!

The turtle, inspired by the courage of muskrat, volunteered to bear the weight of the new creation on his shell. Those on and around the log placed the dirt on turtle's shell and implored Gitchie Manito to create Earth once more. The noodinoon (four winds) began to blow and the dirt on turtle's back grew until it formed a minisi (island). The animals and Waynaboozhoo pulled themselves onto the land and continued to sing as the land continued to grow; and turtle miraculously never buckled under the weight.

The new land was named after the turtle and became the home of all of those who survived the great flood. The muskrat's self-sacrifice is remembered by his descendants, each of whom build their homes in the shape of the small ball of earth. They teach anyone willing to see about the Earth's cleansing and the sacrifice of one small creature that saved us all. New tales were created by the peoples of Turtle Island until, one day, others from the direction of the eastern wind arrived in giant logs of wood.

These foreign people of the eastern wind ignored the ancient names of the land of Aninishinaabe, Waynaboozhoo, the noble muskrat, the proud wolf, and Gitchie Manito. They cared little for turtles, they had stories about their own gods that didn't see muskrats as noble. These strangers began calling everything ... America.

This is just one of countless creation stories, one of the innumerable stories passed down through generations - stories of the Great Creator who spoke the world into existence, stories about an Original man from whom all people could trace their roots, stories of a sacred garden and the naming of the beasts, stories that signified the number seven as sacred to the creation account, ancient stories of fratricide and a humanity so evil that only a great flood could cleanse the earth, stories of one humble creature's sacrifice in order to begin a new creation.

And it was these very stories, despite their numerous and obvious connections to the Bible, that were deemed too pagan by 19th and 20th century Christians. These stories were no longer allowed to remain within Canadian Christendom.

The words of this Ojibway creation story don't represent a large collection of Indigenous stories, but it is an important one. It was loaned to me by a former student who thought it would help me understand better the beliefs of her and her husband.[1]

This one Ojibway creation story is also a matter of debate. Some scholars challenge how authentic or ancient stories like this one are based on the clear parallels between it and biblical concepts. Some might believe this is a white-washed creation account clearly influenced by Christianity, a story that has little to do with an authentic Indigenous worldview. It is entirely possible—likely even—but those very tensions are what make this creation account so important.

We will return to this story again at the end of this chapter because this story, and what it represents, might be in jeopardy of disappearing again if we're not very careful.

---

1   The creation account is a redacted re-telling of material found in Edward Benton-Banai's *The Mishomis Book: The Voice of the Ojibway*, (Hayward: Indian Country Communications, 1988), chapters 1-5.

RECONCILIATION

David MacDonald sat in a Halifax church reflecting upon Isaiah 58:12. He would later write that a biblical understanding of reconciliation necessitates "recognizing and responding to the hurt and the need. Years of alienation and oppression resulting from Indian residential schools requires a concrete response. Without that, reconciliation is nothing more than hollow words without meaning. The challenge of reconciliation is both to know and do the truth. These are not separate functions, but part of the same reality."[2] Building on that idea, he reminded believers of this century that we are "being granted an enormous opportunity...to learn the whole truth of Indian residential schools and to share that truth with one another... to live out the various apologies we have made...to walk with Aboriginal women, men, and children who share this land with us."[3]

This chapter is about how churches, in the name of Christ, became the devil to this land's first inhabitants. Reconciliation is a concept that sounds good on paper but is much harder to enact in the real world. I cannot tell the story of Canadian Christianity without including the churches' treatment of the First Nations.

Theologically, reconciliation is the teaching that sinful creatures are reconciled to their Creator through Jesus' sacrifice on the cross. This is at the heart of all Christian belief, even if we disagree with the ensuing teachings of various churches. However, reconciliation between humans is a beast of a different stripe. Gentle reader, the effects of violent colonization and residential schools on the Indigenous, and Christian churches' role in such tragedies, is a true darkness within the soul of Canadian Christianity.

The contents of this chapter are the most sensitive and important treated in this book. It is easy, compelling even, to

---

2   David MacDonald. "A Call to the Churches: 'You Shall Be Called the Repairer of the Breach,.'" In *From Truth to Reconciliation: Transforming the Legacy of Residential Schools*. Prepared by Marlene Brant Castellano, Linda Archibald, Mike DeGange, 341-360 (Ottawa: Aboriginal Healing Foundation, 2008.), 342.

3   MacDonald, "Breach," 343.

picture the architects of the residential school system as a group of wealthy white men sitting around a well-furnished room, tenting their fingers evilly and plotting gleefully the destruction of the First Nations. What might offend our present-day sensibilities is the notion that no such event actually occurred.

Though such a stance could invite criticism of this work, we learn more by examining those people involved with the residential school system who believed they were helping. Those who thought changing Indigenous culture to that of the rest of Canada was the right thing to do. They didn't consider that forcing Indigenous people to conform to Canadian society and Christianity would result in intergenerational trauma and the destruction of Indigenous communities and culture. We will also address those who had clearly diabolical motivations, but we are better served by exploring the trajectory of this time that is often overlooked. The trajectory shows a definitive shift from benevolent cooperation between churches, government officials, and Indigenous people to malevolent coercion.

In order to examine this shift, let's rename the points of the Atlantic Triangle we looked at in chapter one. Let's change that triangle from an external symbol of international relations to an internal description of power dynamics at play within Canada. Rather than it being composed of America, Britain, and Canada, let's replace America and Britain as the dominant points with the terms "government" and "the church." In the place of Canada on the Triangle, let's put the term "Indigenous communities" in relation with the culture of the other two (placing these diverse communities under one identifying banner is an issue we will explore in this chapter). The difference is that, in chapter one, we saw a more benign blending of American and British ideas that helped develop Canadian culture. Now, we acknowledge that the church and the government forced culture upon many First Nations, Metis, and Inuit. The story of Canada would be a much different one if America and Britain had acted towards Canada the way Canadians acted towards these Indigenous communities.

That's the point of this chapter: the history of Canadian Christianity is much different when an Indigenous perspective is included in the story.

Map from Wikipedia. Triangle drawn by author.

We have already witnessed how 19th and 20th century views celebrated the ethnic superiority of Anglo-Saxons. This was not in contrast solely with First Nations, but also included views towards Chinese, Japanese, Indian, African, Italians, and Irish Catholics. While we have rightly condemned such teachings as racist, bigoted, and lacking any merit, they can still teach us and keep us from falling into similar traps. To think that our current views about, and treatment of, the First Nations, Metis, and Inuit is somehow removed from the historic views of the past is naïve and dangerous.

There were many church and government officials who espoused and printed ideologies of racism designed to destroy entire people groups. The residential schools were created by those who saw nothing of value in Indigenous culture. Canadians of the present age are right to condemn such beliefs and teachings as racist.

However, the greater danger in labelling these people without understanding their world is that we effectively distance them from current racist attitudes. We effectively silence these long-dead Canadians' abilities to teach us because we see ourselves as more enlightened and therefore incapable of condoning such deplorable ideologies. The architects of residential schools become remnants of a bygone age, muted villains we can denigrate in order to signal our own superior views, caricatures and strawmen no longer able to shine a light on our own similar attitudes. Such beliefs are ignorant and arrogant and have profound ramifications for today.

I have stepped away from this chapter more than any other. I have stopped working on it for weeks at a time. I have done so because the contents of this chapter are very disturbing. This topic scares me and I want to handle it as well as I possibly can. I will fail in such goals. My own blind spots will be revealed in this chapter and I will possibly cause harm. I do hope this chapter can inspire conversations and hopefully do some good. My great fear is that it won't and that fear, along with a desire to do as much research as I can, has pulled me away from this chapter more than any other.

Then, as I researched Indigenous voices on this issue, I became personally confronted that my ability to walk away *is* a blind spot. I only have to deal with this when I want to deal with it. Despite my belief that this is an important topic, I must admit that it can be an "out-of-sight, out-of-mind" experience for me. Indigenous in this nation have no such luxury.

As an outsider to the Indigenous experience of Christianity, I have nothing to offer in the way of suggestions for moving forward. However, from a historical perspective (the only perspective I can offer) I have grave concerns because present-day attitudes around First Nations—some that I see within myself as well—are not as far removed from the past as we may like to think.

In order to explore such thinking more, this chapter is going to look at the following:
1. The White Man's Burden
2. Language around First Nations
3. Residential schools were not boarding schools

4. Christian Residential Schools

5. Dismantling, apologies & aftermath

6. Ongoing arrogance

7. A truer reconciliation

THE WHITE MAN'S BURDEN

This term comes from Rudyard Kipling's 1899 poem to America, encouraging citizens to take up the imperial mantle in the Philippines as Britain had done around the world. In it Kipling wrote the following: "Take up the White Man's burden—And reap his old reward: The blame of those ye better. The hate of those ye guard." This poem asserted that the white man's role was to bring stability and civility to the less civilized cultures of the world.

The poem acknowledges that such actions frequently yielded the displeasure of the Indigenous recipients of imperial attention. The idea of bettering others is the frequent claim of all empires and any resistance is chalked up to the ignorance of the conquered, rather than the arrogance of the conquerors. The white man's role on earth was a burden because his benevolence and Christian duty was rarely celebrated by those he came to save.

Disagree with this all you want, gentle reader, but please understand that such thinking was a *de facto* setting for most people, and many ethnicities, during that time. When Theodore Roosevelt first read Kipling's work, his only criticism was the poor writing; the sentiments within the poem were celebrated as sensible.

While we might desire to challenge this flawed thinking, we do so because history has shown us where such thinking leads. I believe we gain greater insight into genuine reconciliation by first looking at the intentions of these people before wrestling with their impact. We can do so by revisiting themes we have already explored in this book:

1. Canada was called to maintain a Christian character focused on missions and evangelization.

2. Christianity and civilization go hand in hand. And the ultimate expressions of both are found in the British Empire.

3. Education—both secular and religious—was the key to advancement.

Such themes formed the backdrop and motivation for not only the residential schools, but most interactions with First Nations. While most today would view the second point as problematic (to say the least) I would argue many Christians still value points one and three. Historically, Canadian Christians believed evangelism needed to include converting and educating Indigenous people if the nation desired to claim a Christian character. This point was even advocated by our first prime minister, John A. Macdonald, when he created the residential school system and defended the church's role within the system.

While we are tempted to think of Christianity as a religion forced upon the various Indigenous groups, the truth is, before 1870 substantial numbers accepted the faith with surprising rapidity and vigour. From the beginning "native preachers played a prominent role"[4] in Christianity's warm reception as they guided their brothers and sisters through Christian thinking and behaviour. Most Indigenous were aware of the numerous forms of Christianity and weighed out their options carefully.

Once again, we must return to the theme of power that began this book. While many believe the superior fire power of these European Christians forced the Indigenous people into religious submission, history shows us that is not the case. In Canada, each brand of Christianity promised similar European advantages, so the Indigenous people examined which group best addressed their respective needs. Despite present-day myths about this time period, history shows us that Indigenous groups were not helpless victims of Christianity, but intelligent and active participants in their adoption, or rejection, of the faith.

---

4 John Webster Grant, *Moon of Wintertime: Missionaries and the Indians of Canada in Encounter since 1534*, (Toronto: University of Toronto, 1984), 76.

The Methodists' focus on the mystical and emotive elements of the faith granted them great success, notably among the Mississaugas and Ojibwas. These missionaries were strict in their calls that Indigenous people needed to leave behind their old ways and follow the new path of Jesus Christ. While this is usually taken to mean they needed to adopt European sensibilities, the actual message was more nuanced. The Methodists taught that everyone, regardless of race, needed to make such changes. Conversion was the heart of Methodist teaching and the Indigenous people were treated as "sinners rather than as inferiors."[5] From this perspective, there was no difference between Indigenous and white people; both needed the saving grace of God.

Such beliefs meant that Indigenous people could alter their worldview with dignity because they were no different than the white people called to do the same. They were given positions of leadership within the churches based on piety and merit, and moral failings were seen as part of the universal human condition, not a condemnation of their heritage. Methodist missionaries were also resourceful farmers (as we saw in earlier chapters) and their ability to teach Indigenous people new farming techniques endeared them to some Indigenous groups.

Anglicans stressed the importance of belonging to the religion of the realm and brought with them the substantial blessings of Imperial connection. From the Indigenous perspective, Anglicanism was closely tied to the various agents charged with ministering to the Indigenous groups. Anglicans argued that connection to their church had the potential to bring greater financial and social benefits than the Methodists could offer. I'm not saying that is what happened; I am saying that is what they said because that is what Anglicans tended to say in order to undermine Methodist influence.

Less emotional than the Methodists, Anglicanism offered a calmer version of the faith that seemed to align the Indigenous

---

5 Grant, *Moon*, 90.

people with more conservative whites. You will remember that 19th century Anglicanism dominated the political world and many Indigenous people saw the benefit of aligning with a church better positioned to effect real change. This church was the path to the center of British civilization whereas the Methodists could only offer a small corner. The British respect for hierarchy also granted prestige and influence to Indigenous leaders who, in turn, led their people into the Anglican fold.

However, familiar Anglican issues presented themselves to numerous First Nations' Christians as well. In April of 1842, some leaders of the Tuscaroras wrote to Governor General Charles Bagot explaining when they "left the Church of England and united ourselves to the Baptist Church" they had been "deposed from their offices." This didn't seem correct to them and they voiced concerns strikingly similar to the Reformers of 1828. Threats had been uttered against their leaders if they continued to support any Protestant Church other than the Anglicans. The leaders asked "whether we shall be deprived of our privileges as Indians because we have thought proper to act 'according to the dictates of our consciences' in merely changing the form of our Religious Worship." This again shows a critical understanding of worship, a preference for certain styles of Christianity over others, and concern over how worship was legislated. They didn't see themselves as passive recipients of Christian teaching. These "Chiefs and Warriours [sic] of the Tuscarora Nation"[6] were critical thinkers on matters of faith and policy who took their preferred style of worship seriously.

Catholics were the first Christian voice many Indigenous people heard. Like the Methodists, Catholics had space for the mysterious and mystical and, because of their own second-class status, seemed more sympathetic to Indigenous concerns. The Jesuits in particular had a proven track record of service and were well-versed in numerous Indigenous languages and cultures.

---

6   Charles M. Johnston (ed), *The Valley of the Six Nations: A Collection of Documents on the Indian Lands of the Grand River*, (Toronto: University of Toronto, 1964), 264.

Unlike the Methodists—or Anglicans for that matter—the Catholics were not vested in supporting certain cultural norms. They were (largely) French adherents of Rome and put much less pressure on Indigenous people to view their faith through a British lens. In this, the Catholic version of the faith left more room for Indigenous expressions. Their clear teachings about what was secular and what was sacred helped the people carve out a faith that was both Christian and Indigenous. Their own ecclesiastical rivalries with the Protestants helped Indigenous people with Catholic faith differentiate themselves from those Indigenous people who were Protestant; this also helped create a valued and distinct identity for certain Indigenous Christians.

In these varieties I hope you can see that the white man's burden was not applied uniformly or even necessarily with much coercion in these early interactions on Turtle Island. The growth of Christianity was thanks to Indigenous initiatives as well as missionary endeavours. Sadly, such mutually beneficial relationships between church missionaries and Indigenous people were not destined to last. The collapse of this cooperative spirit happened for the most benevolent of reasons: education.

LANGUAGE

"The Jesuit Mission: A Chronicle of the Cross in the Wilderness," written in 1916 by Thomas Guthrie Marquis, provides just one example of early 20th century attitudes and language around First Nations:

> *To such dens of barbarism had come fresh from the civilization of the Old World—men of learning, culture, and gentle birth, in whose veins flowed the proudest blood of France. To these savages, indolent, superstitious, and vicious, had come [Jesuit priests] with a message of peace, goodwill, and virtue.*[7]

Sentiments like the ones expressed by Marquis are greeted

---

7   This quote is found in Stephen McGregor, *Since Time Immemorial: "Our Story" The Story of Kitigan Zibi Anishinabeg*, (Maniwaki QC: Kitigan Zibi Education Council, 2004, 74.

with contempt in our age. Rightly so, but if we focus only on the words we can miss the deeper and more instructive picture. Marquis was penning a religious hero's tale. Think back to our earlier chapter on Neville Trueman and remember how important these frontier adventure tales were for religious groups and their legitimacy. They used this caricature of the Indigenous people as a rhetorical tool to further highlight the successes of the missionary endeavours. Like all hero tales, it required seemingly insurmountable obstacles for the heroes to overcome. In the case of "The Jesuit Missions" the obstacles were the threatening character of the soon-to-be-converted Indigenous people as well as the harsh wilderness. In Marquis, we see how the First Nations were viewed in contrast to the historical reality.

In chapter four we learned how language creates worlds of understanding and one of the first steps towards reconciliation is proper terminology. Understanding that even the word "chief" so synonymous with Indigenous culture in this part of the world, is actually a European word underlines how quickly foreign terms and ideas were superimposed onto Indigenous people.[8] Using terms like "First Nations" and "Indigenous" instead of the term "Indian" is also important. So is the term "Settler" to indicate those of us whose ancestry traces back to other parts of the world.

The term Settler doesn't mean "guest" because few seriously entertain the idea that non-Indigenous ethnicities are going to return to their ancestral homelands. It does acknowledge that many of our ancestors settled on land already inhabited by others. Such distinctions can help Settler Canadians realize that for many people in this land, Canada is "a nation that violently displaces others for its own wants and desires, a state that

---

8 "Please note that 'chief' is a European term. Traditional leaders can go by many titles, including headmen/women, clan leaders, and heads of villages or groups of people." Bob Joseph and Cynthia F. Joseph, *Indigenous Relations: Insights, Tips & Suggestions to Make Reconciliation a Reality*, (Indigenous Relations Press, 2019), 21.

breaks treaties and uses police and starvation to clear the land."[9]

During the same time "loyalty" was being used to remove Methodists from the realms of higher education, another word was being employed to force education upon the First Nations. By the middle of the 19th century, Indigenous people were increasingly excluded as "active partners in their own evangelization."[10] In order for the residential schools to become a reality, men of influence needed to assign a group identity to the Indigenous people so that their "white man's burden" could be enacted most effectively. That meant systematizing and legitimizing what we would rightly call racism into universally accepted doctrine. In the words of Thomas King: "[O]ut of ignorance, disregard, frustration, and expediency, North America set about creating a single entity, an entity that would stand for the whole."[11]

The expansive and varied First Nations and communities were simplified and "communitized" in ways that served the rulers of the age—both secular and religious. The differences between each cultural community were minimized and dismissed to such a point that many whites believed all Indigenous people were the same. Despite their different languages and cultures spread out over this vast land, First Nations people were corralled, both ethnically and literally, on reserves within their own lands. Each of these multiple cultures and unique expressions was placed under a singular designation: Indian.

Thus communitized under a single word, the next step was apparently to moralize the designation. Frequently attached to the front of the term "Indian" were even more harmful terms like "Savage, Pagan, Ignorant, Violent, and Vice-ridden." These secondary terms were so frequently attached that they moved from adjective to synonym in a very brief amount of time.

9   Emma Battell Lowman and Adam J. Barker, *Settler: Identity and Colonialism in 21st Century Canada,* (Halifax: Fernwood Publishing, 2015), 1.

10   Grant, *Moon*, 95.

11   Thomas King, *The Inconvenient Indian: A Curious Account of Native People in North America*, (Toronto: Anchor Canada, 2013), 82.

Such terms became accepted premises that empowered and equipped a national atrocity. Despite the fact Christianity was an established religion within numerous Indigenous communities by that point, the churches of the later 19th century—Catholic and Protestant—became the eager tip of this new ideological spear.

Bob and Cynthia Joseph's *Indigenous Relations: Insights, Tips & Suggestions to make Reconciliation a Reality* challenge their readers to remember "language has the power to respect and honour or hurt and offend."[12] For those who desire reconciliation, we must take the words we use seriously. A substantial portion of the Josephs' book is dedicated to awareness around, and correction of, numerous phrases because ignorance of the "historical context of certain phrases" can prevent moving forward in reconciliation.[13] The shift in power dynamics of the mid 19th century couldn't have happened without a shift in vocabulary and definitions.

The word "Savage" harmed First Nations people arguably the most because it allowed Canadian leaders to ignore Indigenous concerns they deemed contrary to their own goals. Any complaint voiced from an Indigenous mouth was summarily dismissed as the kind of "blame" Kipling said all uncivilized people demonstrate. Hear the nuance in what I am saying: the words didn't just excuse such actions; the actions were supported by particular definitions of words believed to be true.

Returning to David MacDonald's call for people to learn the "full truth" means a better understanding of the worldviews of that time. We must recognize the multifaceted nature of Christianity's involvement with First Nations before we can move forward. We can't just find new words; reconciliation necessitates finding better understandings and a shared vocabulary. Changing terms and definitions was one of the most effective ways the 19th century whites were able to construct

---

12 Joseph and Joseph, *Relations*, 161.

13 For more on this, see Joseph and Joseph, *Relations*, with special attention paid to 161-176.

a residential school world in Canada. One way to avoid doing something similar is to recognize that our beliefs are a product of our culture and contain within them blind spots, just like the beliefs of the people we are studying.

For example, let's look at missionaries. Missionaries find people, tell them about Jesus, and set about converting them from their previous (sinful) worldview into a new (saved) worldview. That is what conversion is and, Indigenous or not, conversion necessitates replacing one worldview with another. Conversion remains a large part of the Canadian Christian world today and most churches measure their worth based on their ability to convert the so-called lost. Lack of conversions also forms the backdrop for most Canadian Christians' concern over secularization. As it pertains to this chapter, the missionaries were (and are) calling Indigenous peoples to leave their understandings of the world and replace such understandings with a Christian one.

Such endeavours are lambasted as tools of colonialism in our present age and there is substantial evidence to support such a stance. However, if we take just a moment more to look deeper into their world, we might see the lingering darkness in our own a little better.

Were these missionaries able to jump forward in time and see our beliefs that Indigenous culture needs to be respected and returned to a pre-Christian way of being, they would be horrified. Not because they are evil or racist or because they hate Indigenous people. Many of those missionaries would see such ideas as hard-hearted and lacking compassion. I'm not talking about the malevolent clerical and administrative abusers who later signed up for residential schools out of clearly insidious and predatory motives, but those who genuinely were doing what they believed was right.

They struggled to find connections and many risked their lives. They did so out of the belief that it was their calling to bring these people out of pagan superstition into true faith. They offered material and spiritual incentives and worked hard to understand the people. While supremacy was definitely a part of their worldview, they also believed that Indigenous lives could be vastly improved—in all areas—by Jesus.

Present-day attitudes that Indigenous culture should return to pre-Christian states would be viewed, from a 19th century vantage, as damming all those people to hell. I'm not condoning such beliefs, but I am saying they would condemn our choices as evil in much the same way we do theirs. That should, at the very least, give us pause to reflect.

RESIDENTIAL SCHOOLS WERE NOT BOARDING SCHOOLS

As we have already seen, education was a frequent and contentious issue, reflective of its importance within the minds of leaders and citizens alike. Therefore, educating young Indigenous boys and girls took primary place as Indigenous peoples became wards of the state (more on that in a moment). While some have argued that residential schools were a version of British boarding schools (given the Imperial background of leaders like Macdonald) there are some crucial differences between residential and boarding schools that negate such beliefs.

As early as the 1830s, the boarding school model was not seen as an opportunity for Indigenous parents, like their British counterparts, to send their children away for education, community, or advancements for future careers. Rather, residential schools were established to intentionally sever relationships between parents and their children.

Missionaries noted in great and frequent detail the importance of removing children from their parents' instruction in order to ultimately Christianize the Indigenous people. The Upper Canada Commissions from the 1830s-1850s advocated separation and clearly targeted children as the gates through which all Indigenous peoples could be civilized.

Their barbaric rituals, it was argued, would be transformed over a generation into activities more suited to western society. Their language would be traded for the King's English. Their pagan, demonic religions would succumb to the light of Christian teaching. The children would parent the adults into the ways of advanced society and its incumbent gifts of medicine, science, law, and religion. But first, the old ways had to be removed, and education was the best way to achieve such a goal. These were some of the arguments used to advance the mission of residential schools.

Egerton Ryerson, one of the most influential architects of Indigenous education, lived for many years in various Indigenous communities. His father recalled visiting his son one day and found him "about half a mile from the village, stripped to the shirt and pantaloons, clearing land with between twelve and twenty little Indian boys, who were all engaged in chopping and picking up brush." Ryerson was a known and respected educator for most of his career. Many of his innovations in Canadian education came from his time as a teacher among Indigenous peoples. Ryerson was no distant academic but an involved teacher who seemed to enjoy spending time with the people he was called to teach. His father would go on to report that Egerton "spent an hour or more every morning and evening in this way, for the benefit of his own health and the improvement of the Indian children."[14]

As we have already noted, Methodist farming abilities had endeared them to several communities. As the educational program developed, this notion increased in popularity as "the manual labour school...found increasing favour."[15] Ryerson drew inspiration from his Methodism and proposed teaching Indigenous children manual trades as well as reading, writing, and arithmetic. Much of Ryerson's writing on this topic detailed the numerous ways in which Euro/Canadian culture and technology would elevate the status and financial independence of Indigenous people. This model—developed first by Presbyterian missionary Gideon Black—was greeted with

---

14   J. George Hodgins. *Historical and Other Papers and Documents Illustrative of the Educational System of Ontario, 1853-1868.* (Toronto: L. K. Cameron, 1911), 99.
15   Grant, *Moon*, 86.

enthusiasm in Settler and even some Indigenous communities.[16]

While flowery words can sometimes conceal darker truths that are only discovered after a careful reading between the lines, this is not the case with Ryerson. Sadly, he was also repeatedly up front, vocal, and dismissive of Indigenous children's intelligence and aptitudes. Returning to the Upper Canada Commission, Ryerson clearly stated that he could find little redeemable within Indigenous culture. His recommendations were clear as he too advocated residential schools as a necessary tool to remove children from their parents' influence.

Despite such claims (or because of them), other reports felt the need to celebrate Indigenous children who were doing well in the white man's schools. Clergy and educators marveled and celebrated the ways in which Indigenous youth took to education. Although this strains our modern ears, Indigenous children were frequently viewed and celebrated as equal to Settler children in most regards. One 1870 report went so far as to record: "I inquired from their Teacher...whether, in receiving instruction, there was any appreciable difference between the children of the two races. He thought that, of the two, the Indians were the quickest."[17] These early, though statistically small, successes convinced leaders to adopt the residential model.

In the first decades of residential education, much like in the first missionary endeavours, there was a sense of cooperation and collegiality that had the potential to grow. Although such facts don't find support in many present-day narratives around the residential schools, we should note that some Indigenous parents intentionally requested English education for their children. Let me be very clear with what I am

---

16 1839 Report: "[I]t is not unusual for the [Indigenous youth] to enter the collegiate institutes and high schools side by side with the whites, and advance thence through the colleges of the Dominion, taking high rank in the classes there. And while attention is thus paid to mental training, many of the pupils are carefully instructed in industrial trades, such as shoemaking, tailoring, blacksmithing, plastering, carpentering, and printing." *Historical papers*, 98. It must be noted that, as the quote indicates, this was in regards to collegiate schools and not residential schools. The quote was included to display an example of the type of quote I am referencing.

17 *Historical papers*, 104.

saying: these parents weren't requesting residential schools—or boarding schools for that matter—for their kids, neither were they denigrating their own language. They believed, in much the same way English-speaking parents enroll their kids in French immersion programs today, that bilingualism would open up opportunities for their young that they never knew. They believed that children fluent in both languages would have an advantage in future employment. They could create new connections between their people and the whites and help their entire community grow and succeed.

However, much like the missionary endeavours, this collegial attitude increasingly shifted so much that by the 1850s, European educational values were imposed upon Indigenous children with or without the consent of their parents.

CHRISTIAN RESIDENTIAL SCHOOLS

Arguably the main reason behind the shift in earlier attitudes is that Canada grew more urban, industrial, and financially prosperous in the Dominion days of the 19th century. In the decade before Confederation, the government enacted the 1857 legislature known as the Gradual Civilization Act.

Like similar offerings to western provincial leaders, the Metis government in Manitoba, or the Hudson's Bay Company, the Act sought to entice Indigenous people to join in with the newly forming union of provinces. By 1869 (two years after Confederation—not a coincidence) such gradual entreaties turned into Compulsory Enfranchisement, which did exactly as the title states. Such acts, along with the sale of the Hudson's Bay territory, fueled Louis Riel's rebellion as Canada began to use its growing power to force ideals upon Indigenous people who had yet to assimilate in ways the leaders deemed appropriate.

The mission of Canada toward Indigenous people was officially legislated in 1876 under the Indian Act. In essence, this act gave the government control over almost every facet of Indigenous life and treated them as wards of the state with little autonomy. One year later, Nicholas Davin issued his famous

Davin Report that was one of the first fully articulated pleas for the residential school system. Davin wanted to have Regina and surrounding territories granted Provincial status and utilized his beliefs about Indigenous peoples to help achieve this end.

Davin's report didn't include any mention of the churches, but his report did inspire Prime Minister John A. Macdonald to officially advocate for the schools. Macdonald would develop the plans further and build partnerships with various Protestant and Catholic Churches that would see them eventually running the entire enterprise on behalf of the Canadian government. The Protestants were needed because they were already building Canadian Christendom and civilizing the Indigenous fit their goals perfectly. The Catholics were also courted because they were more numerous, already had deep inroads in the growing west, had centuries-long relationships in some Indigenous communities, and were seen to be skilled frontier educators.

It took three more years but, by 1880, 11 residential schools were opened. 1883 saw the beginning of western residential schools and 1884 saw an amendment to the Indian Act that made it mandatory for Indigenous youth to be enrolled in school. One year later, the railroad was completed, Canada was joined from coast to coast and the building programs we have previously discussed went into full gear.

By 1892 Protestants and Catholics were given control over the residential school contracts. The Canadian government was pleased to hand the expensive and logistically problematic contracts over to the churches because they believed church leaders would require very little oversight.

According to John Milloy, the government would always remain the senior partner in this deal, but the churches were largely responsible for the day-to-day molding of Indigenous youth into upstanding and moral members of Canadian society.[18]

18 "Essentially, the residential school system was a creature of the federal government even though the children in the schools were, in most cases, in the immediate care of the church." John S. Milloy, *A National Crime: The Canadian Government and the Residential School System*, (Regina: University of Manitoba), 2017, Kindle Introduction.

For its part, the government would offer the majority of the financing that assisted the churches with the financial load. Despite numerous fights between various churches and the government over budgets—the former believing they were being underfunded and the latter believing the former were spending too extravagantly—overall this system seemed much cheaper for the government. And just like that, Indigenous education was outsourced to the most reputable social organization the land had to offer.

The churches got to work and by 1896 there were 45 residential schools across Canada. A study of the Treaties between the Canadian government and various Indigenous peoples shows that as the railway moved in, the local Indigenous communities were moved out. They were sent into more obscure and undesirable locations far removed from the economic and social gains the railway brought.

Catholic priests, missionaries, and nuns remained in such arduous assignments because their vows made it impossible for them to refuse these increasingly undesirable placements. Knowing this, the government utilized these Catholics to help move numerous communities when the First Nations were deemed to be blocking progress. Citing concerns that white vices (like alcohol or gambling) would harm the Indigenous faithful (strange they weren't too worried about the impact on the white faithful), many of these Catholic missionaries organized the separations of Indigenous communities from their locations close to white settlements. This arrangement worked well for the Catholic missionaries' goals as well. It was more expedient for them when their Catholic Indigenous adherents moved into smaller and more contained geographical locales. In places like Atlantic Canada, which housed large Indigenous Catholic populations, the church was frequently called on to help select new lands for the people and then explain to the people why they were being forced to move.

Worse still, no one ever questioned why some missionaries and priests actually volunteered to be placed in such challenging

CHAPTER 7: RECONCILIATION | 277

and remote locations. These men and women were celebrated as heroes of missionary zeal and lauded as champions for Christ. Later records would reveal the chilling fact many Indigenous children had known for decades: these people signed up to abuse and assault children without fear of being caught. Countless children were the victims of neglect, rape, forced abortions, forced sterilizations, beatings, tortures, and murder at the hands of both Catholic and Protestant churches.

Along with the vicious assaults came the insidious demoralizing of Indigenous children for their intelligence and abilities. Despite earlier rhetoric about the benefit of teaching Indigenous children practical skills, most schools turned into glorified sweatshops. Boys' education consisted mostly of menial labour and the girls were taught skills needed to serve in the homes of wealthier citizens. The academic elements of their education were increasingly disregarded and more time was spent in the field than in the classroom.

Standardized test scores for Indigenous children were consistently below the national average, consistent with the sub-par education they were receiving. Rather than altering their pedagogy, these scores were used to advance ideas that Indigenous children were lazy and stupid. The earlier reports of Indigenous intelligence were swallowed up in the myth of the inferior Indian perpetrated by their own teachers.

Such abuse and practically non-existent education was also joined by criminal negligence. A 1908 medical report began to raise some red flags when it found that children in residential schools suffered from influenza and other contagious diseases at a much higher rate than children anywhere else. Some statistics cite the almost unbelievable mortality rate as high as 60% and yet neither the church nor the government voiced concern.

Such medical reports had the potential to reveal the criminal neglect these children were experiencing. Therefore, a truly heinous plan was hatched to make sure such potentially damning testimony never came to light. Gentle reader, I present to you Duncan Campbell Scott, a pioneering voice in Canadian poetry, Superintendent of Indian Affairs, and as true a villain as ever existed during this period of time. Scott found the quickest way to solve concerns about the health of residential school attendees: he abolished the role of medical inspector. Beginning in 1919 and extending for the next 50 years, Scott ensured there was almost no medical or ethical oversight in any capacity for residential schools.

In contrast, medical examiner Dr. Peter Bryce risked his health and career fighting against Scott. He repeatedly and creatively attempted to sound the alarm as to what was happening in these schools. His work was silenced time and again but that didn't stop Dr. Bryce. He went to publisher James Hope and, in 1922, published *The Story of a National Crime*. In it, he not only lambasted Scott's policies and called Canadians to action, he also offered practical solutions.

Dr. Bryce argued that easy correctives to ventilation and sanitation would greatly curb the spread of infectious and fatal diseases like tuberculosis. He noted the amount of money the city of Ottawa spent on healthcare was three times the amount spent on all Indigenous people nationwide. His life was one spent in frustration and heartbreak as neither the government nor the churches cared enough to intervene. Dr. Bryce's true merit was not valued in his own lifetime, but future generations can safely say he was a true hero in a very dark period.

For those children who survived and graduated their residential schools, they entered into a nation that had little to offer them. They had been traumatized and many found it difficult to return home. But neither were they prepared for the Canada that awaited them. The one thing residential schools claimed they were doing was assimilating Indigenous children into the larger Canadian culture. Once again, this was a bold-faced lie.

Just a few examples from around the time of Scott and Bryce will suffice to show residential schools as only the first in a series of degradations the Indigenous peoples of Canada were forced to endure. The First World War saw over 3500

Indigenous people enlist to fight for Canada. In order to do so, they had to renounce their Aboriginal citizenship and become citizens of Canada alone (the same was true in WWII). This was a policy no other people group had to experience in this land. Despite such clearly racist restrictions, numerous Indigenous peoples renounced their homeland in order to have the honour of fighting for Canada. Indigenous religious observances and feasts were made illegal during this time, which impeded the ability of Indigenous people to learn their stories (like the ones that began this chapter). The 1940s saw a dramatic increase in the forced relocations of numerous communities from Newfoundland (which had only officially joined Canada in 1949) all the way over to Vancouver Island and up into Inuit territory as well. It would not be until years after WWII that any sort of changes in this downward trajectory began to occur.

DISMANTLING, APOLOGIES & AFTERMATH

"I've been thinking about institutionalization. I got institutionalized by the church, the Indian day school, and the residential school. Then I took it to the next institution: jail. Its followed me all my life."[19]

By 1958, the idea of closing residential schools was officially being entertained. The process was painfully slow and allowed for damage to continue, largely unabated, for decades more. By 1969, with countless testimonials coming forward about the abuses suffered at the hands of clergy, the Canadian government removed residential schools from the churches. By 1979, 1200 Indigenous youths remained in the system and it would take until 1984 for the last B.C. residential school to close.

It would be 1996 before the final school shuttered its doors for good. That year also saw Roman Catholic Bishop Hubert O'Connor convicted for the rape of two young Indigenous girls in the 1960s. To this date, this is one of the more public examples of justice but it only looms large in the Canadian story because

---

19 Meshake and Anderson, *INJICHAAG*, 118.

convictions have proven tragically rare.

The 1990s ushered in an era of apologies that began with the Oblates who, in 1991, officially apologized to the Indigenous people for their role in the residential school system. This was followed in 1993 by the Anglicans, 1994 the Presbyterians offered their own apology, and in 1998 when the UCC finally acknowledged their role and asked forgiveness.

In 2001, the Aboriginal Healing Foundation began and in 2004 the RCMP—largely employed to hunt down children seeking to escape these hellish schools and return to their parents—finally apologized. Four years later, the Federal Government yielded to intense public pressure and apologized. By 2010, the Truth and Reconciliation Commission began to investigate concrete actions to bring about healing for the innumerable victims of the residential schools and ensure that such travesties never happen again.

While some Indigenous have recorded some positive experiences in these schools, the horrors many other children experienced at the hands of clergy are too awful and too numerous for me to report accurately. Many Canadians speak proudly about the lack of overt racism in this land. We frequently laud our involvement in the underground railroad. We celebrate Canada's support of the North in the American Civil War. In recent memory, American President Donald Trump's use of detainment centers on their southern border, the clear abuse of children, and the forced sterilizations of non-documented immigrant women were greeted with horror in Canada.

However, such attitudes of Canadian moral superiority are destroyed when we remember the last residential school closed in 1996. This is not just a Christendom problem of a previous age, this is a reality of the enlightened and modern Canada of the late 20th century. Perhaps you, gentle reader, were alive at a time when residential schools existed; I was. Let that sink in. Because the sinking in of that point might explain why this topic, as important as it is, is greeted with defensiveness by some and outright hostility by others. It is an uncomfortable truth to recognize how complicit many of us are in this national crime.

I took pains to demonstrate the benevolent and beneficial relationships that both Settlers and Indigenous peoples enjoyed for a long part of our shared history. Indigenous people were valuable allies to the French and the Catholic Church can log among its martyrs those who were killed alongside their Indigenous friends.

Indigenous also embraced the later arrival of English Protestant settlers and proved just as willing to engage in mutually beneficial relationships. However, as David MacDonald notes "a critical line was crossed at some point which resulted in a disastrous change in that [mutually beneficial and cordial] relationship. Aboriginal people were no longer seen as equals, no longer accepted as compatriots in the adventure of knowing and benefiting from this land; instead they were treated as wards of the state."[20] I argue that while such harmful ideologies were present in the first half of the 19th century, the isolated nature of Canada prevented forcible assimilation on any substantial level. A strong argument can be made that MacDonald's "critical line" was crossed after Confederation when the churches began to build a Dominion.

Civilizing and Christianizing the vast collection of "pagans" within the borders displayed Canada's Christian character. Their so-called backwards ways were seen as a threat to their own souls and an impediment to the advancement of Canada. Combine such ideologies with the Treaties and Settlers' desire for more land, and you see why there were precious few concerned about residential schools, let alone critical of them.

Thus were the agents of the residential school systems able to, in the name of Christ and charity, perpetuate countless atrocities upon children they claimed to be saving.

ONGOING ARROGANCE

"Justice to the native peoples, however, demands

---

20   MacDonald, "Breach", 345-6.

acknowledgement not only of the long reign of the spirits of the land but of the traumatic effects of their displacement by Christian missionaries who in their zeal were frequently insensitive to the cultural wounds they were inflicting."[21]

I want to return to Thomas King's *The Inconvenient Indian* right now because he articulates an important idea with skill and wit. He demonstrates that Settlers don't actually have a problem with dead Indians (his words) but Live and Legal Indians present an entirely other dilemma. He argues convincingly that dead Indians are silent and can be easily placed into several convenient tropes, many of which are frequently reiterated through art, literature, and cinema. Live and Legal Indians, on the other hand, frustratingly refuse simplistic categorization.

There is the familiar—though condemned—trope of the brutal savage terrorizing the frontier, a favourite theme of many older Hollywood films and literature. Again, this is an idea most modern people condemn.

More problematic is the trope of the noble Indigenous warrior, or guide. Audiences are called to mourn this tragic figure of a soon-to-be-gone age. One common character is the helpful First Nations warrior (or a woman, like Pocahontas, as King writes about the fetishizing of Indigenous women as well) who assists the white protagonist through a quest, even at the expense of his own survival.

There is also the wise older guide or shaman who seems to speak only in powerful and mythical riddles, usually while sitting in a Teepee with a face partially obscured by smoke. These embodied tropes will be dressed in very familiar clothing like headdresses, beads, are frequently adorned with face paint, and are almost always shirtless.

At some point the audience will witness the Indigenous warrior heroically and tragically riding his horse off into the sunset as the modern world closes in. The music will be sorrowful and cinematic and will call us to lament how our

---

21 Grant, *Profusion*, 221

technologies and consumerism forced such a noble human being literally out of sight. While this second trope seems more sympathetic and more able to inspire change, King reminds us: "In the end though, neither the Indian as savage nor the Indian as hero changed the dynamics of racism."[22]

Such tropes are troubling because they, once again, put Indigenous people into simplistic categories. Categories that are believed to be totally different from, but are clearly still connected to, the ones that created the residential schools in the first place.

In this age, the categories are more benign and seemingly complimentary as they celebrate and seek to reclaim Indigenous culture from the past. Gurus and naturalists respond to the lament of the vanishing warrior by co-opting so-called Indigenous culture for the benefit of people who want to feel more connected to "Mother Earth" or "Shamanism" and can afford the products that will help them achieve just that. We can purchase pseudo-spirituality and feel better without ever understanding how little the product has to do with actual Indigenous culture.[23] If we think back to the previous chapter, we can once again see just how pervasive spiritual consumerism is well beyond the confines of church shopping. This trope inspires white people from around the world to dress up like "dead Indians" in order to—they would argue—prevent the loss of these ancient peoples and their customs.

The problem as King sees it, is that such mentalities leave no room for actual Indigenous people or their criticisms of such practices. Ironically, he writes, such clubs and products would be "better served if Live Indians and Legal Indians somehow disappeared...there's nothing worse than having the original available when you're trying to sell the counterfeit."[24] That is a problem that persists within Canadian Christianity today as

---

22 King, *Inconvenient*, 30.

23 It's "as much to do with Indians as Eskimo Pie has to do with the Inuit." King, *Inconvenient*, 74.

24 King, *Inconvenient*, 75.

well.

The problem with present attitudes around condemning the Christianization of the Indigenous is that it is well-meaning but reiterates similar damaging tropes. Even the most liberal and compassionate among us tend to view the missionaries as active agents of colonization and the Indigenous people as passive recipients—or victims—of a message that swept away their former beliefs. Not only is that historically inaccurate, it is also another well-intended marginalization of Indigenous peoples. It is a trope of King's "dead Indian" that affords precious little room to recognize the legitimacy of Indigenous Christians; many of whom can trace their faith roots back dozens of generations.

Prior to 1870, numerous First Peoples in the land we call Canada chose to become Christian for a variety of reasons. To see them merely as victims is to belittle these people for lacking the wisdom to make choices for themselves. They made a variety of conscious choices based on their understanding of the world and what they believed Christianity had to offer. Some saw the gods of their parents growing weaker and believed a powerful spiritual presence had come from across the water that could help. Others added this new and clearly powerful God to a pantheon of their existing deities. They worshiped their ancestral gods and Jesus and benefited from European connections without upsetting their ancestors.

Of course some were conned, some were tricked, and some were even bribed. Others converted for some stated reason, got what they wanted from a local official, and then were later "caught" by missionaries still practicing their former religion. Whatever the reason, whatever the choice, and however long such choices remained formative, the point is the historical record of Indigenous conversions to Christianity is as complex, contrary, and multifaceted as any other account. Indigenous Christians come from a variety of places and backgrounds and hold to a variety of different Protestant and Catholic teachings interpreted through a variety of cultural lenses.

The image of Indigenous being tricked, conned, forced, and

coerced by Christianity is a sympathetic one but it also lumps all Indigenous people into one experiential category. It is more reminiscent of King's Noble and Tragic Dead Indian trope than the messy and often confusing historical record. I want to be very clear here: this is not an apology for former Christian attitudes towards Indigenous people; it is a call for a better assessment of our present ones.

TRUER RECONCILIATION

And this brings us back to the creation account that began this chapter.

If you were a fly on the hull of the ship that brought the first missionaries to the land that centuries later would be called Canada, you could have easily overheard the following conversations. Perhaps the missionaries would've been discussing the heretical English King Henry VIII and his recent divorce of Catherine to marry that Boleyn girl. You might have overheard them discussing the scandalous teachings of that upstart Augustinian monk Martin Luther who was causing such chaos among the Germanic Provinces. Perhaps, if the priests were especially attuned to politics, you heard their concern about a Parisian academic who was reputedly working on a systematized collection of heresies. He had fled Paris right before the missionary ship left because the French government had finally clamped down on such scandalous thinking. You may have heard them struggle to remember his name. Perhaps one of them finally snapped his fingers and shouted "*Calvin! Il s'appelle Jean Calvin!*"

I'm not saying that is what the first missionaries to Canada spoke about on their journey to new lands. I'm merely giving you an idea of what was happening in the global Christian world when the stories of Jesus were first told on these shores. Despite such ancient roots, few Canadian Christians seem to respect the wisdom centuries of Indigenous Christianity has to offer. Canadian Christians should pause to ask why Indigenous theology isn't granted the respect afforded to Catholic Thomism, or Reformed Theology, or Wesleyanism, or even centuries younger Pentecostal theology?

The story from the beginning of this chapter might offer a clue. It is entirely possible that the story that began this chapter is a blend of one Ojibway creation account with Christian thinking. Some might consider it too European to be considered authentically Indigenous. Others might argue it is too Indigenous to be taught in a Bible-believing Canadian church. In such tensions resides something beautiful and something powerful and something overlooked.

For starters, it reminds Canadian Christians that we haven't traversed as far from our national ancestors as we may like to believe. Sure, we don't use the same words for our Indigenous brothers and sisters anymore. I would go so far to say that many Canadian Christians likely have more respect for Indigenous culture as well. However, such words and respect—important as they are—haven't opened up theological space for Indigenous Christian thinking either. Thinking that has been part of this land's culture much longer than most other forms of the faith. Given the role geography has played in the history of Canadian Christianity, I hope you see how profound an oversight that is.

To be honest, I stand in bewildered awe that some Indigenous people actually found a relationship with Jesus in spite of their experiences with Canadian Christianity. I think of people like Dr. Terry LeBlanc, Director of NAIITS (formerly this stood for "North American Institute for Indigenous Theological Studies" but the leadership reference it as an Indigenous Learning Community, rather than explaining the acronym) and Executive Director of Indigenous Pathways, who has spent decades highlighting the interpretive value Indigenous culture brings to western biblical studies. Others like him have found paths that are moving past bridging Indigenous and Christian cultures into embracing the importance and uniqueness of Indigenous understandings of the Gospel. Messages that have the power to reconcile the historical abuses of the past and offer exciting new understandings of Jesus; but only for those who have ears to hear them.

One of the strange elements any historical study reveals is the wisdom and insights maligned communities gain through their suffering. Much of John Calvin's thought came from the time he spent as a pastor to French Protestant refugees fleeing their Catholic homeland. Martin Luther's 95 theses that sparked the Protestant Reformation were largely inspired by the poverty he saw the church inflicting upon his fellow Germans. This is not a veiled attempt to find some silver lining in these dark clouds. I am arguing that such wisdom exists much closer to Canada than anything written by either Calvin or Luther. I am arguing that Indigenous interpretations of Jesus—so often overlooked or rejected as not Christian enough—aligns Indigenous faiths with prophetic and liberating messages found in the Gospels. Settler faith—both Protestant and Catholic—possesses no such wisdom because Settler faith has always operated from a place of worldly power, even in Canada.

I am not arguing that Catholic and Protestant Indigenous Christians are going to agree on doctrine; that would be naïve and argue against literally everything this book has been about. I am saying that this whole book is about looking at the overlooked stories of Canadian Christianity. There is power in being overlooked and if Canada is an overlooked nation, and Christians believe they are an overlooked element within that overlooked nation, then Indigenous Christians, whatever branch of the faith they claim, are the most overlooked of us all. And there is transformative power in that.

Settler Christians must acknowledge that, as it pertains to Canada, we occupy the role of the crucifiers not the crucified. But, just like the humble Cornelius, or the Centurion who asked Jesus to heal his servant, or even the soldier at the foot of the cross, if we acknowledge our station and, in humility, seek after God from those we have maligned, we can be opened to a fresh outpouring of God's Spirit. That humility comes from acknowledging the actions of our churches offend a God of justice. The ongoing sin comes from our inability to see that

Settlers still benefit from these historical abuses, even if we aren't the perpetrators of them.

As we move from apologies into action we must educate ourselves about the systemic issues that remain today because of residential schools. These schools and the ongoing suffering of numerous First Nations people reveals to us the most dramatic and violent outworking of Canadian Christian arrogance; the evil of Canada's Christendom. To borrow from the Bible: a stiff-necked people we were, until we engage with, and learn from, our Indigenous brothers and sisters, a stiff-necked people we will remain. And we will remain so no matter how enlightened our motives may seem.

We recognize the importance of land acknowledgments and school units on Indigenous peoples and their cultures; yet few lessons validate Christianity as a part of ancient Indigenous cultures. I don't say that as a Christian, I say that as an historian. Indigenous Christianity was born in 1534 and is almost 500 years old; how much older does a worldview need to be before it is considered authentic?

Some Indigenous Christians have belonged to faith communities that are as old, if not older than, every single form of Protestant Christianity. Yet the theology of Dr. Leblanc and men and women like him remain almost unheard in most Canadian Christian circles. Where does this ignorance come from if not from an ongoing and deeply embedded belief that Settler Christianity is still superior? Canada is a land comfortable borrowing from the teachings of other lands and yet we still seem unwilling to borrow from these other nations located much closer.

Perhaps we overlook Indigenous Christianity because the forms of Jesus worship may not look like the forms of Christianity most Settlers practice today. They may have different ways of understanding familiar Gospel stories, they may concern themselves less with the scandals and ideas that we have detailed in this book. In that, they may also reveal to us a new picture of our shared faith.

For those concerned about the future of Christianity in Canada, Indigenous Christians are also immune to the criticisms of the Canadian unchurched who see the faith as a tool of oppression. A version of Christianity few in this land recognize and, what concerns me more, even fewer seem willing to learn from. We might ask fellow Indigenous Christians to teach us about their experiences, but are we willing to see them as theological teachers as well?

True reconciliation, whether on a micro or macro scale, can only begin when one party acknowledges that they have harmed another. Our actions can only be called reconciliation if we willingly engage in actions of restoration, no matter the cost, for the sake of reclaiming harmony.

Christians of today can look to our predecessors in order to learn a valuable lesson. There are numerous accounts of early missionaries to this land stating they would have died or gotten hopelessly lost without Indigenous guides to direct and save them. In the spiritual wilderness of our present age, similar arguments could be made. Indigenous faiths that have navigated away from "looking like us" can offer guidance to the modern Christian Canadian narrative. However, if we only use surface-level rhetoric regarding Indigenous Christians to convince unchurched Canadians that we are progressive, then we are simply re-iterating the old patterns of Canadian Christian thought that made residential schools a reality in the first place.

What can actually separate us from our colonizing ancestors is the simple recognition that God is active within Indigenous cultures. Just as evangelicals saw God at work in teen culture, or the myriad other ways that Christianity has brought a spiritual lens to all aspects of Settler culture, we need to see in the Indigenous world the face of Christ. Reaching out respectfully and patiently to Indigenous Christians can also be a way to acknowledge the sovereignty of these First Nations. A concrete way to honour similarities as well as celebrating and honouring differences. Actions that embody an antithesis to our Christian ancestors who forced Indigenous people into being wards of the state. An acknowledgement that these are separate nations with unique cultures, and different languages that can also shed light on elements of the faith unique to this land that have been overlooked and rejected in the past.

Reconciliation is an important and rich term used throughout the New Testament. Paul teaches that the body of Christ is supposed to be filled with competing and antagonistic social groups. After all, Jews and Greeks had just as complicated a history as Settlers and First Nations (and a much longer history of violence at that). He taught when a diverse collection of people, people the world believes shouldn't be together, unite with one another under the banner of Christ, they present a very intriguing picture to those outside the faith. In such ways the church doesn't do evangelism, the church is evangelism. The church doesn't have to talk about the body of Christ because the church is displaying the body of Christ.

The great saint of early Christianity reminded followers of Jesus that, thanks to his sacrifice, we are all one family united in Him. That is not rhetorical flourish, Paul reminds us that unless we value people over our perceived personal rights and differences, we have yet to experience true reconciliation. As if that is not difficult enough, he goes on to communicate a message as important to Canadian Christians of today as it was to the Colossians of biblical times: if you are not reconciled with each other, how can you believe you are reconciled with God?

Reconciliation truly is the hardest element of the faith to genuinely live out. However, if you believe Paul, it is also the most important.

RESOURCES

John Webster Grant. *The Moon of Wintertime: Missionaries and the Indians of Canada in Encounter since 1534*. Toronto: University of Toronto, 1984.

- A comprehensive history of Christian and Native missionary connection with very practical and profound recommendations for Christians to consider.

Emma Battell Lowman and Adam J. Barker. S*ettler: Identity and Colonialism in 21st Century Canada*. Halifax: Fernwood Publishing, 2015.

- This book taught me the nuance and importance of proper language and how that can shift a paradigm to increase conversation.

Rene Meshake. *INJICHAAG: My Soul in Story-Anishinaabe Poetics in Art and Words*. Winnipeg: University of Manitoba, 2019.

- A collection of beautiful poems, essays, and "word bundles" about Meshake's life. His is a modern tale of the residential school system from a man who has found art a compelling way to both heal and tell his story.

Thomas King. *The Inconvenient Indian: A Curious Account of Native People in North America*. Toronto: Anchor Canada, 2013.

- A brilliant, funny, and profound examination of the ways in which First Nations people have been, and are, viewed in North America. *The Globe and Mail* called King "our Twain" and that is an accurate assessment of the man's humour and insight.

Terry LeBlanc. "Native American Theology." YouTube Accessed at https://youtu.be/5UyMhwYN0jM.

- Dr. LeBlanc explains the unique interpretive abilities his Indigenous culture brings to understanding the Bible for post-Christendom North American Christians.

---

1 IDEA

Indigenous Christianity is the oldest form of Christianity in this land. Why don't other Christians see it as a viable expression of the faith from which we can learn?

CONCLUSION: A HIP CHURCH

Everything is bleak
It's the middle of the night
You're all alone
And the dummies might be right
You feel like a jerk...
Avoid trends and cliches
Don't try to be up to date
And when the sunlight hits the olive oil
Don't hesitate
— "My Music @ Work,"
The Tragically Hip

I was born, grew up, and have lived most of my life
in a country that many of my fellow citizens...
regard as beneath consideration as a
locale for new and significant ideas,
of new hope for the human species.
— Tom Wayman,
A Country Not Considered, 1.

History...does not refer merely, or even principally, to the past.
On the contrary, the great force of history comes
from the fact that we carry it within us,
are unconsciously controlled by it in many ways,
and history is literally present in all we do...
it is to history that we owe our frames of reference,
our identities, and our aspirations.
— James Baldwin

A HIP CHURCH

At the age of 19, I found myself walking through a cemetery in Kalispell, Montana late in the evening ("Why on earth were you doing that?" you ask). I was trying to impress a pretty American girl I had just met (that's why). During the course of conversation two young people have in a cemetery late at night, we discovered similar tastes in music. However, one band I mentioned stymied her. Despite being a music aficionado with cosmopolitan tastes, she had never heard of The Tragically Hip. Flabbergasted, I tried to explain who they were and why I liked their sound, but then decided to let her ignorance add to my mystique. What I assuredly was not thinking about, was that I had just discovered a cultural divide between America and Canada.

The Tragically Hip were pretty much a staple of every CD collection in the 1990s. Most younger Canadians had at least two of their discs in our portable CD binders (if you don't know what a CD binder is, congratulations, you're young...or older. Either way, congratulations). Canada is over 9,000,000 square kilometers and you would be hard pressed to find anyone in that space—even the remote places—that didn't have at least some working knowledge of the band. Yet here I was, just two hours south of my home, and they were totally unknown.

Therein lies the lesson Canadian Christians can learn from The Tragically Hip.

The first thing you should know about this Canadian band is that they performed more in America than they did in Canada. According to Allan Cross' *Ongoing History of New Music* series, they played 561 shows in America and 549 shows in Canada. That is a shocking statistic for most Hip fans.

The Tragically Hip has been called Canada's band and I think many of us would agree that accurately describes their influence over this land. But they didn't receive it for a lack of trying to make it on the American music scene. In the 1990s, when they first became popular here, they couldn't make it in the States because they weren't really Grunge. Throughout their long career, their sound never fit into the dominant musical trends of America at any time. Other Canadian bands like Rush or The Barenaked Ladies found tremendous success south of the border, but that never happened for The Hip.

Why were The Hip subpar musicians with poorly produced songs and vapid lyrics? Absolutely not. They were excellent musicians creating fantastic songs with an engaging frontman who was a true showman and poet. The Tragically Hip made music for decades and many of their songs were specifically about Canada. Perhaps such a Canadian focus contributed to their lack of American success, but that's not the point I want to raise.

They told Canadian stories through song whether they sold a million records or not. They told us about the strange death and legacy of Bill Biralko, and conjured up the mystical elements of Bobcaygeon, they taught us our history, both sublime and terrible. Their songs were our stories and many Canadians sang our stories at campfires around this land thanks to them. If you grew up in Canada, there is a good chance you have screamed out some of the lyrics printed throughout this book at some point in your life. If not, I highly recommend you do so, their music is very cathartic.

While not everyone can relate to this and not everyone is a Hip fan, they truly were Canada's band. Their tour in the summer of 2016 proved that point for generations of Canadians. Their final show in Kingston was broadcast live by the CBC and an estimated 11 million Canadians tuned in to watch the band perform live for the last time. By then, it was widely known that lead singer Gord Downie had terminal brain cancer and didn't have long to live. Many tears were shed as we watched the seminal Canadian poet sing and cry and scream and dance around as only he could, knowing we weren't going to see his theatrical presence again.[1]

---

1   Gord Downie died on 17 October, 2017. I read one tweet that day that demonstrates my point about the cultural importance of the band and the man (it still gets me emotional): "Canada closed. Death in the family."

I watched the final show at an outdoor venue in Burlington, Ontario and the emotion of that day will not soon leave me. His final legacy was one of bravery, refusing to let the sickness define his last days. He was compassionate and used his remaining influence to champion the cause of First Nations. At that televised concert, he directly called on Prime Minister Justin Trudeau to right the wrongs the Canadian nation had perpetrated against our Indigenous brothers and sisters. Downie was truly a legend and Canadians should be proud to call The Tragically Hip "our band."

That is precisely what The Tragically Hip can teach Canadian Christians about their own irrelevance. If we approach secularization more like The Hip, we can see our current experience in an entirely new light and discover a strength. The Tragically Hip struggled to influence the coveted American music scene; Canadian churches are struggling to influence the Canadian cultural scene. The Tragically Hip offers an interesting case study of success in the face of perceived failures.

Gentle reader, The Hip are Canada's band *because* they didn't make it in the States.

AN OVERLOOKED GIFT

There is freedom in being a Canadian Christian today, a freedom previous generations never experienced: a freedom to do and be whoever or whatever we want to do or be. Churches are set free to do whatever they want to do for one simple reason we tend to overlook: no one else cares.

I don't know what your church wants to do or what your church thinks is important but all I can say is that you should do whatever brings your community joy. Be an authentic, unapologetic, and creative Catholic (English or French speaking), Pentecostal, United, Baptist, Orthodox, or whatever other Christian tribe you claim. Celebrate the freedom in this age because there is very little pressure to succeed. Even if your experimentation is a total disaster, it's not like you're going to make the numbers decline any faster. Most Canadians don't care about your church so all you can really do is pleasantly surprise them.

Be set free to, like The Hip, bring the sound of your faith to as many places as possible, but don't let the rejection of others define you or your faith community. The Hip were overlooked in America and that made us more proud of them. They were our brilliant secret and we loved them for teaching us our own stories and for being unapologetically Canadian.

Christianity can likewise be great because of rejection. Jesus operated from the periphery and his earliest followers extolled the virtue of weakness. Only when weak could humans get out of the way of Kingdom work. Weakness brought genuine dependence and that always beats power in the economy of God.

The good news is Canada has given the church all the tools and experience it will ever need to operate as a "not considered" entity. A huge part of Canada's identity—not just church identity—is wrapped up in the fact almost no one thinks about us. Not even our closest national friend, with whom we share a border, gives us much serious thought. Yet, Canadians have been able to find purpose and meaning and even a strange pride in that reality.

We really only have to contend with two questions as we move forward. The first question we should ask ourselves is: what is the Gospel?

Is it a proclamation? Is it a name for a series of stories? Is it the key to salvation? Is it a collection of morality tales? Is it a useful social ethic? Is it a tool the government should use to guide policy? Is it historically accurate? Is it theology? Is it myth? Is it the lens through which we understand the world? Is it the property of Christians alone or do all religions have a part of it? Is it irrelevant? Is it a writing that inspires shame? Guilt? Joy? Is it made up? Is it Divine?

The Gospel has been all those things in Canada at some point or another and, depending on who or when you're asking, it's usually a combination of several of those answers.

Therefore, the second question we need to ask becomes:

what is the Gospel in Canada?

What is the Gospel you want to communicate to others? What is it about the Gospel that you believe is so important? How can you share those beliefs with the people of this nation, knowing what you know about the culture? Can you talk about Jesus in ways that are true to the Gospel and to Canadians? How has your own experience in Canada shaped your understanding of the Gospel? And, most importantly, which elements of your beliefs are Gospel and which elements are Canadian? Which are both?

Answer these questions and you discover your "sound." Leave the reception of your sound to the uncontrollable market of popular opinion and be content to tell the stories you think are worth telling. If you remove the concern about numbers or even influence from your church, you will be better equipped to serve the Canadian scene. Remember, the only element of this nation that is truly big is our geography, in all other areas, Canadians thrive in the small.

The Hip were largely overlooked by the world, and that is what set them free to become huge in Canada. We loved them because they were overlooked.

AN OVERLOOKED CONCERN

Many of our attempts to correct the trajectory of secularization focus on reaching out to the unchurched. Most churches seem opposed to cannibalizing other faith communities and genuinely want to inform the uninformed about the wonders of faith. Churches plan outreach events and desire to be known as a positive space in their respective communities. They believe Christian community can be an antidote to the increasing isolation many Canadians are feeling.

Alpha groups invite people to eat together and learn basic elements of the faith. Many churches host AA, NA, and AlAnon meetings to help those impacted by addiction. Food banks, Inn from the Cold, and shelters all use churches to feed and shelter marginalized and homeless fellow Canadians. Historically and morally speaking, these are noble pursuits because churches that provide Canadians with practical assistance do earn respect.

Also historically speaking, that respect doesn't always translate into adherence; and that can cause frustration. Much of the literature from recent years focuses on finding new and compelling ways to enhance the appearance of the church for those beyond its walls. I wonder if this increased Christian irrelevancy isn't also highlighting some of the deep-seated fears believers have about their own faith. For all the Christian rhetoric around Jesus being the truth, we have no ability to validate our claims. Christian or not, we live in a scientific age that demands evidence.

If approximately 20% of Canadians are active Christians and 20% are No Religion then, statistically speaking, Canadian Christianity is just as likely to be wrong as it is to be right. I think it is important to acknowledge the doubt this land creates in its Christian citizens. This land doesn't allow a Christian monopoly and, as we have seen in this book, things weren't perfect when it did. This speaks against many of the teachings we have traditionally received about Christian nations.

Canada hasn't collapsed into degradation or vice, despite the arguments of many believers. Birth control and legal divorce didn't destroy families or undo the fabric of society. Taking prayer out of school didn't create Satanic centers of evil indoctrination, and non-believing neighbours can be good people with active ethics who appear to live full lives. If Christianity is about finding purpose and a wonderful life, most Canadians have proven you can do that without ever setting foot in a church.

So, what is the gospel in Canada? Whatever it is, it's clearly not as demonstrably important to life as Canadian Christians have been told it is, and our nation has the numbers to prove such an uncomfortable statement.

Historians never talk about the future. If we were a character in a heist movie, we would be the guy sitting in the back seat looking out the back window and telling the rest of the crew what's behind us; we're not the drivers and we don't ride shotgun where all the action is. Humans are profoundly complex (and a little chaotic) so predicting what will happen next is seen as a fool's errand by most in my discipline. Historians make lousy fortune tellers.

However, you and I have walked together for quite a long time so perhaps I can offer some reflections on what we can do with this information. In order to do that, I want to focus on the themes we covered in each chapter.

POWER

Power has always been a nebulous idea in Canada. This is a nation in which conquerors don't make the conquered look like them (First Nations, Metis, and Inuit after 1870 being the painful exception). This is a land that, from the beginning, legislated amicable relationships and saw the financial blessings of cooperation. From the 18th century, Canada was populated by those familiar with loss and occupying the underside of power. A nation of losers, so to speak.

Various Indigenous communities, the French, and the UEL (Black and White) each experienced being on the losing side of history. Canada's relationship to power is complicated and nuanced and a lot of that comes from our relationship to America. The States are seen to be the powerful ones in this North American relationship and Canadians have remained suspect of overt displays of strength from the beginning. Because of this, I remind churches to approach all their interactions, both internally and externally, with a light touch.

Larger churches have more work to do in this regard for a couple of reasons. First, those communities who genuinely enjoy larger numbers and the power that goes along with that, I point your attention to the Anglicans and their experiences in early Canada as just one example. They were the dominant Christian voice in the halls of power for many years. They had money, land, influence, and government support. However, belief in the power of power also brought them down and their ecclesiology prevented them from reaching most Canadians of their time.

Second, larger communities often require a more homogenous culture in order to flourish. Despite their numbers, such churches tend to have a unifying brand (or ideological flag) around which their people can gather. Remember our examination of the Family Compact's use of the term "loyalty" and the damage that inflicted upon others. The word itself is virtuous but, like all words, how it is being defined (and by whom) is of the utmost importance. Larger churches can likewise create a culture that values loyalty to the church's message, or brand, over other important virtues like truth, or accountability. Power dynamics within a large church can lead to the valuing of leaders or ideas over the legitimate concerns, or complaints, of their own members. Strict definitions of what— or who—is loyal, good, or worthy can create an unchristian and toxic culture. In such cultures, homogeneity can trump holiness, and the leaders' character is less important than their charisma.

In such a top-down, power-based culture like the one the Compact was trying to establish (for all the right reasons, they would argue) weaker denominations like the Methodists and Baptists and Catholics (who were superior numerically but lacked governmental power) were able to effect real change. Their smaller size, more flexible ecclesiology, and willingness to enfranchise the disaffected made them a real David to Anglicanism's Goliath. In Canada, the Church of England provides an important cautionary tale about church power.

From more recent and nonreligious memory, is the tale of Target. The massive chain of retail stores rivals Wal-Mart in size and economic success and yet was unable to survive in Canada due to the massive geography and smaller population. Think about that for a moment if you belong to a bigger church, or desire to lead a large Canadian Christian movement. If Target can't make it work here—a business with much more appeal to the Canadian culture of the present age—what chance does a church really have?

POWER AND RIVALRY

Rivalry reminds us that this land has always been a place of numerous expressions and many Christians fought each other for dominance over the religious landscape. Those battles shaped church tensions for generations and, as we look to the formative 20th century, we are struck with how much those distinctions remain today. While Christians have always called for a revival throughout the history of this nation, this chapter reminds us that revivals were suspect in the early days of Canada and, strangely enough, that suspicion never really left our mindset.

Despite the advent of Pentecostalism, or the Hamilton revivals, or the Toronto Blessing, or the revivalist tones of the Prairies, or the success of evangelicals in Atlantic Canada, or even Aimee Semple-McPherson's success, revivalism has never been as formative for Canadians. As a novel experience it might draw people in but it will do next to nothing for long-term solutions. Even the most compelling of these churches faded in Canada unless they were able to calm down and organize.

I feel I should be clear because I am an historian, not a heretic (although, admittedly, the line between the two can appear blurry from time to time). I'm not advocating against revivalism; I am cautioning how Canadians define revivalism. If we define it as the Holy Spirit driving up numbers and influence of the church, then we're going to remain sadly disappointed. However, if Canadian Christians see revival as the Spirit working in quiet and surprising ways, we are getting closer to the historical impact revival has had in this nation.

Remember, the Methodists gave up their camp-meetings, the Baptists distanced themselves from Alline, and even Pentecostals' longevity in Canada (so far) owes more to their organization than revivalism. The Anglican and Presbyterian focus on sober logic, as well as the size of Catholicism in Canada, tempered the revivalist spirit. America had a different experience and this is important for Canadians to remember; the vast quantities of revivalist material coming from the States is less useful up here. Attitudes towards revival are one of the most important cultural differences between Canadian and American Christianity.

If we feel the need to borrow materials from other nations (another true Canadian pastime), might I suggest looking to places like New Zealand, England, Ireland, or Australia for more culturally suitable information. However, as the previous chapter suggested, Indigenous Christian literature and teachings in this area would likely be the most helpful.

Combining the themes of power and rivalry reminds us how important ecumenical movements have been in Canada. Churches do better when they have solid working relationships with the other faith communities located nearby. Competition has kept churches isolated from each other due to theology, traditions, polity, and fear. Once again, a focus on numbers can hamper the cooperative spirit each church is supposed to exhibit. Struggling communities have much to learn from larger churches but will avoid them out of concern their people will abandon them for a bigger church. Larger churches can alleviate such concerns by adopting the aforementioned attitude towards power. Bigger churches have plenty to learn from their smaller brothers and sisters but can only do so when they don't cannibalize them.

Imagine the impact a collection of churches could have over a community if they rejected the spirits of rivalry and power that have dominated many of our faith communities.

POWER, RIVALRY, AND INFLUENCE

In case such recommendations sound theologically problematic and antithetical to growth, remember the chapter on influence and the Canadian Christendom we encountered there. The advent of the railroad and Confederation enabled churches to have a powerful presence across the vast breadth of this nation. The idea of Dominion gave Protestantism a formative role over Canadian nationalism, and they believed God was instructing them to build a Christian nation.

During this time, we saw churches advancing the ecumenical growth I was just talking about, but they did so from a place of power and control. These churches also strengthened racist ideologies, encouraged restrictive immigration policies, attacked Catholics, and used their power in damaging ways. They did so believing they were using their power in God-honouring ways; history shows us the problems with such thinking. Despite Protestant leaders' new relationship with power, and the ecumenical movement of this time, the demography of Canadian Christianity changed surprisingly little.

The size and mosaic nature of this land make it almost impossible for the exclusive claims of Christianity to be enforced. From its inception, the geography of this place has provided numerous paths to the same location and that trickled into our psyches over time. Even when Christianity was the dominant religious expression, the fragmented ethos of Protestantism taught the people that for every opinion, another one was just around the corner. This is a land that learned from the Anglican priest, the Methodist itinerant, and the Catholic missionary even though each saw the others' worldview as un-Christian. For believers who think that Jesus is the only way to heaven, you are going to have a real problem selling that idea to Canadians outside your doors.

POWER, RIVALRY, INFLUENCE, AND LANGUAGE

The 20th-century world necessitated new language for many Christians and those new words created new worlds for subsequent generations. Terms like inerrancy and creationism and modernism turned many of the earlier rivalries into bitter contests that changed Canadian Protestantism forever. Advances in science and literature, coupled with world wars created crises for the ancient understandings of the faith.

Christians attempted to address these new concerns and, in so doing, split the faith yet again and created jargon that grew increasingly out of touch with the culture. While issues of biblical authority are important to Christians, it was the care many churches provided during the Great Depression that Canadians remembered. The birth of Pentecostalism seemed for some to be a corrective to mainline churches' focus on the academic elements of the faith. Increasingly, two camps formed in order to defend the church in the changing world of the 20th century. One camp sought to defend traditional and fundamental teachings of the faith. The other believed social action and ethical teachings were the best way forward. Such myopic focuses weakened the message of both sides.

The new language of those days allowed Christians to dismiss fellow believers as heretical based on words and ideas that are barely 100 years old even now. Others accused their rivals of being out of touch and too doctrinally focused; so heavenly minded they were no earthly good. French and English tensions within Catholicism brought division to the largest body of Canadian Christianity that likewise weakened its impact.

Language matters and I brought up the linguistic issues of the past to help us see the linguistic issues of the present a little clearer. We talk about secularization and post-Christendom as if they are facts without taking the time to ask what we mean by these words. We received many of our definitions and concerns because of the struggles of the early 20th century. Do you frame secularization as a loss in regular church attendance? Is post-Christendom due to the shrinking of Christian institutions or Christian influence? Do you think kids should learn the Lord's Prayer in school or that stores should be closed on Sunday? Does a person have to pray the Sinner's prayer in order to be a Christian? Do believers need to hold to a literal seven-day creation account or can they believe in evolution?

These concerns were created by the words of the early 20th century and will dictate how Christians of today react to the Canada in which we live. What is the Gospel in Canada and what words do we use to describe it? The painful lesson of this chapter is that the multiple ways such questions were answered helped create the secularism we are trying to correct today.

POWER, RIVALRY, INFLUENCE, LANGUAGE, AND FREEDOM

Canadians no longer look to the church as their moral guide and we have to accept that. But this is not simply indicative of this age's secularism, it is a notion Christians have experienced since the dawn of the faith. I hope this book opens you up to the breadth of valuable historical voices well beyond Canadian ones. As James Baldwin noted in the 1960s, history guides and influences us whether we know it or not. For example, the female mystic Teresa of Avila wrote the following in the 16th century, but her views are so relevant they could have been penned yesterday:

> Let us look at our own shortcomings and leave other people's alone; those who live carefully ordered lives are apt to be shocked at everything and we might well learn very important lessons from the persons who shock us. Our outward comportment and behaviour may be better than theirs, but this, though good, is not the most important thing: there is no reason why we should expect everyone else to travel by our own road, and we should not attempt to point them to the spiritual path and perhaps we do not know what it is. Even with these desires that God gives us to help others we may make many mistakes, and thus it is better to attempt to do what our rule tells us—to try to live ever in silence and in hope, and the Lord will take care of his own.
>
> If, when we beseech this of his majesty, we do not become negligent ourselves, we shall be able, with his help, to be of great profit to them.[2]

As Christendom crumbled, Canadians began to enjoy new freedoms that concerned many churches. The government created a new and more modern version of Canada that intentionally broke Protestantism's control over the religious landscape. Former codes of morality and decency altered through changes to the criminal code and the introduction of

---

2   Teresa of Avila. *Interior Castle*. Translated and edited by E. Allison Speers. (New York: Image, 2004), 49-50.

immigration. Protestants were no longer in charge because Canadians understood, as they had generations earlier, the nation grows in strength when it allows more voices to be heard.

Expo '67 highlighted the ongoing tensions within Protestantism as the Christian Pavilion and the Sermons from Science Pavilion cemented earlier conservative and liberal Christian tensions. Catholicism was decimated in the 1960s when the Quiet Revolution pretty much removed religion as a dominant societal factor throughout Quebec. If ever there is a lesson for all churches of Canada to take from the 1960s, it is the Quiet Revolution. This event proved in its dramatic removal of the church from society that this land can survive, and thrive, after any form of secularization. The 1960s took the tensions birthed at the end of the second world war and turned them into the norms of the nation going forward. This is the decade that Canada moved away from desiring to be a Protestant nation and decided to become a modern one.

If we can let go of our judgment claims as it pertains to the non-religious I think we find the better path forward in this so-called spiritual crisis. As we learn from the mistakes and triumphs of our spiritual ancestors in Canada, we come face to face with our own lack of vision. I hope this book has shown you that we never really know the long-term impact of our decisions; that should humble us. Therefore, let us trust Teresa's wisdom and just quietly go about our lives. If we reframe secularization and move it away from power dynamics or belief in the church's need to influence society and see this land for what it actually is, then I think we are actually set free to do whatever we want and be whoever we want. And Canada will benefit from that.

POWER, RIVALRY, INFLUENCE, LANGUAGE, FREEDOM, AND REALITY

Reality can be a harsh, and difficult term to define. The reality for the churches of the 1980s and on was that they were operating from the wings of Canadian society even if many of them refused to admit it. Televangelism from the States shaped the church world and some churches were accused of watering down the faith for the sake of bigger numbers. Reginald Bibby told us Canadians shop for church like they shop for shoes because religion, like most things in the upper 2/3 of North America, had become a consumer commodity.[3]

The loss of numbers was, for some, an indication of bad times ahead but for those coming to age in this generation, it was the beginning of a new period of the faith. The flashiness of the past needed to be replaced and some began to argue that the church needed to fundamentally change if it hoped to survive.

The skepticism of the 1990s began to undo the seeker-sensitive service in much the same way the youth movements of the 1960s undid Christendom. Like all cultural reversals, it was messy and didn't happen overnight. Many still hold to some version of the seeker model because it was the only system that temporarily reversed the downward trajectory of church attendance. This was the decade of the Toronto Blessing and Canada's turn as a dominant global Christian force. For the impressive duration and impact of the Blessing, it did little to change the demographics of Christianity within Canadian borders. Churches across the nation were birthed thanks to the Blessing but the more dominant story is one of increased skepticism and inattention to even this most Charismatic of Christian expressions.

By the 1990s, the great cultural experiment that removed exclusivist faith from the public sphere had been tested for a while and proven sustainable. Church assertions of power and claims to authority were immediately dismissed as outdated and suspected of corruption. The internet brought even more alternative voices that built on the spiritual smorgasbord of the 1960s. Such ideas further marginalized Christianity as one voice among many. However, the Christian narrative is too strong to be

---

3 Bibby begins *Fragmented Gods* by stating that the main challenge to ongoing faith in Canada is that religion "has become a neatly packaged consumer item—taking its place among other commodities that can be bought or bypassed according to one's consumption whims." Bibby, *Fragmented*, 1-2.

outright rejected and many Canadians still view God as tenable even in this age.

For all the concerns around secularization that took place in that decade, most people fail to see it for what it truly was. The reality of Canada in the last decade of the 20th century was that coercive faith no longer had any merit. Creative and socially-minded faith still had some intrinsic value but evangelism that focused on avoiding hell or condemning certain behaviours fell on deaf ears. Canadians had moved on theologically (though most wouldn't define their thoughts as such) and rejected any form of faith-based-fear-mongering.

POWER, RIVALRY, INFLUENCE, LANGUAGE, FREEDOM, REALITY, AND RECONCILIATION

While the other topics in this book discuss the foibles and follies and successes of Christianity in this land that are open to interpretation and challenge, this chapter forces us to recognize the profoundly anti-Christ nature of Christians that continues to harm the First Nations. The type of Christianity that allowed the residential school system to happen has no place in the Kingdom of God, even though it was welcomed on the landscape of this nation. This is something we must accept and the ongoing marginalization of Indigenous people is something Christians of this land must combat if we ever hope to be taken seriously as a voice for positive change.

This chapter challenges present-day beliefs about the people of the past. Historically, Canada has treated Indigenous people with a velvet gauntlet. Soft words and pretty rhetoric have covered the harsh policies and violent actions of Settlers toward Indigenous people; history reveals such abuses with painful clarity to Settler eyes and ears. We believe using terms like "First Nations" and "Settler" proves our enlightened stance. We fail to see the ways in which our words, once again, betray us. Believing the people of the past were racist (which, of course, is supported by evidence) gives us permission to remove ourselves from them as if our own worldviews are better. Yet, I know of few Christians today who recognize Indigenous Christians as learned members of the faith who have much to teach us.

Those who are concerned with this issue still tend to look down upon First Nations' Christianity as not quite Christian enough. Those outside the church see First Nations Christians as not quite Indigenous enough. Thus are our Indigenous brothers and sisters marginalized all over again, only with nicer language this time. I argue, in that tension lies an incredibly exciting sweet spot. Understandings of the Bible that are both rooted in this part of the world and that offer legitimate interpretations of the Gospel which are new to many of us. Interpretations that might excite life-long believers because they help reframe familiar stories. The acceptance of such wisdom might actually model for the rest of this nation practical steps towards actual reconciliation.

Even though it is the oldest form of Christianity in this land, there are few churches who access this as a learning tool to help us grow in our own faith. Canadians are happy to draw from American and European sources but there is little demand for Indigenous Sunday School lessons or Indigenous church planting techniques or Indigenous theologians or preachers to help us. While we, historically, have been more than comfortable seeking out the Christian resources and perspectives of other nations, we overlook the resources of these separate nations within Canadian borders.

Let me be very clear, using Indigenous teachings in order to breathe new life into stale Christian interpretations for the sake of reclaiming Christian influence over this land is just another form of colonialism. However, learning from Indigenous voices on matters of the faith out of a sense of their inherent value is closer to reconciliation.

To overlook these fonts of ancient Christianity proves that Settler attitudes towards the first inhabitants of this land remain dismissive and more connected to the reprehensible attitudes of the past than we may care to admit.

A MISSIONAL CANADIAN CHURCH

"A society grows great when old men plant trees whose shade they know they shall never sit in."

-Greek Proverb-

I would argue Canadian Christians can only move forward after recognizing the spiritual wilderness we currently inhabit. If secularization is defined as a loss of the Christian voice in Canada then, from the Christian perspective, this conjures up images of desolation and removal. Perhaps we are better served by picturing secularization as something else entirely. Perhaps in obsessing over what has been lost, we have overlooked what has been growing.

We have a massive forest of presuppositions and opinions about Christianity that we simply can't ignore. Like a forest, the term secularization is a complex ideological ecosystem that, as this book has shown, didn't spring up overnight. The issues of today are the results of conducive growing conditions and seeds that were planted much earlier. Some seeds grew because of the actions of those beyond the church but, as we have seen, some of the trees in the "secularization forest" were grown by Christians. Some are mere shoots that have only been growing for a relatively short amount of time, others are hundreds of years old. Some can be pruned, others can be chopped down, but many have deep and strong root systems that extend into the structures upon which our nation rests.

Now, asking you to visualize secularization as a forest may seem like pointless metaphorical nitpicking, but hear me out on this. Altering imagery, like altering vocabulary, creates new ways to understand and operate in the world. You may never have understood secularization in agricultural terms, but such an allegorical interpretation can remind concerned Christians who see secularization as a concerning loss and decline, other Canadians see it as growth and beauty.

With this in mind, Christians of today can cast themselves in the role of pioneer, called to explore and cultivate a vast, rugged, and untamed landscape. Throughout the course of this young nation's history, the ground has been cleared and ideas have been planted that have, metaphorically speaking, given rise to a spiritual topography as daunting as the physical topography was to earlier inhabitants. The obvious difference being the latter is more visible and physical than the former, making the work easier in some ways. But, like those pioneers of old, our job is still to assess the landscape honestly, decide how we want to cultivate this wilderness, and then begin the hard work of re-forming it into something new.

However, Christians of today must also contend with the fact that the trees we see as obstructions will be viewed as shelter by others. Trees we think are secular others will see as sacred (another lesson we need to learn from our Indigenous brothers and sisters). The ground we believe should be cultivated or cleared will be defended by detractors as pristine and worth protecting. Clearing ideological landscapes create similar tensions for some as clearing physical landscapes do for others.

Once again we look to the pioneers of old for wisdom. Our work will be fatiguing, unrelenting, full of risk, measured in small increments, and likely will not yield many results for the foreseeable future. But, like the farmers of old, the value in such work is to be found in benefiting the generations to come. The value in such work is the application of patience and humility and the willingness to fail and start again. If we ignore our egos and accept irrelevance as a challenge rather than a failure, the meager crops of today might actually prepare the spiritual ground of Canada for an impressive crop in the future.

So what could healthy, missional, Canadian churches look like? Organizations like The Flourishing Congregations Institute argue they look a lot of different ways.[4] Therefore, I want to dedicate the remainder of our time together unpacking a few elements. I am indebted to Drs. Patrick Franklin and Victor Shepherd for explaining these ideas that I have put into visual

---

4 For more see flourishingcongregations.org

form below:

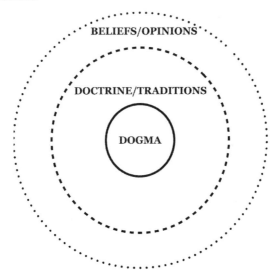

So, let's talk about a Canadian, missional church. I chose the term missional for a couple of reasons. First, it's a good word that contain a sense of purpose and urgency. Second, terms like "missional" and "emerging" became more popular during the 1990s as many young Canadian Christians navigated the shifting landscape. Such terms are not unique to Canadian Christianity, but the ways in which we define them can create an interesting Canadian conversation.

The first thing early Canadians did was clear a small patch of land in order to build shelter (there's no point in clearing acres of land and planting crops if you die of exposure). Thus, Christians of today must likewise begin small by defining that which is absolutely essential. Historically and theologically, such essentials are known as Dogma. Simply put, Dogma is the word we give to the ancient, core teachings of the faith. Ideas that are non-negotiable.

Teachings handed down through generations that are rooted in the New Testament and the earliest followers of Jesus. Ideas that other men and women—whom the church universal has recognized as profound and genuine thinkers—have communicated to us. Names like Tertullian, Clement, Macrina, The Cappadocians, Augustine, Jerome, Athanasius, Hildegard, Aquinas, Alopen, Catherine, Luther, Calvin, Erasmus, Zwingli, Wesley, Bonhoeffer, Von Balthasar, or Barth make this list. They have argued that for Christianity to be truly Christian it must recognize Jesus of Nazareth as Divine, it must see God as a Trinity, it must recognize that Jesus' death on the cross took away condemnation and that his literal resurrection granted salvation to wayward humanity. These people have consistently taught that Jesus is God and allegiance to Him is the path to eternity. These are core attributes of historical Christianity.

With that in mind, let's return to the "Descent of the Modernists" comic strip from chapter four. That cartoon raises legitimate criticisms about some early 20th-century Christian thinking. Some Christians were too quick to abandon core Christianity—Dogma—in order to maintain relevance on the Canadian scene. While these ideas were jettisoned out of a desire to remain conversant with the culture, ironically such choices actually diminished these churches' voice. Without language rooted in historic Christian thinking, such churches found they had precious little to say.

For a while, many of these churches became intellectual hubs for mostly middle-class Canadians that were exciting and innovative. However, over time and thanks to developments like the post-war suburbs, the growth of marketing, increased spending money, and a multiplicity of competing events, many churches devolved into little more than social clubs. They retained some trappings of spirituality but lost the teachings Christians have been rooted in for more than two millennia. They ended up having little value to society at large, or even their own members.

In this regard, and for some of these reasons, the Fundamentalists were correct in their assessment that the 20th century possessed some seductive dangers. 2000 years of teaching that has been tested repeatedly throughout history should not be cast aside for the whims of the day. If a Christian can toss out teachings like Jesus' Divinity, the Atonement, miracles, or the character of God as revealed in Christ, and neuter Jesus' challenging teachings into simple morality tales, the question "are you actually a Christian?" is a valid one.

The next, and wider, circle above shows Doctrine or Tradition. Traditions are the ways in which we bring Dogma into the world and can incorporate theology as well as ecclesiology. Doctrine can include ideas around biblical inerrancy, ordination, what kind of music your church plays, liturgy, polity, the Eucharist, and the role of missions. Doctrine is incredibly important because Doctrine helps faith communities find identity and purpose through their interpretation of Dogma.

It is in the realm of Doctrine and Tradition where the Fundamentalists fell down. They treated their Doctrines as Dogma. While vital, Doctrines are not as central to Christianity as Dogma. Many of these conservative Christians mistook their Traditions for core teachings and were thus unwilling, or unable, to be flexible in some crucial areas. They failed to see how their lack of self-awareness created a rigidity that, likewise, lessened their ability to manifest the Kingdom. Their Traditions were considered canon when some could have been jettisoned much easier and earlier to serve this nation.

Finally, we have Beliefs or Opinions and they, like Doctrine, matter but they are even further removed from core tenets of the Gospel. As their name indicates, these are thoughts and ideas we all have about faith and, like all opinions, some of them are good and others are not. This raises the question: how do we tell the difference between a good or a bad idea? History provides one solution. Some ideas are revealed to be either good or bad based solely on how well the idea holds up over time. However, that isn't helpful in the short term so what other criteria could we use? Community provides a more immediate answer. Good theology is done in community. Sacred community offers an antidote to the individualism of our age and challenges the belief that we can figure out God on our own. Despite some Christian focus on the individual in matters of salvation, critically discerning your own beliefs is an impossible intellectual and spiritual burden to bear on your own. A theological community offers a sound defence for the importance of church that has nothing to do with numbers. Your faith community is there to protect you from yourself, to pray for you when you can't even pray for yourself, and to remind you that your salvation is not dependent on you alone. A sacred community literally embodies the maxim that multiple heads are better than one.

It is not my place to tell you what elements of your faith should be considered Opinions and what elements are Doctrine. What I will say is this: Opinions and Doctrine have a porous boundary and ideas about which is which will travel back and forth. Like the Canadian/American border, Opinions can easily become Doctrine over time and then, depending on life experiences, return from whence they came. Rather than seeing such changes as denying the Gospel—which is what many Fundamentalists did—we can see them as the natural outworking of spiritual growth. There is risk in such moves but, again, the role of community is to help safeguard and mitigate such risks. Rarely is the world comprised of straight paths and the ability to pivot and navigate is a skill to be celebrated and sought after.

An honest assessment of the spiritual ground we inhabit begins by acknowledging the criticisms many Canadians have about the church are valid. We have to see that the church's traditional treatment of women, our inability to calmly address the shifting moral norms of our society, our pandering, or our obsession with certain church models and church language has worked against us. We have to admit Christianity has been used as a tool of oppression. The picture above displays a balanced theological mindset that gives room for deconstruction, challenge, and change as well as assistance to remain connected to historic faith.

No matter what decisions your community makes in regards to Tradition or Beliefs, any Canadian missional church will face tensions that are unique to this land. Some might argue any church that doesn't support women in leadership or isn't affirming of same-sex and trans identities can't consider itself missional in the Canadian setting. These churches believe it is important to find space within the church for more progressive teachings around gender and sexual identity because that is how Canadian culture tends to treat such issues.

However, for other churches, such stances betray the morality as described in the Bible. Fair enough, many missional scholars and thinkers argue that missional Christianity should offer challenges to cultural norms. Depending on how your community defines terms like missional, doctrine, or beliefs will determine how your community interacts with, reacts to, and is shaped by the Canadian culture.

If (for lack of a better term) more conservative views around sex and gender are central to your practice of the faith, then stick with it. This book is not counselling any Christian to betray the dictates of his or her conscience. What this book cautions and explains is that Canadian churches who hold to such beliefs likely have chosen the hill upon which their church will die.

Canada settled these issues long ago and no Canadian is going to betray his or her own conscience about such moral issues in order to join a church; such a move would be considered unethical. Again, I don't say this to be condemnatory at all, everything has to die and I think most of us would rather die on a hill of our choosing than betray our beliefs. What I am saying is that a church with such stances has chosen to define missional as a critique of the Canadian moral context.

On the other side, the UCC offers a missional church to Canada that seeks to affirm many of these cultural elements. This is a church with adherents who would be comfortable in Fundamentalism as well as a church possessing a professed atheist as a pastor. This is a church that has honoured same-sex attraction since the 1980s, has been vocal on First Nations' issues, and led the pack in female ordination. Yet, this church is also numerically dying and that fact has been used by more conservative churches as proof that the UCC's missional character has earned the disapproval of God.

To be honest, I'm not sure why the UCC continues to disappear; it could be argued that it is too Canadian and therefore has lost its unique voice. What I can tell you is that the UCC is viewed more positively than most evangelical churches by unchurched Canadians. The UCC may be doing little to grow Canadian Christianity but it is also doing little to harm it.

The UCC is pleasantly regarded (like a sweet grandparent) and easily disregarded (like a sweet grandparent when visiting time is over); a true example of Canadian Christianity if ever there was one. These are just a couple of examples that could possibly fit under the term missional but there are plenty more that also deserve more attention and study.

What I am calling us all to understand is, once again, words have meanings that are fluid and because of that fluidity, we must constantly investigate and adapt our vocabulary in ways that are faithful to the history, syntax, context, and definition of the word. However, we must also take seriously the connections and differences between Dogma, Doctrines, and Beliefs. We have room to be flexible without betraying the faith but, again, this requires vigilant self-awareness and humility. A willingness to let go of what we like in order to be all things to all people but also a willingness to communicate unapologetically the core tenets of the faith.

I think the model of the three circles could be an overlooked antidote to the increasingly divisive world in which we live. The 21st century seems concerningly rigid in the realm of Beliefs but has little at the heart of such beliefs. There is precious little room to disagree or debate and few seem to have much of a working knowledge of the historic and time-tested origins of their beliefs. Ironically, if Christian communities would look to historic models of missions and theology, we could model a generous humility regarding our own beliefs without losing the core of what makes us distinct.

Again, as this book has demonstrated repeatedly,

Christians have a storied past of disagreements and divisions. Yet, ecumenical movements have challenged the faithful to find common ground in Christ with each other, and even appreciate the different ways the Body of Christ functions. If we simply took seriously the famous maxim "In Essentials Unity, In Non-Essentials Liberty, In All Things Charity" Canadian Christians might actually model a way of embracing those with whom we disagree. Perhaps such actions would be a better use of our time than simply addressing the moral norms of the day.

So, what could a Canadian church look like? Here are a few final suggestions:

- It needs to be only moderately concerned with numbers.
- It needs to handle its beliefs and its models with a light touch that is open to adaptation.
- Churches that engage in genuine conversation with other churches close by, and share resources and swap preachers with those of different denominations, will serve their respective areas with greater efficiency. Such churches will also learn more about their own beliefs and will model a unity that celebrates, rather than minimizes, the traditions that differentiate us.
- Canadian churches should pray for leaders but also take limited interest in advancing political interests; no matter how important such interests are believed to be.
- They should be intentional about their language to help build shared understandings of the faith without slipping into overused jargon.
- They would do well to focus more on deepening the faith of their existing communities, rather than obsessing over reaching the unchurched.
- They will focus less on the morality—or immorality— of others and instead build communities dedicated to advancing clear, intelligible, fun, and compassionate faith.

- They will invite Indigenous leaders to help guide them in such complex times.
- In fact, Indigenous interpretations of the faith are likely the most interesting and authentic way to breathe new life into Christian beliefs.

Many Canadian Christians have overlooked the excitement of our time and place and I hope this book gives you cause to celebrate and have hope. If both "Canada" and "Christian" are a series of constructs and concepts, then we live in a double blessing. Both of these are worldviews deeply familiar with being overlooked and unconsidered. Canadians and Canadian Christians are reasonably comfortable occupying such a humble position and we should lean on that as we navigate our ways forward in this scary, challenging, and exciting world.

***

The ending of this book is somewhat disappointing.

It's an ending that lacks a definitive plan. Despite being a book for concerned Christians, it offers no multiple and clearly defined steps to success. Some might argue it's a non-committal ending (though I would prefer to call it flexible). It's an ending that provides no singular roadmap for the future. An ending that advances no goal as the correct goal.

It's an ending that simply calls you, gentle reader, to see the freedom, the beauty, and the power in being overlooked. An ending that calls you to see that as a Christian virtue. It's a modest ending. For those very reasons, I hope you can see that this ending is also very Canadian.

WORKS CONSULTED

PRIMARY SOURCES

Bell, D.G. (ed.) *Newlight Baptist Journals of James Manning and James Innis.* Hantsport NS: Lancelot Press, 1984.

Beverley, James and Barry Moody (eds.) *The Journal of Henry Alline.* Hantsport NS: Lancelot Press, 1982.

Bryce, P.H. *The Story of a National Crime: An Appeal for Justice to the Indians of Canada.* Ottawa: James Hope & Sons, 1922.

Francis, R. Douglas and Donald B. Smith (eds). *Readings in Canadian History: Post-Confederation 3rd Edition.* Toronto: Holt, Rinehart and Winston, 1990.

_____. *Readings in Canadian History: Pre-Confederation 4th Edition.* Toronto: Harcourt Brace, 1994.

Henderson, J.L.H. (ed). *John Strachan Documents and Opinions.* Toronto: McClelland & Stewart, 1969.

Hodgins, J. George. *Historical and Other Papers and Documents Illustrative of the Educational System of Ontario, 1853-1868.* Toronto: L. K. Cameron, 1911.

Johnston, Charles M. (ed). *The Valley of the Six Nations: A Collection of Documents on the Indian Lands of the Grand River.* Toronto: University of Toronto, 1964.

Joseph, Bob and Cynthia F. Joseph. *Indigenous Relations: Insights, Tips & Suggestions to Make Reconciliation a Reality*. Indigenous Relations Press, 2019.

King, Thomas. *The Inconvenient Indian: A Curious Account of Native People in North America*. Toronto: Anchor Canada, 2013.

McGregor, Stephen. *Since Time Immemorial: "Our Story" The Story of Kitigan Zibi Anishinabeg*. Maniwaki QC: Kitigan Zibi Education Council, 2004.

Meshake, Rene. *Injichaag: My Soul in Story-Anishinaabe Poetics in Art and Words*. Winnipeg: University of Manitoba, 2019.

Moodie, Susanna. *Roughing It In the Bush Or Forest Life in Canada*. London: T.N. Foulis, 1913.

Morris, Alexander. *The Treaties of Canada with the Indians of Manitoba and North-West Territories Including the Negotiations on Which They Were Based, and Other Information Relating Thereto*. Toronto: Belfords & Clarke, 1880.

Ovid, *Metamorphoses*, Book 8, Trans. By Brookes More (accessed 18/11/2021) http://www.theoi.com/Text/OvidMetamorphoses8.html Metamorphoses.

Rawlyk, George A. (ed). *New Light Letters and Spiritual Songs, 1778-1793*. Hantsport: Lancelot, 1983.

Robertson, J. Ross (ed). *The Diary of Mrs. John Graves Simcoe the Wife of the First Lieutenant-Governor of the Province of Upper Canada, 1792-6*. Toronto: Prospero, 2001.

Sansom, Joseph. *Travels in Lower Canada With the Author's Recollection of the Soil, and Aspect; the Morals, Habits, and Religious Institutions of that Country*. London: Sir Richard Phillips & Co., 1820.

Teresa of Avila. *Interior Castle.* Translated and edited by E. Allison Speers. New York: Image, 2004.

SECONDARY SOURCES

Abella, Irving and Harold Troper. *None Is Too Many: Canada and the Jews of Europe 1933-1948*. Toronto: Lester & Orpen, 1983.

Adams, Michael. *Fire & Ice: The United States, Canada and the Myth of Converging Values*. Toronto: Penguin, 2009.

_____. *Sex in the Snow: The Surprising Revolution in Canadian Social Values (10th Anniversary Edition)*. Toronto: Penguin, 2006.

Airhart, Phyllis. *A Church with the Soul of a Nation: Making and Remaking the United Church of Canada*. Montreal & Kingston: McGill-Queen's University Press, 2013

_____. "Ordering a New Nation and Re-Ordering Protestantism: 1867-1914." In *The Canadian Protestant Experience:1760-1990*. Edited by George Rawlyk. 91-138. Montreal & Kington: McGill Queen's University Press, 1990.

Armstrong, M.W. "Neutrality and Religion in Revolutionary Nova Scotia," *New England Quarterly* (Mar. 1946), 50-61.

Beaman, Lori G (ed.). *Religion and Canadian Society: Contexts, Identities, and Strategies, 2nd Edition*. Toronto: Canadian Scholars' Press, 2006.

Benton-Banai, Edward. *The Mishomis Book: The Voice of the Ojibway*. Hayward: Indian Country Communications, 1988.

Berton, Pierre. *The Comfortable Pew: A Critical Look at Christianity and the Religious Establishment in the New Age*. Toronto: Hodder & Stoughton, 1965.

Bibby, Reginald. *Fragmented Gods: The Poverty and Potential of Religion in Canada*. Toronto: Irwin Publishing, 1987.

Blatchford, Christie. *Helpless: Caledonia's Nightmare of Fear and Anarchy, and How the Law Failed Us All*. Toronto: Anchor, 2010.

Bourdieu, Pierre. *The Field of Cultural Production: Essays on Art and Literature*. New York: Columbia University Press, 1993.

Brant Castellano, Marlene and Archibald, Linda and DeGagne, Mike (compilers). *From Truth to Reconciliation: Transforming the Legacy of Residential Schools*. Ottawa: Aboriginal Healing Foundation, 2008.

Bucke, Richard Maurice. *Cosmic Consciousness: A Study of the Evolution of the Human Mind*. Philadelphia: Innes & Sons, 1905.

Canniff, William. *The Settlement of Upper Canada*. Belleville: Milka Screening, 1971.

Careless, J.M.S. (ed). *Colonists & Canadiens 1760-1867*. Toronto: Macmillan, 1971.

Choquette, Robert. *Canada's Religions.* Ottawa: University of Ottawa, 2004.

_____. *The Oblate Assault on Canada's Northwest.* Ottawa: University of Ottawa, 1995.

Christie, Nancy. "Sacred Sex: The United Church and the Privatization of the Family in Post-War Canada." In *Households of Faith: Family, Gender, and Community in Canada, 1760-1969.* Edited by Nancy Christie. Montreal & Kingston: McGill-Queen's University, 2002.

_____. *Transatlantic Subjects: Ideas, Institutions, and Social Experience in Post-Revolutionary British North America.* Montreal and Kingston: McGill-Queen's University Press, 2008.

Christie, Nancy and Michael Gauvreau. *A Full-Orbed Christianity.* Montreal and Kingston: McGill-Queen's University Press, 1996.

Clarke, Brian P. and Stuart Macdonald. *Leaving Christianity: Changing Allegiances in Canada Since 1945.* Montreal and Kingston: McGill-Queen's University Press, 2017.

Cook, Ramsay. *The Regenerators: Social Criticism in Late Victorian English Canada.* Toronto: University of Toronto, 1985.

Creech, Joe. "Visions of Glory: The Place of the Azusa Street Revival in Pentecostal History," *Church History* 65, no. 3 (September, 1996).

Cuccioletta, Donald and Martin Lubin. "The Quebec Quiet Revolution: A Noisy Evolution." *Quebec Studies* (Vol. 36): Fall-Winter 2003.

Cuthbertson, Brian. *The First Bishop: A Biography of Charles*

Inglis. Halifax: Waegwoltic Press, 1987.

Douville, Bruce. *The Uncomfortable Pew: Christianity and the New Left in Toronto*. Montreal & Kingston: McGill-Queen's University, 2020.

English, John, Richard Gwyn and P. Whitney Lackenbauer (eds). *The Hidden Pierre Elliot Trudeau: The Faith Behind the Politics*. Ottawa: Novalis, 2004.

Epp, Frank H. *Mennonites in Canada, 1786-1920: The History of a Separate People*. Toronto: Macmillan, 1974.

Fay, Terrence J. *A History of Canadian Catholics*. Montreal & Kingston: McGill-Queen's University Press, 2002.

Grant, John Webster. *A Profusion of Spires: Religion in Nineteenth-Century Ontario*. Toronto: University of Toronto, 1988.

_____. *The Church in the Canadian Era*. Vancouver: Regent, 1988.

_____. *The Moon of Wintertime: Missionaries and the Indians of Canada in Encounter since 1534*. Toronto: University of Toronto, 1984.

Gray, Charlotte. *The Promise of Canada: People and Ideas That Have Shaped Our Country*. Toronto: Simon & Schuster, 2016.

Heath, Gordon L. *A War with a Silver Lining*. Montreal & Kingston: McGill-Queen's University Press, 2009.

Hughes, Aaron W. *From Seminary to University: An Institutional History of the Study of Religion in Canada*. Toronto: University of Toronto, 2020.

Hughes, Everett C. *French Canada in Transition.* Chicago: University of Chicago, 1943.

Joblin, Kingsley. *Servant to First Nations: A Biography of Elgie Joblin.* Downsview, ON: Northern Spirit Publications, 2002.

Joseph, Bob and Joseph, Cynthia F. *Indigenous Relations: Insights, Tips & Suggestions to Make Reconciliation a Reality.* Port Coquitlam: Indigenous Relations Press, 2019.

Klosterman, Chuck. *Sex, Drugs, and Cocoa Puffs*.* New York: Scribner, 2004.

Knowles, Norman. *Inventing the Loyalists: The Ontario Loyalist Tradition and the Creation of Usable Pasts.* Toronto: University of Toronto, 1997.

Leibbrant, Gottlieb. *Little Paradise: The Saga of the German Canadians of Waterloo County, Ontario, 1800-1975.* Kitchener: Allprint, 1980.

Letto, Irving. *Sealskin Boots and a Printing Press: Piecing Together the Life of Canon J.T. Richards.* Victoria: Friesen Press, 2012.

Lowman, Emma Battell and Adam J. Barker. *Settler: Identity and Colonialism in 21st Century Canada.* Halifax & Winnipeg: Fernwood, 2015.

Mack, D.B. "George Monro Grant and the Bow of Ulysses: An Ecumenical Vision in Victorian Canada." Published on Academia.edu

Marsden, George M. *Understanding Fundamentalism and*

Evangelicalism. Grand Rapids: Eerdmans, 1991.

McLaren, Scott. *Pulpit, Press and Politics: Methodists and the Market for Books in Upper Canada.* Toronto: University of Toronto, 2019.

McGregor, Stephen. *Since Time Immemorial: Our Story-The Story of the Kitigan Zibi Anishinabeg.* Maniwaki QC: Kitigan Zibi Education Council, 2004.

McLaurin, C.C. *Pioneering in Western Canada: A Story of the Baptists.* Calgary: Armac Press, 1939.

Miedema, Gary R. *For Canada's Sake: Public Religion, Centennial Celebrations, and the Re-Making of Canada in the 1960s.* Montreal & Kingston: McGill-Queen's University, 2005.

Mika, Nick and Helma Mika. *United Empire Loyalists: Pioneers of Upper Canada.* Belleville: Mika Publishing, 1976.

Miller, Thomas William. "The Canadian Jerusalem: The Story of James and Ellen Hebden and Their Toronto Mission Part 1," In *A/G Heritage*: 5-22 [Fall 1991].

Milloy, John S. *A National Crime: The Canadian Government and the Residential School System.* Regina: University of Manitoba, 2017.

Moir, John S. *The Church in the British Era: From the British Conquest to Confederation.* Toronto: McGraw-Hill, 1972.

Moodie, Susanna. *Roughing It In the Bush Or Forest Life in Canada.* London: T.N. Foulis, 1913.

Morgan, Cecilia. *Public Men and Virtuous Women: The Gendered*

Languages of Religion and Politics in Upper Canada, 1791-1850. Toronto: University of Toronto, 1996.

Noll, Mark. *A History of Christianity in the United States and Canada*. Grand Rapids: Eerdmans, 1992.

_____. *What Happened to Christian Canada?* Vancouver: Regent, 2007.

Parkman, Francis. *Montcalm and Wolfe: The Riveting Story of the Heroes of the French and Indian War*. New York: Modern Library, 1999.

Phillips, Dorrie. "Early Years of the Black Loyalists." *Loyalists in Nova Scotia*. Hantsport: Lancelot Press, 1983.

Power, Michael and Nancy Butler. *Slavery and Freedom in Niagara.* Niagara-on-the-Lake: Niagara Historical Society, 2000.

Rawlyk, George A. (ed). *The Canadian Protestant Experience 1760-1990*. Montreal & Kingston: McGill-Queen's University, 1990.

Rayburn, Alan. *Naming Canada: Stories About Place Names from Canadian Geographic*. Toronto: University of Toronto, 1994.

Semple, Neil. *The Lord's Dominion: The History of Canadian Methodism.* Montreal & Kingston: McGill-Queen's University, 1996.

Smith, W.G. *Building the Nation: A Study of Some Problems Concerning the Churches' Relation to the Immigrants.* Toronto: Canadian Council of the Missionary Education Movement, 1922.

Stackhouse, John G. *Canadian Evangelicalism in the Twentieth Century: An Introduction to its Character*. Toronto: University of Toronto, 1993.

Stewart, Gordon and George Rawlyk. *A People Highly Favoured of God: The Nova Scotia Yankees and the American Revolution*. Toronto: University of Toronto, 1972.

Symons, Harry. *Ojibway Melody*. Toronto: Ambassador Books, 1946.

Thompson, Andrew. "Slow to Leave the Bedrooms of the Nation" in *The Hidden Pierre Elliot Trudeau: The Faith Behind the Politics*. Edited by John English, Richard Gwyn and Whitney Lackenbauer. Ottawa: Novalis, 2004.

Wayman, Tom. *A Country Not Considered: Canada, Culture, Work*. Concord ON: Anansi, 1993.

Webb, Todd. *Transatlantic Methodists: British Wesleyanism and the Formation of an Evangelical Culture in Nineteenth-Century Ontario and Quebec.* Montreal and Kingston: McGill-Queen's University Press, 2013.

Wetmore, Donald and Lester B. Sellick (eds.) *Loyalists in Nova Scotia: Biographies of Loyalist Settlers*. Hantsport NS: Lancelot Press, 1983.

White, Richard. *The Middle Ground: Indians, Empires, and Republics in the Great Lakes Region, 1650-1815.* New York: Cambridge University Press, 1991.

Wilkinson, Michael and Linda M. Ambrose. *After the Revival: Pentecostalism and the Making of a Canadian Church.* Montreal & Kingston: McGill-Queen's University, 2020.

ABOUT THE AUTHOR

Dr. James Tyler Robertson's research and publishing explore the Canadian context of the Christian faith. He works with church planting/missionary groups from around Canada and the United States highlighting the importance of historical awareness. He has published extensively in the areas of Canadian Church history and speaks frequently at popular and academic presentations. In addition to this, Dr. Robertson teaches the development of Christianity around the world, with a focus on the development of the faith during the Reformation and into the Modern Age. His focus on Church and War has brought him into dialogue with the military, inter-faith groups, and various peace organizations. He is also a past president of the Canadian Society of Church History.

James also serves as the Director of Tyndale's Distributed Learning Department. In this role, he oversees the development of online content and pedagogy for the entire University.

He pastors two rural churches in southwestern Ontario, so the study of history is much more than an academic exercise to him. He sees the value of bringing the voices of the past into discussions around hope for the future.

New Leaf Press

amplifying innovative Canadian voices

WHO IS NEW LEAF NETWORK PRESS?

Starting something new is hard, and when you are breaking new ground you often feel alone. In those moments of loneliness, finding someone else who is on a similar journey is so important - many of us have found encouraging voices in books that we have read. Yet, in the publishing market of resources for the Canadian church, there is often a gap where distinctly Canadian stories and resources should be. That's where New Leaf Network Press comes in.

We are a small-scale imprint committed to offering the work of Canadian authors to a Canadian audience. We are part of the *New Leaf Network*, and all of our publications seek to support the broader network.

The *New Leaf Network* is a collaborative, relational, and creative missional organization that supports, equips and connects church-planters, spiritual entrepreneurs and missional practitioners in post-Christian Canada.

Whether you're starting from scratch or leading an existing community, we want to help you start something new right here on Canadian soil.

We've got a hunch that our ever-increasing post-Christian culture is begging for new forms of Jesus-centered cultural engagement, neighbourhood connection, and mission innovation. We believe it's time for Canadian Jesus followers to unite together, equip each other, cultivate our voice, and start something new from coast-to-coast.

Through online collaboration spaces, interactive learning workshops, events, story-telling, and specialized coaching, this growing collective of Canadian, Jesus-centered leaders is a community of innovators, both church and lay leaders, working to lead from the emerging future.

For more information visit www.newleafnetwork.ca/newleafpress

Manufactured by Amazon.ca
Bolton, ON

25625864R00195